HIDDEN VOICES

Key Issues in Social Justice: Voices from the Frontline

Series Editors: **Kalwant Bhopal**,
University of Birmingham,
Martin Myers, University of Nottingham,
Karl Kitching, University of Birmingham
and **Kenzo Sung**, Rowan University

How do issues of social justice, inclusion and equity shape modern day society? This series delivers a forum for perspectives from historically marginalised and minoritised communities to challenge contemporary dominant discourses about social justice, inclusion and equity in the social sciences and aligned disciplines.

Forthcoming in the series:

*Transformative Teaching and Learning in Further Education:
Pedagogies of Hope and Social Justice*
By **Rob Smith** and **Vicky Duckworth**

*Low-income Female Teacher Values and Agency in India:
Implications for Reflective Practice*
By **Ruth Samuel**

Find out more at
bristoluniversitypress.co.uk/key-issues-in-social-justice

HIDDEN VOICES

Lived Experiences in the Irish Welfare Space

Joe Whelan

With a foreword by
Fred Powell

First published in Great Britain in 2022 by

Policy Press, an imprint of
Bristol University Press
University of Bristol
1-9 Old Park Hill
Bristol
BS2 8BB
UK
t: +44 (0)117 954 5940
e: bup-info@bristol.ac.uk

Details of international sales and distribution partners are available at
policy.bristoluniversitypress.co.uk

© Bristol University Press 2022

British Library Cataloguing in Publication Data
A catalogue record for this book is available from the British Library

ISBN 978-1-4473-6092-6 hardcover
ISBN 978-1-4473-6094-0 ePub
ISBN 978-1-4473-6095-7 ePdf

Cover design: Liam Roberts
Front cover image: © Mark de Jong/Unsplash
Bristol University Press and Policy Press use environmentally responsible
print partners.
Printed in Great Britain by CPI Group (UK) Ltd, Croydon, CR0 4YY

For Deirbhile and Sadhbh

Contents

List of tables

Glossary

List of abbreviations

BTEA	Back to Education Allowance
DA	Disability Allowance
DSP	Department of Social Protection
DWS	Developmental welfare state
GP	General practitioner
HRC	Habitual residence condition
IB	Illness Benefit
JA	Jobseeker's Allowance
JB	Jobseeker's Benefit
JST	Jobseeker's Transitional Payment
OPFP	One-Parent Family Payment
PUP	Pandemic Unemployment Payment
SWA	Supplementary Welfare Allowance
UBI	Universal Basic Income

Words written in the Irish language and their meanings in English

Cumann na Daoine	Association of People (widespread national community group).
Dáil Éireann	The lower house, and principal chamber, of the Oireachtas, which currently consists of 158 members. Equivalent to the British House of Commons.
Oireachtas	The Irish legislature and houses of parliament.
Tánaiste	Second most senior member of the Irish Government
Taoiseach	Foremost member of the Irish Government. Equivalent to the British Prime Minister.
Teachta Dála (TD)	An elected representative of Dáil Éireann. Equivalent to a British Member of Parliament.

About the author

Joe Whelan is an assistant professor and researcher in the School of Social Work and Social Policy at the University of Dublin, Trinity College. His main area of research interest focuses on exploring the nexus of work and welfare. He is particularly interested in exploring and understanding lived experiences in the context of welfare recipiency, focusing on the processes and effects of welfare conditionality. As a working-class and first-generation scholar, he is also someone with lived experience of being a welfare recipient over many years, and this part of his biography strongly underpins his research interests.

Acknowledgements

I would like to thank all those who took part in the research that underpins much of what is presented in this book. Their words permeate these pages, and, in doing so, offer life to experiences that would otherwise remain hidden.

Foreword

Fred Powell

Joe Whelan has written a very important book that breaks new ground in Irish social policy discourse. He brings a fresh voice that represents a new generation of Irish scholars willing to take up more critical approaches to analysing Irish social policy. That is a very exciting development that should be welcomed with enthusiasm. The remarkable scholarship of the work marks the book out as a seminal contribution to Irish and international social science. This book captures a 'bottom–up' perspective on the lived experience of the Irish poor.

Irish social policy has been historically shaped by two conservative forces: first, the Catholic Church, which resisted a welfare state in order to maintain religious hegemony over Irish civil society, through the principle of subsidiarity; and second, the initiative to create a new post-revolutionary society, envisaged in the Marxist Democratic Programme 1919 and quickly suppressed. Nationalists favoured a residual welfare model that retained poor law attitudes towards those in need. The new leaders of Ireland developed what the distinguished Irish commentator and public intellectual, Fintan O'Toole, has characterised as 'a half-baked Welfare State, a chaotic and enormously inefficient mix of public, private and charitable provision' (*Irish Times*, 25 April 2017). Universalism had no place in the post-revolutionary social contract.

The Irish Revolution produced a residual welfare system, ideologically shaped by the belief that government should play a limited role in the distribution of benefits and services. Religious charity, in the form of a very conservative mixed economy, would have a central role in what Joe Whelan calls the 'welfare space'.

The theocratic phase in Irish social policy began to disintegrate following the beginnings of modernisation in the 1960s, albeit that the Catholic Church still controls almost 90 per cent of primary schools. Modernisation was led by foreign direct investment, over the decades turning Ireland into a tax haven for multinational corporations. Ireland's 12.5 per cent corporate tax rate has recently become the subject of international criticism and is likely to be modified. That will probably be a beneficial policy development that enables Ireland to refocus from wealth generation to poverty alleviation.

The legacy of historical abuse perpetrated by the Catholic Church against children and single mothers in institutional care has undermined clerical power in both civil and political society. It was also a damning judgement on the ethical role of charity. This has led to a step-change in Irish social policy, ushering in a more inclusive, rights-based society. It has led to major changes in social legislation that have legalised contraception, divorce and homosexuality. Two constitutional referenda have subsequently approved same-sex marriages and abortion by two-thirds majorities. It is an overdue recognition of women's reproductive rights and gay people's rights to equality, and a rejection of traditional patriarchal society embodied in clerical power over citizens' lives in a republic.

Ireland's road to social equality has been slow and painful in a society that professes republican rhetoric but fails to articulate republican values. This may be due to the dominance of nationalism that defines republicanism in terms of the historic achievement of independence. Ireland since independence has been dominated by two nationalist political parties. They have alternated in government but offered little that differentiates one from the other. Currently they are in coalition in an increasingly multi-party parliament. Membership of the European Union is gradually reshaping Irish politics. These new horizons have led to an academic discussion of the Irish welfare state. The discussion has an existential dimension. Some commentators cast doubt on the existence of an Irish welfare state. The National Economic and Social Council in 2005 concluded that the Irish welfare state is both 'complex and hybrid'. Joe Whelan deftly opts for the term 'welfare space'. He may have captured the essence of the Irish welfare zeitgeist.

What is clear is that the condition of the Irish poor continues to be a seminal question in Irish social policy. The condition of the Irish poor is a historic legacy shaped by the experience and memory of the Great Famine (1845–51). It is a spectre hanging over Irish culture and identity. Over one million died. At least a million more emigrated in the Irish diaspora over the following century. Hope lay elsewhere in the United States, Canada and Australia. Irish population decline has only begun in recent decades to be arrested, after more than a century of population outflows. The historic tragedy of the Great Famine was that it was the product of a denial of rights – particularly the right to poor relief that existed in England but was deemed unsuited to the scale of Irish poverty.

What Joe Whelan has done in his remarkably innovative book is to translate the condition of Irish poverty question into the 21st century. He has democratically asked the poor for their view on their condition. He calls it a 'snapshot'. Whelan's book is in reality an exploration of the lived experience of the Irish poor, revealing what working-class life in contemporary Ireland is about. Whelan represents the poor as living 'a marginal and liminal social existence'. He poses the question: 'What does it mean for people to exist in this space?' That is the central issue confronted by this powerful and challenging book.

Series editors' preface

Kalwant Bhopal (Series Editor), Martin Myers,
Karl Kitching and Kenzo Sung

Debates about social justice, inclusion and equity in the early 21st century have become increasingly more contentious and problematic. This should not come as a surprise and reflects Western social, economic and political climates driven by neoliberal narratives; the rapid expansion of European Union membership followed by signs of its impending potential dissolution, such as the election of Donald Trump as 45th President of the US in 2016; and the growing populism of nationalist political parties in almost every Western democracy. At the same time, the Global South has seen economic expansion on a scale that would have been inconceivable a generation ago and that threatens to undermine the hegemony of the West.

This original book series delivers a forum for marginalised and minoritised perspectives in the social sciences. It challenges contemporary dominant discourses about social justice, inclusion and equity from the perspective of marginalised and minoritised communities. Drawing on the work of researchers, theorists and practitioners from Europe, the US and the Global South, the series adopts a broad interdisciplinary approach spanning disciplines such as education, sociology, social policy and childhood studies. The titles in the series are published on wide-ranging topics, underpinned by research and theory.

The series draws on definitions of social justice that identify the marginalisation and exclusion of groups and communities of people based on their difference from the majority population, and seeks to understand how such processes should be disrupted and subverted. Social justice in this respect is both the subject matter of the book series but also its practical contribution to academic scholarship. By providing an outlet for scholarship that itself emerges from under-represented voices, the books published in the series contribute to addressing rather than simply commenting on social justice issues. The series centres social justice, inclusion and equity; gives voice to those from marginalised communities and groups; places a spotlight on the work of under-represented (minority ethnic, religious, disabled, female, LGBTQ) academics; and challenges hegemonic narratives that underpin Western discourses about how best to reach a socially just world.

A key strength of the series is its broad range of topics from different disciplines in the social sciences including education, sociology, social policy, gender studies, migration and international relations, politics and childhood studies. The series draws on themes that include race/ethnicity, gender, class, sexuality, age, poverty, disability and other topics that address and challenge inequalities. It includes a range of different theoretical perspectives including addressing intersectional identities.

Hidden Voices: Lived Experiences in the Irish Welfare Space by Joe Whelan provides a unique contribution to the series. It critically explores the policy discourse in the Irish context by focusing on and giving voice to a marginalised group: poor people in Ireland in receipt of welfare benefits. Drawing on powerful and compelling empirical research with those living in poverty, Whelan is able to bring the real experiences of respondents to life. Each chapter eloquently draws on the Irish context, which is contextualised with relevant literature. Additional chapters focus on empirical research, highlighting marginality and liminality, the work ethic, welfare conditionality, compliance and impression management, and concepts of deservingness, othering and reciprocity. Whelan expertly brings together all themes exploring the 'welfare imaginary' and finally examines the research within the context of the pandemic. This book provides an original contribution to debates on poverty within the Irish context. Clear, sharp and hard-hitting, it centres the importance of why a socially just society is one that must be seen as a moral right, rather than a simple obligation.

Introduction

About this book

This is a book about lived experiences in the context of welfare recipiency in Ireland. As such, my primary wish as an author is to present, unblemished and unvarnished, the experiences of others. Through the construction of several themes that form the empirical chapters of this book, I hope to have done this in a way that offers both depth of understanding and some useful lenses to help guide and contextualise that understanding without 'over-theorising' it. Therefore, it is hoped that readers will gain a real and visceral sense of the everyday lived realities of those whose words describe that reality. I think that this is an important and worthy undertaking, not least because lived experience as a form of knowledge is something that I wish to champion and something that can often be overlooked or measured against criteria that miss the inherent nature and value of what a knowledge of lived experiences can offer. The idea of lived experience as a valid and valuable form of knowledge is something that is growing in the context of scholarly work concerned with welfare and welfare states, and this will be made evident through the rich variety of literature referenced in this text. It is the hope that what is offered here adds to this growing cannon.

The research presented here is drawn from the Irish example and is very much presented as a 'case study' that stands on its own. The empirical materials presented further on are the outcome of a study that offers a 'deep dive' into a relatively specific and 'slow-moving' social milieu. Therefore, this text is not strictly intended to be comparative. However, the materials used to ground this study come from a variety of jurisdictions, and so the book will have relevance to international readers. Moreover, I argue that the experiences presented are potentially 'shared typical' in nature, and so have resonance in other jurisdictions and particularly in jurisdictions where cognate welfare systems persist. The vast majority of empirical material presented in this book comes from data that were gathered after the 2007-08 global financial crisis and before the 2020 global COVID-19 outbreak, and therefore reflect experiences of welfare recipiency that predate the changes seen in welfare states both at the onset and during the pandemic. Nevertheless, this does not dilute the veracity of this study on the basis that it represents experiences in a welfare state that has developed across many decades, with features that have remained largely unchanged despite the pandemic. It should also be noted that, at the time of writing, many of the emergency welfare features introduced in Ireland during the pandemic are being slowly retrenched while simultaneously many of the pre-COVID-19 policies are being reinstated. This book, therefore, is not presented as a contribution to the 'COVID-19 literature'; rather, through the lens of lived experience, it deals with themes that are perennial in the context of welfare. Therefore, for the bulk of the book, the COVID-19 pandemic is of little relevance. However, it is briefly visited in Chapter 8, which also introduces some empirical materials gathered by the author and colleagues in a separate study that was carried out during the pandemic.

Following this Introduction, Chapter 1 provides a brief history of the development of the Irish welfare state. This chapter is intended to offer context, to give a sense of how the Irish welfare state has developed, what makes it different from other welfare states and how it has ultimately become the modern welfare apparatus it is today. From here, the book moves through a series of chapters (Chapters 2–7) that present empirical materials in thematic form. Each chapter is introduced, contextualised and grounded in a literature where this is necessary or possible. The empirical materials are then introduced and conveyed at length. The first empirical chapter, Chapter 2, introduces the ideas of marginality and socially liminality, showing how these phenomena are threaded through the contemporary welfare experience for recipients of multiple payment types in Ireland. Chapter 3 introduces the concept of the work ethic and shows how this both permeates experiences in the day to day lives of those who took part in the study and how it is threaded through the policies and practices of the Irish welfare state. Chapter 4 moves to explicate the area of lived experiences in the context of welfare conditionality, showing how conditionality practices affect participants across different payment types. Chapter 5 begins to document some of the practices and behaviours that those interviewed for the study spoke about engaging in and interrogates the areas of maintaining compliance and engaging in impression management. Chapter 6 stays in the area of practices and behaviours and looks, in particular, at the concepts of deservingness, othering and the norm of reciprocity. Chapter 7 concludes the empirical section of the book by bringing together previously visited themes and focuses on how a changing 'welfare imaginary' has come to define welfare as something implicitly or inherently bad, meaning that those who receive it are tainted by proxy. Chapter 8 considers the COVID-19 welfare landscape and introduces some empirical materials from a survey study that aimed to capture the lived experiences of welfare recipients in Ireland during the pandemic. Finally, the Conclusion Chapter presents some closing thoughts on what welfare could and should be are offered.

A note on the research

Before moving into the main body of this work, it is important to offer some context for the research on which it is largely based. The experiences documented in this book are drawn from a set of empirical materials that resulted from a qualitative study carried out in the Republic of Ireland in 2019 and which used in-depth interviews as a mode for data collection. In particular, this study focused on those who either were or had been in receipt of the following core groups of Irish welfare payments:

- Jobseeker's Benefit (JB) and Jobseeker's Allowance (JA);
- Illness Benefit (IB) and Disability Allowance (DA);
- One-Parent Family Payment (OPFP) and Jobseeker's Transitional Payment (JST).[1]

In terms of the first two groups of benefits, the intention was to capture a sample of people who were or had been receiving social welfare in order to meet the same basic needs but who may have had very different experiences due to the nature of the payment. In this respect, it should be noted that JB is a social insurance-based payment, whereas JA is a means-tested or assistance-based payment. It was also entirely possible that some participants may have had experiences with both as JB is only paid for a limited time, after which those recipients who have not found employment in the intervening period are expected to apply for JA and submit to a means test. It is also possible to receive both payments at once, with JA acting as a top-up payment in cases where insurance contributions alone are not sufficient to meet the base rate for a qualified adult. In the case of IB and DA, the same logic is followed, with IB functioning as a limited insurance-based payment and DA functioning as a means-tested, assistance-based payment. Certification via a medical professional is also needed in order to qualify for these payments. OPFP is a payment targeted at people who are either caring for a child or children on their own, or who are co-parenting but in the position of primary carer[2] for the child or children. They may or may not be in receipt of maintenance. It is a means-tested payment and it is possible for recipients to work for a limited number of hours before the payment becomes affected. JST is targeted at those who are in receipt of OPFP and whose youngest child has turned seven, lasting until the youngest child has turned 14, at which point claimants who still have a welfare need are expected to apply for JA. The underlying ethos of the JST payment scheme is preparation for and transition to the workplace and, as such, obligatory attendance at workplace preparation training is expected, with the potential for sanctions for those who do not engage. Unlike JA, the recipient does not have to be available for or genuinely seeking work to continue to receive JST. It is also possible to continue to pursue higher education while on this payment, and this has the potential to extend the duration for which the payment is made, although, even then, activation measures such as compulsory attendance at workplace preparation events may still apply.

These particular payment schemes were chosen as they provide a comprehensive cross-section of working-age welfare state service users in Ireland who are in receipt of direct payments. In this respect, the sample group was selected on the basis of a desire to potentially uncover a wide range of experiences along with the potential differences and similarities between these.

Inclusion criteria

To be included in the research, participants simply either had to have been in, or still be in, receipt of any of the payments listed in the previous section. There were no exclusions based on age, ethnicity, gender and so on. This was because the core research interest was broad representation of lived experiences across core working-age payments related to unemployment as opposed to an attempt to test whether there were differences in experiences according to other aspects of identity (gender, ethnicity, age and so on). The breakdown of participants whose transcripts were selected for analysis is detailed in Table 0.1.

As can be seen from the table, a total of 19 interviews, from 11 female and eight male participants, were included for analysis. As well as payment type, data on gender, approximate age bracket, duration of time on a payment, approximate geographical location and some minor biographical details were also gathered. This is both to ground the empirical materials and to give readers a sense of whose stories and experiences are drawn on throughout. Three additional interviews (from one male and two female participants) were carried out, but these were not included as they failed to meet the inclusion criteria due to the fact that the experiences of the individuals concerned related to other payment types. The names given in the table are pseudonyms and are referred to in the empirical chapters further on. All other information has been suitably anonymised.

A note on interviewing

The interview technique used for this study is best described as existing somewhere on a continuum between semi-structured and fully open. For clarity, the method used is described as a 'structured conversation' interview technique. This was not as strictly structured as semi-structured interviewing in that a repeatable question schedule was not used. Neither was it as unstructured as a fully open interview technique in that some thematic

Table 0.1: Participant attributes

Pseudonym	Gender	Age group	Welfare category	Duration spent on current scheme	Region	Other details
Jane	F	40–49	JST/OPFP	10 yrs approx.	Cork city area	Single m* of two. In higher ED**
Patricia	F	30–39	JSA/BTEA	5 yrs approx.	Town in Tipperary county/ Cork city area***	Single individual. In higher ED
Clive	M	50–65	JSA	10 yrs approx.	Town in Cork county	Single individual. Fully unemployed
Olive	F	40–49	JSA/BTEA	10 yrs approx. (periodically)	Rural Clare/ Kerry	Single individual. Currently on Tús[3] scheme
Mary	F	18–29	JSA	3 months full time/ 9–10 months on and off	Cork city area	Single individual. Suffers from diagnosed anxiety disorder. Fully unemployed
Scarlett	F	18–29	OPFP	4 yrs approx.	Town in Cork county	Single m of two. Also works part time
Lisa	F	30–39	JSA/BTEA	6 months approx.	Cork city area	Works part time
Grace	F	18–29	OPFP	5 yrs approx.	Cork city area	Single m of one. Fully unemployed
James	M	50–65	DA	20+ yrs	Cork city area	Single individual. Suffers from severe and diagnosed psychological illness
Martin	M	30–39	JSA	2 yrs approx.	Town in Cork county	Single individual. Fully unemployed
Gail	F	30–39	DA	15 yrs approx.	Town in Cork county	Single m of one. Significant mental health and diagnosed mental illness issues. Fully unemployed

(continued)

Table 0.1: Participant attributes (continued)

Pseudonym	Gender	Age group	Welfare category	Duration spent on current scheme	Region	Other details
Trevor	M	30–39	DA	12 yrs approx.	Town in Cork county	Single individual. Significant mental health and diagnosed mental illness issues. Fully unemployed
Trish	F	40–49	JSA	3 yrs approx.	Cork city area	Single individual. Fully unemployed
Alan	M	18–29	JSA/BTEA	2 yrs full time then 3 yrs on and off	Cork city area and rural Kerry	Single individual. Now fully employed
Peter	M	30–39	JSA	2 yrs full time plus 1 yr part time	Cork city area	Single individual. Works part time
Graham	M	50–65+	JSA	10+ yrs	Cork city area	Fully unemployed
Harley	F	18–29	IB	5 months	Town in Cork county	Recent mental breakdown. Currently receiving treatment
Frank	M	50–65+	DA	8 yrs	Town in Cork county	Suffers from poor mental health. Experienced recent marital breakdown. Children are in state care
Jennifer	F	30–39	OPFP	16 yrs approx.	Cork city suburb	m of two; also has long-term chronic health condition

Notes:

Breakdown: F (11); M (8). JSA (10); OPFP/JST (4); DA (4); IB (1).

*m = mother.

**ED = education.

***Some people have had experiences in more than one geographical area.

guidance was utilised (Leech, 2002). In real terms, after a period of rapport building, the researcher entered into a conversation with each participant that visited specific themes and contexts consecutively. Each participant was first asked about their experiences in the context of making an initial claim for welfare as well their experiences of subsequently maintaining their claim. Following this, participants were asked to talk about how they felt they were viewed by other people in the context of their welfare recipiency. Finally, participants were asked how they felt about themselves in the context of welfare recipiency. Each interview was thoroughly unique, although each covered the same broad themes. With respect to the practice of entering into a 'conversation', the active voice of the researcher varied according to each participant. Participants were generally encouraged to tell their own story with the researcher acting as a facilitator in this respect. Nevertheless, as some participants were more reticent than others, I did enter into the role of a more active conversant where this was necessary in order to better 'draw out' the thoughts, feelings and experiences of those more reluctant participants. Use of this method was arguably more labour-intensive than 'straight' semi-structured type interviewing in that I had to be able to 'improvise' in practice. However, it can be suggested that the benefit or 'return' for this more intensive style of interviewing was the resultant richly detailed data.

A note on analysis

This study employed a latent thematic analysis (TA) that draws on a reflexive model of TA, as developed and described by Braun and Clarke (2006, 2012, 2013, 2016, 2020, 2021a, 2021b). In the first instance, TA as an overall approach was seen as being suitable as it could potentially provide a 'rich and detailed, yet complex, account of data' (Braun and Clarke, 2006: 78). However, there are different orientations or approaches within reflexive TA, and the approach used here is best described as latent TA, wherein coding and theme development aims to report and unpack the concepts and assumptions underpinning the data. The opposite of a semantic thematic analysis, wherein the researcher simply constructs themes based on what is inherent in the explicit or surface meanings of the data and nothing beyond that, Braun and Clarke (2006: 84) note that a latent thematic analysis 'goes beyond the semantic content of the data, and starts to identify or examine the underlying ideas, assumptions, and conceptualisations – and ideologies – that are theorised as shaping or informing the semantic content of the data'.

Therefore, the analysis undertaken has sought to use data to construct themes that capture particular types of form and meaning, and the concepts and assumptions that underlie these. For clarity, the stages of analysis undertaken by the researcher can be seen in Table 0.2, which has been adapted from Braun and Clarke, (2006: 87).

While Table 0.2 remains largely true to what was originally prescribed by Braun and Clarke, (2006: 87), the process has been tailored specifically to the current researcher's approach. In particular, the inclusion of a continued engagement with the extant literature is seen as being key, particularly with

Table 0.2: Phases of thematic analysis

Phases	Process description
Familiarising myself with the data	Immersion in the data, re-reading data. Noting initial ideas. Re-reading key literature.
Generating initial codes	Open coding for interesting features and experience types across the data set. Note taking and early comparison to extant literature.
Constructing initial themes	Theme building: collating codes into potential themes and gathering relevant data to each potential theme. Continuing to engage with the literature.
Reviewing themes	Checking if themes work in relation to coded extracts; checking if themes work in relation to entire data set; reviewing data for additional themes; generating a thematic map of the analysis. Continuing to engage with existing cognate literature alongside the theme-building process.
Defining, refining and naming themes	Ongoing analysis to refine themes. Generating clear theme names and definitions.
Producing the report	Selection of vivid/compelling extract examples; final analysis of extracts; relating analysis back to research questions and couching the finding within the broader literature.

Source: Adapted from Braun and Clarke (2006: 87).

respect to the concept of 'shared typical', which is elucidated further on. It should also be noted that stages set out above take cognisance of Braun and Clarke's later work (see 2012, 2013, 2016, 2020, 2021a, 2021b) and in particular, their clarification that researchers do not 'search for' themes in the sense of themes being within the data, simply waiting to be found. Neither do themes organically or magically 'emerge'. Rather, the construction of themes is a type of intellectual labour through which the researcher imbues the data with meaning, remaining reflexive in doing so. This was very much the approach taken here. The six themes that were developed via this process and which form the basis for the bulk of the observations presented in this book are as follows:

- **Marginality and social liminality:** the sense of being on the margins while also being in an 'in between' space underlies experiences in the context of welfare recipiency.
- **The work ethic (enforcement and experience of):** the continuous intrinsic and extrinsic societal enforcement of the work ethic, and how this is experienced, underlies and contributes to experiences in the context of welfare recipiency.
- **Welfare conditionality:** the conditions attached to being a welfare recipient deeply affect lived experiences.

8

- **Maintaining compliance and engaging in impression management:** the feeling of a need to maintain compliance with what it means to be a 'good' citizen along with what it means to be a 'good' welfare recipient, and the impression management engaged in as a result of both, contribute to and underlie experiences in the context of welfare recipiency.
- **Deservingness:** societal narratives surrounding deservingness shape experiences of welfare. They are often actualised in:
  - **othering and self-justification (as a result of othering):** othering coupled with self-justification represent an internal and external struggle in the context of deservingness;
  - **social reciprocity:** the sense that welfare recipiency is 'taking while not giving' contributes to and underpins experiences in the context of welfare recipiency.
  - **Welfare is bad:** an overarching theme, the sense that it is 'normal' to feel bad about receiving welfare and that welfare itself is something inherently 'bad'.

Lived experience as a form of knowledge

This book showcases and presents materials that were both gathered and analysed using what may be broadly referred to as qualitative techniques (Bryman, 2012; Gronmo, 2020) which embrace qualitative research with a 'big Q', meaning they embrace qualitative methods, but also, equally importantly, qualitative values (Braun and Clarke, 2021a). In doing so, the intention is to champion the doing of qualitative research as a means of arriving at real, distinctive and meaningful social scientific knowledge. To make this case, rather than justifying qualitative research as an approach to knowledge generation by comparing it to more quantitative, or 'small q' qualitative approaches, I deal briefly with what I feel are the strengths of qualitative research as well as some of the misconceptions.

First, there are difficulties with the term 'lived experience' and this is something that has been picked up by researchers working in this space, with McIntosh and Wright (2019: 450) noting that '… we have found the idea of lived experience both intuitive and useful, but have become increasingly perplexed by its potential to seem vacuous or contradictory – what is any experience if it is not lived?'.

Ultimately, through documenting the complexity of 'lived experience' as a term with particular meanings in particular contexts, McIntosh and Wright (2019: 463) argue that presenting lived experience as a form of knowledge can offer a 'sharp critical edge' and can, therefore 'be associated with an empathetic immersion in the lives and concerns of people affected by and involved in policy processes and outcomes, including elite policy makers and influential context creators, managers and front-line workers as well as disempowered and oppressed groups'.

This effectively captures how lived experience as a form of knowledge is being presented here, both in terms of its form and effect (empathetic immersion), its potential (affecting policy makers and so on) and those whose stories it has the power to transmit (disempowered and oppressed groups, in this case, welfare recipients). Approached in this way, lived experiences as a form of knowledge can be particularly powerful when the knowledge they offer is transmitted in the vocabulary of those who have 'lived the experience' because, to paraphrase the philosopher Richard Rorty (2007), we come to new forms of sympathy and understanding when we come to know something of the life history of persons. I would argue that sympathy and understanding as the building blocks of social policy seem like a good place to start.

There are also arguments that suggest that research based on lived experience lacks a 'generalisability' factor (Smith, 2018), making it somehow 'less valuable' and I wish to briefly address this further misconception. In the first instance, this critique somewhat misses the point of 'big Q' qualitative research, which aims for depth over and above probability and breadth (breadth in the general sense, that is, regarding sample size and so on) and can in fact be strengthened by the deep focus permitted by smaller sample sizes (Crouch and McKenzie, 2006). Indeed, Crouch and McKenzie (2006) have suggested that small sample sizes are often preferable in forms of exploratory research, qualifying this by noting that such research would ultimately be grounded or embedded within existing and ongoing cognate research (see the section on 'shared typical' forms of knowledge) and this is very much the approach taken here. On generalisability, Smith (2018: 138) notes: 'Qualitative research does lack generalizability when it is understood only through one particular type of generalizability, that is, statistical-probabilistic generalizability.'

This is undoubtedly true, and therefore statistical-probabilistic generalisability is not the goal here nor in 'big Q' qualitative work in general. To clarify the type of generalisability claimed here, I draw on Lewis and colleagues (2014: 351), who note that:

> Qualitative research cannot be generalised on a statistical basis – it is not the prevalence of particular views or experiences, not the extent of their location within parts of the sample, about which inferences can be drawn. Nor, of course, is this the objective of qualitative research. Rather, the value of qualitative research is in *revealing the breadth and nature of the phenomena under study*. [Emphasis added.]

The empirical materials introduced from Chapter two onwards therefore aim to illustrate both depth and breadth (breadth in the sense of complexity of phenomena) in the context of welfare recipiency as a social phenomenon. Because qualitative data is 'messy' by nature, structure is 'imposed' upon it through the construction of themes. This involves separating out and distinctly presenting aspects of a common experience and the things that underlie them, which, in reality, are intimately intertwined.

'Shared typical' forms of knowledge

A term that will be referred to continually throughout the empirical chapters of this book, doing quite a bit of heavy lifting in the process, is 'shared typical' and I therefore wish to explain what I mean by this and what I am claiming for it. It is arguably well known that lived experience is an often neglected or demoted form of knowledge and this is true across multiple contexts, usually devolving on arguments suggesting that knowledge based on lived experience cannot be generalisable in the same way as knowledge based on quantitative research, which captures or utilises big datasets (Bryman, 2012; Parker and Northcott, 2016; Gronmo, 2020). Such an approach to or understanding of qualitative research may be said to favour research values synonymous with a 'small q' lens, thus eschewing the values associated with 'big Q' qualitative research. Yet, examples of research that draws on lived experiences in the context of welfare specifically and within the social sciences in general, abound (examples are too numerous to be inclusive here; nevertheless see Patrick, 2012, 2014, 2016, 2017, 2019; Boland and Griffin, 2015a, 2016; Garthwaite, 2015a, 2015b, 2016; Wright, 2016; Whelan, 2020a, 2020b, 2021a; Finn, 2021 for just some examples). In many of these examples, similar themes, narratives and descriptions of experiences are found. The similarity in these experience types constitute what I argue here to be 'shared typical' aspects of lived experience, which are less about jurisdictional and procedural differences and much more about everyday lived realties despite the former and the latter. In employing this concept, I follow other scholars who I would suggest work in the 'big Q' qualitative space and in the context of welfare by taking up the work of McIntosh and Wright (2019) and Wright and Patrick (2019) in particular. Drawing on C. Wright Mills (1940) and the idea of a constellation of motives as a way to 'pick out' sources of motive or action that may not be wholly individual or structural, McIntosh and Wright (2019) have argued that social policy, as a discipline, can and should use lived experience as a window into the 'shared typical'. In particular, they note the potential for identifying 'shared typical' knowledge types in longitudinal work. By aggregating qualitative longitudinal research, Wright and Patrick (2019) take the concept of 'shared typical' further, firmly arguing and arguably establishing its usefulness as a lens. Treanor and colleagues (2021) have since built on this. The research presented in this book differs in its use of 'shared typical' as a demarcation for transmittable knowledge, likely relevant in multiple instances, in that it is based on 'one off' or 'snapshot' research consisting of one-time, long-form interviews. Nevertheless, it is argued here that this also constitutes a valid approach and the 'why' of this is elaborated in the following section. For now, I propose that 'shared typical' experience types become evident when they can be grounded in a cognate literature documenting similar lived experiences under reasonably similar conditions and, as seen above, use of existing literature for just this purpose was heavily factored into the data analysis process.

Temporality in research: the value of a snapshot

The data presented in this book represent a snapshot or rather 19 snapshots of people's lives; a series of fixed moments in time where, in the social context of an interview, one person shared with another some of the complexity of their life. This, I argue, is a strength of this study, as it offers a precise distillation of the themes covered at interview. Were the participants to have been interviewed again, what was offered in the original interview would have taken on a new texture, even a dilution of sorts. This is not to suggest that longitudinal or follow-up interviews are a less powerful or useful form of data gathering. Rather, what I wish to suggest is that they are utilised to perform a different task, a task that aims to capture movement and change in participant circumstances. The research elucidated here aimed to offer a pure, distilled, moment in time in the lives of those who took part in the study, to capture these moments, to scrutinise each one deeply and to relate them to each other and to cognate research. Braun and Clarke (2021a: 28) note that when we interview participants 'we "capture" meaning on and of the moment, and that this is, potentially, shifting and changing'. The data presented in this book stay with or even dwell with the moments captured, avoiding a focus on the shifts and changes that lives necessarily encompass in order to honour a partial story, a 'snapshot', and all the meaning with which that snapshot is imbued, thus fulfilling the task of deep interpretation. In this way, the knowledge claims made here move away from a model of human experience that values consistency, and singularity, over change and partiality in a way that chimes with many post-structuralist critiques (see Henriques et al, 1984; Potter and Wetherell, 1987; Burr, 2002). What emerges is a precise and distilled account of how those interviewed interpreted and articulated their experiences at the time of interview.

Setting the stage: the development of the Irish welfare state and its place in the world of welfare

The purpose of this chapter is to delineate the Irish welfare state and, in so doing, situate it within a broader welfare context. Later in the chapter, I directly address where Ireland 'fits' with respect to the 'doing' of welfare. However, before this, and in order to give a sense of the different and often competing interests that have had a hand in shaping Ireland's welfare state, the primary method of delineation is to offer a history of that development. In this respect, we start by noting that the revolution that birthed the Irish Free State, which officially came into being on 7 January 1922, was not followed by any meaningful social revolution. This has been well documented elsewhere (see Powell, 1992, 2017; Peillon, 2001; Cousins, 2005; Ferriter, 2005, 2013, 2015; Dukelow and Considine, 2017 for just some examples). Reviewing this literature, what emerges is a picture of an Ireland that, after a bitter period of civil war, is conservative and austere, bearing the hallmarks of an emphasis on 'self-sufficiency' that had been propagated by figures like Sein Féin's Arthur Griffith (Lee, 1990; Powell, 1992; Ferriter, 2005; McGee, 2015). When considering the sociology of a newly independent Ireland, it is important to note the emergence of what would ultimately become 'traditional' sites of shame, trauma and stigma arising from the practice of mass incarceration through reform and industrial schools, in mother and baby homes and in asylums (Rafferty and O'Sullivan, 2002). In this respect, the role of the Catholic Church and of Catholic social teaching is hugely important when considering the development of the Irish welfare state. It may be tempting to assume that an immediate and overt role emerged for the Catholic Church, that the Church became the state's conscience on the same day that the state formed. However, this is not entirely accurate and what at least constituted a visage of state secularism, evident in the 1922 constitution, at first remained (Ferriter, 2005; Powell, 2017). However, Powell (1992: 161) has noted that a 'politics of informal consensus' between state and Church meant that Church power was assured, and that early social policy was heavily influenced by the Catholic Church and not the liberal-democratic ideology espoused in the 1922 constitution. The Church held strong moral views on a host of matters relating to particular cohorts and on the policies and services that the state should engage in, views that undoubtedly influenced the doing of welfare and the broad development of the Irish welfare state.

During this early period of Irish independence, despite some measures being introduced, there was no centralised or purposeful welfare state to speak of (Cousins, 2005). However, while welfare state development may have been slow or even non-existent at this time, it is clear that an awareness of the needs of some and of the failures of existing poor relief existed at a political level, with reference having been made to a desire to abolish the poor law prior to independence and as far back as the 1919 Democratic Programme of the first Dáil, which stated that:

> The Irish Republic fully realises the necessity of abolishing the present odious, degrading and foreign Poor Law System, substituting therefore a sympathetic native scheme for the care of the Nation's aged and infirm, who shall not be regarded as a burden, but rather entitled to the Nation's gratitude and consideration.

Clearly, terms used in this passage, such as 'odious' or 'degrading', coupled with an ambition to remove the notion of 'burden' from the idea of caring for those most in need, denotes, at the very least, an awareness in formative Irish political circles of a desire to do welfare differently. In independent Ireland, this ambition became actualised in deliberate efforts to remove the stigma associated with the poor law, via the introduction of Home Assistance payments, which were discretionary, and which were largely administered through the existing, though renamed, poor law infrastructure (Cinnéide, 1970; Powell, 1992; Cousins, 2005). Boards of guardians were replaced or superseded by Boards of Health and Public Assistance and workhouses became county homes. Documenting this, Powell (1992: 176) has noted that: 'The Free State Government sought to reduce the stigma associated with the Poor Law through the Electoral Act, 1923.... The dreaded name "workhouse" was ... replaced by "county home" in another effort to remove the stigma associated with the Poor Law.

Powell (1992) goes on to note that these changes were largely symbolic and did little to change the subordinated status of the poor.

Political pressure to do more in respect of the Free State Government's efforts regarding poor law reform followed, coming most notably from the Labour Party, the result of which saw the establishment of the Commission on the Relief of the Sick and Destitute Poor. Ultimately, the report produced by the commission and published in 1925, was mixed, with three of the ten signatories only signing after adding major qualifications. It arguably contained very little that was favourable towards those experiencing poverty. For example, an excerpt concerning Home Assistance, from paragraph 158 on page 53, reads:

… we believe that institutional relief should only be granted where it is impossible, impracticable or wasteful to relieve in any other manner. To avoid abuse in the administration of Home Assistance without being able to fall back on a test such as the workhouse test requires careful scrutiny of each applicant's case and courage and determination to resist undue pressure to afford relief under circumstances that may not altogether warrant its being given.

There were overt suggestions within the report that many of the poor people availing of Home Assistance were abusing it, that it was open to abuse and that as a result, poor people were seemingly imagined as engaging in a sort of flamboyant largesse. Largely, the report suggested tightening up the system and even proposed further potentially stigmatising measures such as the publication of the names of claimants in each district as a form of deterrence (Powell, 1992).

Early developments

The year 1932 saw the ascension of Fianna Fáil under Éamon de Valera and with it a force that would come to dominant the Irish political landscape throughout much of the 20th and first decade of the 21st centuries (Dunphy, 1995; Whelan, 2011). On entering office, Fianna Fáil immediately began taking decisions – such as repealing the commitment to transmit land annuities to Britain – that would have long-reaching consequences for the populace, particularly the poor (Powell, 1992; Ferriter, 2005). In much the same mould as the previous administration, Fianna Fáil, and de Valera in particular, espoused a vision of 'self-reliance' and 'self-sufficiency' and were decidedly protectionist in their economic outlook[1] (Coogan, 1966; Powell, 1992; Whelan, 2011). However, despite this, some relief measures were introduced early on in the life of the administration such as Unemployment Benefit in 1932 and Widows and Orphans pensions in 1935. While developments during this period did not come close to constituting what could be termed a welfare state, it is nonetheless possible to get some sense of the perceived legitimacy of such schemes. For example, Powell (1992) has noted that Unemployment Assistance, despite the fact that a successful claim came only on the basis of meeting rigorous conditionality requirements, was met with considerable political opposition, particularly among the propertied classes. Arguments against welfare during this period echoed earlier periods and the Ricardian and Malthusian logic that relief had the potential to undermine the incentive to work or to lower wages (Whelan, 2021b). Suffice to say there was not full, or even widespread, political support for the introduction of relief measures despite the clear need for it in the face of burgeoning destitution and unemployment (Powell, 1992). This indicates that state welfare, rudimentary as it was in Ireland at this time, was already suffering from problems of political legitimacy, clearly underpinned by ideological concerns surrounding deservingness and the work ethic (Powell, 1992; Peillon, 2001; Cousins, 2003; 2005; Norris, 2016; Whelan, 2021b; Boland and Griffin, 2021). Undoubtedly then, those who found themselves in need of relief did so in a contested welfare space.

A welfare commons?

Britain, in 1942, saw the publication of the Beveridge Report, which was, for its time, quite radical in tone and called for a minimum standard of income, much of which would be met through social insurance schemes – so being potentially self-funding – with social assistance being made available to those who, for whatever reason, were not in a position to contribute to a social insurance fund. Beveridge certainly envisioned the latter group as being very much in the minority (Page and Silburn, 1999; Page, 2007). More formally known as the *Social insurance and allied services report*, it was generally referred to as the Beveridge Report after its principal author, William Beveridge.[2] Published at the height of the Second World War, part of the report proposed that all people of working age should pay a weekly national insurance contribution. In return, benefits would be paid to people who were sick, unemployed, retired or widowed. The overall goal of the report was to 'slay' what were referred to as 'five giant evils stalking Britain' through a series of 'cradle to grave' welfare measures. In this respect, the five giants to be slain were want, disease, ignorance, squalor and idleness. The report was a bestseller, selling over 70,000 copies in Britain alone (Armstrong, 2017; Whelan, 2021b). The Beveridge Report was certainly available in Ireland where it undoubtedly had a major effect, earning support from several quarters and particularly within the Labour Party (Powell, 1992; Peillon, 2001; Cousins, 2003, 2005). However, the plan set out in the Beveridge Report directly contravened Catholic social teaching and was therefore criticised and delegitimised by the Catholic Church and others (Powell, 1992, 2017). The central argument against it was that the adoption of such a plan would impinge freedom, give the state far too much authority, and ultimately lead to totalitarianism.

However, the term 'welfare state' and the idea of a state that was active in promoting and ensuring the welfare of its populace had now entered the popular lexicon. In 1944, the Catholic Church in Ireland responded with a plan of its own, entitled *Social security: Outline of a scheme on national organisation*, which was authored by Dr Dignan, the then Bishop of Clonfert (Powell, 1992; Peillon, 2001; Cousins, 2003, 2005). Despite earlier criticisms, the plan borrowed from Beveridge. However, the plan also differed significantly in that it suggested a transfer of responsibility for social services from the state to a vocational governing body (Powell, 1992; Peillon, 2001; Cousins, 2003, 2005). The plan was controversial. It was ultimately shelved and, in an uncharacteristic display of resistance to the Church, largely ignored by the state (Powell, 1992, 2017). It nevertheless points to the fact that the need for a comprehensive suite of welfare measures was beginning to enter the discourse with respect to Irish social services.

A department of social welfare

Powell (2017: 129), writing of an emerging welfare state, notes that 'Ireland's road to modernization has been a long and troubled one'. The establishment of a formal Department of Social Welfare in Ireland in 1947 certainly stands out as a milestone in Irish welfare state development. It was an acknowledgement by the state that it had a role in promoting and maintaining the welfare of its populace and it ostensibly created a centralised authority tasked with administering the schemes that fell under the banner of welfare, or more specifically, in Ireland, income maintenance of different types. This development was further consolidated with passing of the Social Welfare Act 1952. Through these two events, Ireland was now officially and formally a European welfare state (Cousins, 2003; Carey, 2003, 2008). Just what type of a welfare state Ireland would go on to be was arguably yet to be decided, and it was not yet a given that it would be governed by a logic closer to its liberal counterparts than to that of the corporate and social democratic welfare states of continental Europe.

Early efforts by the newly formed Department of Social Welfare, which was introduced by the then Fianna Fáil government before it fell in early 1948, focused on exploring options and attempting to devise a coherent welfare system. This effort was characterised by the publication of several white papers (Cousins, 2003). Undoubtedly influenced by Beveridge in Britain, a strong focus on new social insurance schemes, along with the integration of existing schemes, began to emerge (Cousins, 2003). Much of this work was carried out by the inter-party government of 1948, of which Labour leader William Norton – who had, in part, campaigned on the basis of introducing a comprehensive social security plan (Puirséil, 2007) – was Tánaiste and Minister for Social Welfare. As work towards a finalised bill progressed, the release of a draft paper of the purposed bill in 1949 met with considerable political resistance, with many commentators labelling it as too generous. Objections to welfare on the grounds of its effect on the work ethic were, by now, wholly consistent, demonstrating the deep embeddedness of this logic (Powell, 1992; Cousins, 2003; Carey, 2003, 2008; Whelan, 2021b). However, despite objections, work on the bill continued and, despite a further change in government which saw Fianna

Fáil returned to the seat of power in 1951, the bill was finally signed into law on 14 June 1952 and with it the formal birth of the Irish welfare state (Cousins, 2003; Carey, 2003, 2008).

There has been much written, in the context of welfare, about the events that took place between the years 1947 and 1952 in Ireland. In offering one analysis of these events, Cousins (2003) notes that a way of viewing them collectively is as a major achievement of social policy in Ireland and one that continues to shape Irish welfare today. There is no doubt, particularly when the political turmoil surrounding these events is taken into account, that the introduction of these measures at this particular time in history does represent an achievement of sorts and, at the very least, an Irish social policy milestone, ultimately providing a 'unitary framework' for social security (McCashin, 2004). At the risk of damning with faint praise, the introduction of the Social Welfare Act 1952 resulted in a welfare infrastructure that was certainly better than what had existed before it. However, substantial criticisms can and must be offered, and, importantly in relation to the task undertaken in this book, the question of what just sort of welfare state the 1952 Act enshrined, and what this ultimately meant for the experiences of those who would receive welfare under it, must be explored.

Practically speaking, the Social Welfare Act 1952 saw the introduction of some small-scale social reform, but not in all cases. For example, the area of pensions remained largely untouched. It was not an all-encompassing piece of legislation. General reforms were comparatively much less comprehensive than what was being, and had been, introduced internationally, particularly in Britain where much of what was recommended in the Beveridge Report had by now become enshrined in law (Cousins, 2005). It was also much less comprehensive than what had been previously sought domestically by the then Minister of Social Welfare in the Labour/Fianna Fáil coalition government, William Norton. In respect of the exclusionary nature of the 1952 Act, Powell (2017: 164) has noted that 'the Irish Social Welfare Act 1952 excluded farmers, farm laborers and relatives assisting on farms, amounting to 45. 2 per cent of the population'.

The Act concentrated primarily on social insurance type measures along with some unemployment coverage, sickness coverage and coverage for widowhood. Drawing again on the language of Cousins (2003), who has detailed and analysed this period extensively, the events described here may just as easily be viewed as the outcome of a 'compromised project' that can be characterised as a 'failure of politics'. Ultimately, what was made explicit through the Social Welfare Act 1952 did eventually give way to the ad-hoc development of an Irish welfare state. Yet, in many ways, it arguably represents a lost opportunity that, as McCashin (2004: 39) has noted, was ultimately characterised by the fact that 'the 1952 legislation was considerably less comprehensive and redistributive than the grand plans that had simulated debate in the 1940s'.

Importantly, the Act, with its truncated version of social insurance, did very little to offset practice of marking out of the very poor from the rest of Irish society, meaning that social assistance and Home Assistance would continue to have a very significant role in Irish social security (McCashin, 2004). The sociological experience welfare recipiency as an undesirable social condition, much like the receipt of poor relief before it, would still exist, enshrined now in legislation that continues to underpin the Irish welfare system.

Progress and on

The decade of the 1960s, which preceded the enlargement of the European Community, was a period of sustained economic growth in most of Europe and an era of rising living standards and expectations (Ferriter, 2005, 2013). In Ireland, the 1960s was a decade of economic progress after a long history of stagnation. Nevertheless, on joining what was then the European Economic Community (EEC) in 1973 (Ferriter, 2005, 2013), Ireland was still an outlier in respect of social welfare, generally having a lower level of social spending, with the scope and coverage of schemes more restricted and the general structure of social provision more limited. Legislation in this area then was arguably much less advanced than that of many of the Member States (Cousins, 2005, 2016).

The early 1970s was a period of 'rediscovery' in Ireland with respect to poverty, which was becoming a matter of growing concern. This is partly evidenced by the Bishops of Ireland's Council for Social Welfare's hosting of a well-attended conference on poverty in Kilkenny in November 1971 (Dukelow, 2018). This Council for Social Welfare conference is particularly notable for its debate of ideas surrounding what poverty comprises and what kinds of measures should be taken to address it. Séamus Ó Cinnéide, a noted scholar and pioneer of social policy in Ireland, delivered a paper at the conference that attempted to make the case for relative poverty and in doing so estimated that between 20 and 30 per cent of the Irish population were in poverty (Dukelow, 2018). However, there were also several strong papers from attending clergy that were couched in the language of Catholic social teaching and tended to problematise the behaviours of those experiencing poverty over and above potential structural explanations (Dukelow, 2018). Clearly then, the 1952 Act had not 'settled the matter' so to speak, and ideas around the 'doing' of welfare were still being contested. In this respect, also of note in the 1970s was the establishment of a working group on poverty set up in the summer of 1972 by the Labour Party, which produced a detailed report on poverty in Ireland in 1973 (Powell, 1992). The final report of the

National Committee on Pilot Schemes to Combat Poverty (1980) captures much of the discourse surrounding poverty in the 1970s and notes that:

> While Ireland had experienced a long and bitter history of poverty, deprivation and oppression, the growing affluence of the late fifties and sixties afforded an opportunity for many Irish people to conveniently wipe this experience from their minds, forgetting even to the point of denial that such social evils were still present. The fearful stigmatisation and powerlessness of the poor themselves ensured that they remained silent – thus reinforcing the myth that poverty and the poor were no longer a problem in Irish society.

In Ireland, then, the 1970s was not the golden age it was considered to be elsewhere in Europe. The rediscovery of poverty, as demonstrated by the previous quote, was arguably more of a re-acknowledgement than a genuine rediscovery (Dukelow, 2018). Despite this, there was some progress in respect of general welfare provision; for example, the pension age was lowered from 70 to 65, social insurance was made much more inclusive and a number of new schemes such as Deserted Wife's Allowance, Single Woman's Allowance and Prisoner's Wife's Allowance were introduced in the first five years of the 1970s (Powell, 1992; Dukelow and Considine, 2017). There is clearly no denying the gendered and heteronormative nature of these payments as they are obviously all based on the nature of a woman's relationship or non-relationship to a supposed male counterpart. Nevertheless, they are notable for adding to the cannon of overall available payment schemes and for being assistance- rather than insurance-based. A further policy event that was notable in this decade was that Home Assistance, the residual poor law, was formally replaced by Supplementary Welfare Allowance (SWA) in 1975, conferring a legal right to a minimum payment (McCashin, 2004).

If some gains had been made in the 1970s, the 1980s in Ireland saw the onset of recession set against a global context in which 'rolling back the state' became political dogma, having its intellectual heritage in the work of 'new right' intellectuals such as Fredrich Hayek and Milton Friedman and staunch paternalists such as Charles Murray, who each separately attacked welfare states and the Keynesian model of economy that had reigned supreme in the post-war period up until the 1970s (Wright and Patrick, 2019). Describing a country in a state of considerable flux during the 1980s, Dukelow and Considine (2017: 54) have noted: 'The national debt rose from 53.6% of GDP in 1970 to 123.1% of GDP by 1987. In addition, the losses in the manufacturing sector throughout the 1970s and 1980s outstripped the gains made in creating new employment.'

There was also considerable political turmoil in Ireland in the early 1980s with no less than three governments taking office between 1981 and 1982.

During the decade, unemployment approached 18 per cent, emigration resumed on a significant scale, welfare infrastructure saw increasing pressure (Dukelow, 2011) due to high levels of economic dependence and, as Dukelow and Considine (2017: 55) have noted, 'Unemployed people and their children, women, single parent families, older people, people in institutional care and the travelling community were identified as at particular risk of poverty.'

Factoring in a further sizable cohort in Irish society in the form of the 'working poor' who were also affected by and at risk of poverty, it appears that very few sections of Irish society were unaffected (Powell, 1992, 2017; McCashin, 2004; Dukelow, 2011; Dukelow and Considine, 2017).

What then of the 'doing' of social welfare during this time? One possible way to sum up the decade of the 1980s in Ireland in a welfare context is that it was a time of emerging recognitions, few resources and little positive reform (McCashin, 2004; Dukelow, 2011, 2018; Dukelow and Considine, 2017). Recognising that, despite the dire economic outlook, welfare was still up for debate, and, as a practical expression of the need to have that debate, the government established a commission to review the Irish social security system. This led to what was arguably the first major review of welfare infrastructure since the formation of the state and at least since the debates of the late 1940s (Powell, 1992, 2017; McCashin, 2004; Dukelow, 2011; Dukelow and Considine, 2017). By way of background, in 1982 the National Social Services Board[3] in its pre-budget submission had called for the establishment of a commission to carry out a comprehensive review of the Irish social welfare system. A commitment to establish such a commission formed part of the programme of the Fine Gael–Labour coalition government that came into office in December 1982. The Commission on Social Welfare was established in 1983 and its report was published in 1986. Rather than proposing a fully new system for social welfare, the reforms recommended by the commission were centred on adapting the existing system (Powell, 1992, 2017; Dukelow, 2011). The key reforms proposed by the commission concerned payment structure, social insurance, social assistance and financing. The adequacy of payments was perhaps the most important issue considered, and the commission proposed raising them to ensure a sufficient minimum standard: 'The most important issue dealt with is the specification of a minimally adequate income. Social welfare payments should be set at a level that ensures a minimally adequate standard of living relative to incomes and living standards in society generally' (cited in Powell, 1992: 298).

The commission also favoured keeping the social insurance system. It recommended that all income earners should contribute to, and benefit where appropriate from, social insurance, and favoured a widening of coverage for insurance. However, it also recommended that there should be a comprehensive social assistance scheme for those who did not qualify for social insurance (Curry, 1998; Dukelow, 2011). This proposal was coolly received in political circles. This was due in part to the cost implications of its far-reaching recommendations (Curry, 1998; McCashin, 2004). In many ways, due to the economic outlook at the time of the publication of its report, much of what the commission recommended was unimplementable (Curry, 1998). Nevertheless, in terms of ideas, this was an important report in the Irish welfare landscape and was widely endorsed by entities as diverse as the Bishops' Council along with various trade union groups (Powell, 1992; Dukelow, 2011). In actuality, however, what transpired in the Irish welfare space of the 1980s was very different from what was recommended in the report and was characterised by a move towards surveillance, an increased focus on welfare fraud and the introduction of the workfare paradigm via Job-Search (Powell, 1992, 2017; Dukelow, 2011; Dukelow and Considine, 2017). The beginning of an increased emphasis on conditionality is also something that begins to appear at this time. For example, the requirement for jobseekers to be 'genuinely seeking work' in order to qualify for what was then Unemployment Benefit stems from this period (Dukelow, 2011; Dukelow and Considine, 2017). Taken together, these constitute the beginnings of a shift in the Irish welfare space and undoubtedly denote a formative turn towards activation. Ultimately, these are themes that continue to loom large, and that do and have loomed large for the participants whose testimony forms the basis of the research presented in this book.

Where recessions go, austerity follows

Much of what has gone before in this chapter will not have touched the participants of this study directly. Rather, the echoes of what has heretofore been covered will have possibly informed their experiences; the spectres of deep historical practices will have flitted across the canvases of their lives. The last section of this chapter, however, is different. In a chapter that has sought to both offer a context for the original research presented here while also distilling down historical practices that have echoed across the development of the Irish welfare state, these next paragraphs encounter a heretofore absent sense of immediacy. This is because the period towards which the focus now turns is one that begins in the immediate past and one that has wrought policies and practices that continue to shape, underlie and contribute to experiences in the Irish welfare space in a very direct and experiential way. Whereas what has gone before has given detail to how ideas around the 'doing' of welfare in the Irish welfare space has been a matter of debate and contest across decades of welfare state development, what is presented now represents the outcome of much of this debate. It is where we are at, it is the house we now live in, and it has and continues to garner much research interest (see Whelan, 2020a, 2020b, 2021a; Finn, 2021; McGann, 2021; McGann and Murphy, 2021; Murphy, 2021; Boland and Griffin, 2021 for just some examples).

While at the end of the 1980s Ireland was undoubtedly poor by western European standards, the early 1990s to the late 2000s saw an enormous leap in growth and prosperity in Ireland (Ferriter, 2005). The onset of the Celtic Tiger[4] period saw a huge shift in the real economy away from exports and towards foreign direct investment and domestic construction (Dukelow and Considine, 2014a, 2014b, 2017). During the 1990s, there were some significant improvements to Irish welfare state infrastructure, with new assistance schemes, such as DA in 1996 and OPFP in 1997, being introduced. Despite these apparent advances, no singular policy vision for social welfare was offered at this time, and, when viewed in the light of growing wealth and prosperity, it could be argued that the decade approximately represented by the mid-nineties to the mid-noughties (1995–2005) represents a decade of missed opportunity in the Irish welfare space. This is illustrated in real terms by Cousins (2016: 61) in the following passage:

> In 2007, the Irish social protection system – despite significant increases in welfare rates in the period since 2000 – remained a somewhat limited and segmented system.... Although standard welfare benefits were often higher than in the UK ... overall spending on social protection was one of the lowest in Europe.

So, while Ireland may have had relatively generous rates of payments, it was still an outlier in terms of overall social protection spending. This reality arguably devolved on the way in which Ireland, as a welfare state, maintained its emphasis on selective poverty alleviation rather than meaningful redistribution, meaning that the overall structure of the welfare system did not change; groups were still 'singled out' and high levels of means testing remained an integral part of the welfare system (McCashin and O'Shea, 2009; Murphy, 2012). By the autumn of 2008, any opportunity for growth, change or positive development that may have presented itself in the context of the Irish welfare state was lost with the onset of the global financial crisis.

Putting our house in order

> The effect of the economic crisis and its continuing legacy has markedly changed the environment in which social protection policy is made, with constraints and challenges more closely approximating Pierson's (2001) notion of permanent austerity. (Dukelow and Considine, 2017: 194)

This assertion in respect of the Irish social protection policy landscape sums up the new space into which Irish welfare found itself thrust in the wake of the Great Recession.[5] This was a time of now rapidly changing ideas in the welfare space, happening against a backdrop of a painful recession. Providing a statistical context, Eurostat (2019) figures show that Ireland's general government expenditure as a percentage of GDP reached a high of 65 per cent in 2010, two years after the downturn had begun. In terms of spending on social protection, the figure jumped from 15.5 per cent of government expenditure on social protection as a percentage of GDP in 2008 to 18 per cent by 2009. From here the figures begin to fall, to 16 per cent as of 2012 and as low as 9.5 per cent in 2017. There can be little doubt that the government's policies with regard to social welfare provision in Ireland quickly became characterised by austerity and retrenchment. In this respect, Dukelow and Considine (2014a: 56) have noted that 'Ireland's rapid turn to austerity ... was a forerunner of a wider European turn to austerity'.

Social protection in Ireland became increasingly heavily politicised, coming under intense scrutiny and facing repeated criticism for being overly generous and badly managed (NESC, 2011; Dukelow and Considine, 2014a). The threefold dynamic of a failing construction industry, on which the government had been heavily reliant for exchequer returns, rapidly increasing levels of unemployment and exposure to the international bond market meant that Ireland was effectively broke in the face of a burgeoning social protection bill (NESC, 2011; Donovan and Murphy, 2013). Eventually, Ireland would also come under sustained international pressure, and austerity, along with the budgetary measures it wrought, would be implemented with oversight from the Troika, with which Ireland had entered into a bailout programme and which consisted of the European Union, the European Central Bank and the International Monetary Fund (Donovan and Murphy, 2013; Dukelow and Considine; 2014a; 2017).

Rolling back the state: welfare cuts during the economic crisis

As ideas around welfare began to change to reflect the precarious fiscal space that Ireland was in, direct cuts to welfare payments were numerous during the period 2009–14. For example, in December 2010 it was announced by the then Minister for Finance, the late Brian Lenihan TD, that the rate of payment for both JB and JA was to be reduced by eight Euros per week as of January 2011. Reductions of the same amount were also made in respect of both Maternity and Adoptive Benefit. This effectively meant cuts of between 3.8 and 5.1 per cent to the rates for working-age adults. The same year also saw Child Benefit[6] reduced and higher cuts were introduced for the younger unemployed (Department of Finance,

2010). In December 2011, it was announced by the Minister for Public Expenditure, Brendan Howlin TD, that the basic rates of social welfare payments would remain unchanged for 2012. However, other cost-saving measures were introduced, including a reduction in the length of the fuel season,[7] from 32 to 26 weeks, and standardisation of the Child Benefit rate for all children (Department of Public Expenditure and Reform, 2011). Again, in the proposals announced by Minister Howlin for 2013, basic payments remained unchanged, although other cost saving measures were again introduced. These included a reduction in Child Benefit of 10 Euros per child per month and a reduction in the supports available through the Household Benefits Package[8] (Department of Public Expenditure and Reform, 2012). In a particularly blunt measure that arguably amounted to an effort to either activate or encourage emigration, younger people were also subject to specific and particularly harsh cuts. By 2014, the rate of JA and SWA was cut by 51 per cent for people aged 18–24 and by 30 per cent for those aged 25, the only exception to this being young people who had turned 18 and were leaving state care (Dukelow and Considine, 2014a; 2017). OPFP was also restructured. Until 2015 it had been payable until a claimant's youngest child was aged 18, or 22 if in full-time education, arguably recognising the valuable work of those who care in the home while simultaneously reframing as 'deserving' a previously heavily stigmatised group. The payment now ends when the youngest child turns seven and parents face the prospect of gradually transferring to JA via JST, which is much more activation-focused (Dukelow and Considine, 2017).

The punitive turn: the end of ideas in the Irish welfare space?

The cuts listed in the previous section give a sense of the real impact of the period of austerity wrought by the crisis. However, cuts to welfare rates tell only one part of the story. Ultimately, as a result of this intense period of cutbacks and reforms, Ireland has been left with a much tighter and restrictive system welfare system, ushering in the beginning of continuous compulsion (Bonoli, 2011) in the Irish welfare space. Not only that, but social protection and welfare is now arguably ubiquitously discoursed in extremely negative terms in a way that was perhaps not previously the case, or at least not wholly (Boland and Griffin, 2015a, 2016; Devereux and Power, 2019). It is argued here that this represents a 'punitive turn' that has signalled the 'end of ideas' in the Irish welfare space. In a book that is concerned with experiences, this turn towards compulsive activation is of significant import. For this reason, some of the structural changes that have taken place, and the policies they have devolved on, are briefly discussed. In this respect, the Pathways to Work policy agenda serves as a prime example of this changing dynamic in the Irish welfare space. Because of the implications of this type of policy and the ideas that it represents, and because of its very apparent prominence in the original research presented further on in respect of activation, conditionality and compulsion, it is worth discussing here for contextual and illustrative purposes. Furthermore, bearing out the assertion that we have effectively entered a stage of continuing compulsion within the context of welfare in Ireland, it is worth noting that the Pathways to Work policy has recently been renewed (see GOI, 2021) and that while the contents of the newest iteration of the policy may not directly reflect the data presented here, it nevertheless denotes a commitment on the part of government to pursue a particular vision of welfare.

Pathways to Work

As noted, alongside the obvious implications of cuts and reductions to different payments, the uppermost change in the Irish welfare space was arguably one of structure or dynamic. This was particularly true, initially at least, in respect of unemployment-type payments such as JA and JB. Essentially, the Irish welfare system changed from being a predominantly passive system focusing on job creation, education and training, to an active and punitive system focusing on labour market activation and sanctions (Dukelow, 2011; Boland and Griffin, 2015a, 2016; Dukelow and Considine, 2017). In this respect, much of the Irish welfare state infrastructure was at least aesthetically redesigned, particularly with the launch of Intreo[9] in 2012. As previously mentioned, perhaps one of the most profound examples of this change as articulated in policy terms is to be found in the recently renewed Pathways to Work policy strategy, which has gone through several iterations since its inception (GOI, 2012; 2013; 2015; 2016; 2021).

Described by Boland and Griffin (2018) as 'latecomers' to the realm of activation, the Irish government certainly hit the ground running. In the first iteration of the Pathways to Work policy statement, it was suggested that there would need to be 'more regular and on-going engagement with the unemployed' (GOI, 2012: 5). This was the government's attempt to shorten the time spent on the live register by those who found themselves recently unemployed and to activate those who were viewed as being long-term unemployed. The approach was structured around five strands with a specific emphasis on jobseeker responsibility (GOI, 2012: 5–6):

- More regular and on-going engagement with people who are unemployed
- Greater targeting of Activation places and opportunities
- Incentivising take-up of opportunities
- Incentivising employers to provide more jobs for people who are unemployed, and

- Reforming institutions to deliver better services to people who are unemployed.

These strands will ensure that Ireland's greatest resource, its people, will no longer remain on the Live Register for lengthy periods without an appropriate offer of assistance from the State. In return, individuals will be made aware of their responsibility to commit to job-search and/ or other employment, education and training activities or risk losing welfare entitlements.

With respect to the changing nature of ideas around welfare and the shift from passive to active measures, the document also referenced this distinction directly through making international comparisons (2012: 10): 'Activation policies should seek to increase the employability of job seekers and to encourage them to be more active in their efforts to find work. However, in Ireland we have traditionally adopted a passive approach to supporting job seekers compared with other OECD countries.'

Also contained within the policy and consistent with a 'case management' style of engagement was the introduction of 'probability of exit' profiling for all new claimants at this time (GOI, 2012). Claimants were also asked to sign a 'social contract' of 'rights and responsibilities'; and to commit to a 'progression' plan. The policy made no pretence of the very real possibility and intention to deploy sanctions for those seen not to be meeting the required standard of the active jobseeker (Boland and Griffin, 2016), as shown in the following excerpt from an indicative case study (GOI, 2012: 29) contained within the document:

Barry appears on a report after 4 months, that he is still receiving benefits. Barry is asked for evidence that he is genuinely seeking work and is offered access to support services. *Barry is reminded about the possibility of sanctioning if he is not seen to be genuinely seeking work.* A similar process is triggered at two monthly intervals. [Emphasis added.]

The potential for sanctions such as this were given a legislative basis in the Social Welfare Miscellaneous Provisions Act 2013, which provided for sanctions lasting up to nine weeks for a failure or refusal to attend activation meetings. Interestingly, the original policy cites the liberal welfare regimes of Australia and the UK as examples of places where these types of activation measures were deemed to have proved successful and apparently ignored other available research that illustrated the ineffectiveness of activation approaches along with the tendency for such policies to expand precarious employment and the low-wage sector (Konle-Seidl and Eichhorst, 2008). A further point of interest arises from the policy's acknowledgement at that time (GOI, 2012) of the potential to allow private 'job-matching' operators to begin contracting in the Irish welfare space.

In terms of trajectory, the policy strategy continued in much the same vein in 2013, using the same 'five-strand approach' accompanied now by a '50-point action plan' and an ambition to double-down on and intensify activation efforts. Very little changed in the 2015 document, which more or less rehashed what had gone before. The 2016–20 plan, however, added a sixth strand, namely 'building workforce skills'. By this time, Ireland was entering a phase of economic recovery where the mass unemployment of previous years had stabilised, and unemployment figures were beginning to resemble frictional levels. However, despite this, the focus on activation remained strong, and attention turned towards activating new cohorts as the government (GOI, 2016: 14) sought to: 'Increase active labour market participation by people of a working age (including people with disabilities and lone parents) so as to help ensure a supply of labour at competitive rates and to minimise welfare dependency.'

Part of the intent in this statement was actualised by things like the restructuring of OPFP in 2015. It is clear from the approach taken in this document that with the crisis now over, the government was keen to begin focusing on groups or cohorts that had, up until now, not been at the centre of the Pathways to Work policy programme. Furthermore, those to be targeted for labour-force activation were wide-ranging. Lone parents and people with disabilities were not the only cohorts mentioned as potential candidates, with the document (2016: 17) also naming the following groups:

- qualified adult dependants of DSP clients;
- part-time workers;
- people who are unemployed but are not in receipt of a welfare payment;
- people with a disability;
- 'homemakers';
- students; and
- carers, when their caring responsibilities are complete.

Taken together, the measures contained in the multiple Pathways to Work policy suite arguably demonstrate the punitive and compulsive turn in the Irish welfare space. It could also be argued that such policies are indicative of a broader ideological 'attack' on welfare and on the welfare state as well as on those who find themselves at its door. At the very least, policies such as these are illustrative of changed ideas around welfare and the 'doing' of welfare in the Irish welfare space. While it is not the intention here to deeply review the policies in question, it is nevertheless important to critically interpret them on the basis that they constitute an example of the policy paradigm that has gone on to shape experiences in the Irish welfare space.

As noted earlier, a further development of interest, and something that was alluded to as far back the original Pathways to Work document (GOI, 2012) has been the relatively recent introduction of private job-matching services into the infrastructure of the Irish welfare state via the JobPath[10] initiative by two private contractors, Turas Nua and Seetec.[11] Ostensibly tasked with finding employment for people who have been on the live register for a period exceeding 12 months, there has been some analysis – of job matching as a practice both before and since the introduction of private job-matching entities into the Irish welfare space – which suggests that the approach taken, in reality, is something more akin to 'any job is better than none' (Collins and Murphy, 2016; Boland, 2018; Boland and Griffin, 2018; Whelan, 2020a; 2020b). This *is* borne out in the original research presented here, meaning the advent of entities such as these entering the Irish welfare space is particularly notable here, as direct experiences, specifically with Turas Nua, form a sizeable part of the participants' testimony. Drawing attention to them here also serves to further demonstrate the changing nature of welfare and of how it is now governed and delivered in the Irish context. With very few arguments against measures such as these at the level of politics, the birth of the punitive Irish welfare state arguably also represents the 'death of ideas' around the 'doing' of welfare. As Pathways to Work 2021–25 sees the policy suite enter its fifth cycle in the midst of a pandemic, it is, at the very least, a signifier that entrenched ideas are incredibly resistant to change.

So where does Ireland fit?

Taking account of this history, Ireland has undoubtedly come to represent a somewhat unique welfare regime, though it is still commonly cited as a liberal model and for the most part, this simple description still carries a lot of weight. Yet it is worth unpacking for clarity. Drawing, then, on the work of Esping-Andersen (1990), it may be helpful to set out the commonly prescribed welfare state models as follows:

- **a conservative or corporatist model:** strongly based on the concept of social insurance also known as contributory payment schemes;
- **a liberal or residual model:** strongly based on social assistance-type payments, also known as non-contributory schemes; and
- **a social democratic or universal model:** strongly based on universal or non-means-tested payments.

In reality, things are seldom this simple and most welfare states have some of the features of all three types. Ireland, in particular, as will have been made obvious by the complexity of its history, has been difficult to characterise. In this respect, Dukelow and Considine (2014a: 56) note that:

... in social policy terms, while typically linked with the liberal welfare regime, the range of influences on Ireland's welfare development has meant that its position as a liberal welfare state is open to some ambiguity. It has been observed that it 'defies classification' and is better described as a 'hybrid regime', with links in particular to the welfare tradition of the conservative/corporatist regime.

Noting this difficulty, Ireland, along with Britain, Australia, Canada and the US, does still generally tend to be cited as a liberal or residual welfare state and it has certainly increased its emphasis on liberal welfare state mechanics in recent years. This task of modelling welfare state types, particularly in Europe, begins most notably in the work of Esping-Andersen (1990) in his book entitled *The three worlds of welfare capitalism*. It has since been built on by large-scale institutional work concerning welfare attitudes across jurisdictions by authors such as Larsen (2006) and Wendt et al (2011). For its part, the work of Larsen convincingly shows that particular types of welfare state models beget particular types of attitudes and produce particular levels of stigma, ultimately producing particular experience types. Simply put, this rests on the assertion, illustrated here by Dukelow and Considine (2017: 195), that: 'While social security may be represented as quite a technical system of finance, it is underpinned by competing ideological traditions and values, which have different views of the system and its purpose.'

Adapted from Aspalter (2011: 15), who adds a further category in the form of a 'conservative welfare regime', it is possible to get some sense of the complexity of these different ideologies, traditions and values and of how they are reflected in the policies and approaches of different welfare regimes in Table 1.1, which uses four ideal welfare state types for the purposes of comparison.

Drawing on the descriptions in this table and taking the whole of this chapter into account, it could be argued that Ireland, under the influence of Catholic social teaching, certainly has strong historical ties to both corporatist/ Christian-democratic and conservative welfare regimes, favouring the family as the vehicle through which welfare should be administered, albeit this was largely through non-interventionist social policy as opposed to any attempt at preventative social policy (Dukelow and Considine, 2017; Powell, 2017). However, when we consider the contemporary Irish welfare state in the light of Table 1.1, we see that it has continuing and strong links with the liberal model through a reliance on means testing, a favouring of the individual and the market in terms of focus, particularly in the past 20 years or so, and consequently, a weak level of decommodification and redistributive justice. In summary, Ireland as a welfare state is at once a product of religious, political and moral ideology of conservatism and of colonial legacy. It is, generally speaking, best described as a liberal welfare state. Yet it also retains some

Table 1.1: Comparison of ideal-typical welfare regimes

	Social democratic welfare regime	Corporatist/ Christian democratic welfare regime	Liberal welfare regime	Conservative welfare regime
Dominant social policy instruments	Universal social security Public social services Public employment Social transfers (redistribution by way of subsidies, social assistance, and taxation)	Occupational social security Preferential treatment of special interest groups Corporatism in social service provision (especially non-governmental organisations and the Church) Social transfers (redistribution by way of subsidies, social assistance, and taxation)	Means-tested welfare benefits Private savings and insurance Tax programmes (mostly tax cuts benefitting the rich)	Occupational social security Preferential treatment of special interest groups Emphasis on employment-based welfare provision Social investment (investment in education, health, and housing)
Focus in social welfare policy on	Individual State	Family State	Individual Market	Family Market
Degree of decommodification	Strong	Medium	Weak	Weak
Degree of redistribution (effect on stratification)	Strong	Medium	Weak	Weak to medium
Examples	Sweden	Germany	US, UK, Ireland	Japan

Source: Adapted from Aspalter (2011: 15)

corporatist features through limited social insurance. As has been seen, the Irish welfare state is a product of church, state and capital (Powell, 2017) emerging in an ad-hoc way and over many decades. We might therefore finally say that that the Irish example represents a hybrid welfare state with predominately and increasingly liberal features. It has much in common with welfare the liberal welfare states of the UK, the US, Canada and Australia. It has some features in common with corporatist welfare states such as that found in Germany and little in common with the social democratic welfare states of the Nordic countries.

2

Welfare, marginality and social liminality: life in the welfare 'space'

The word liminality undoubtedly conjures the notion of being 'in-between'. Perhaps it is most famously acquitted in the religious domain of the Christian afterlife in the form of 'limbo'. Limbo is that place in-between, that place where persons go when their souls are not pure enough to enter heaven. It is neither heaven nor hell, but something outside of each. You will not experience the torture of the dammed there, but neither will you be privy to the blessed relief that is heaven. It is the first circle that Dante enters after crossing the Acheron. There he finds unbaptised babies and virtuous pagans who, while not deserving of eternal damnation, have chosen, where they could, rationality over the spiritual and so must remain outside of heaven (Alighieri, 1995 [1321]). Liminality then is conceptualised here as being at once 'outside' and 'in-between'. It might be useful to think of it as a nondescript corridor. This corridor is 'somewhere'; it is also between many destinations in the form of adjoining rooms, yet it is also outside of these rooms.

Here, in the first of the chapters presenting the empirical material, I use the concepts of marginality and social liminality within the context of welfare recipiency. In doing so, effectively, what I show is that for many of the people I spoke with, being reliant on welfare begets, at first, an often very marginal existence and that this in turn can lead to social liminality in a number of ways. It is not a hard task to show the presence of marginality for those receiving welfare by looking at available keyline figures. For example, the weekly income threshold for a single adult to stay above the 'at risk of poverty' rate stands at €252.11 approximately (Social Justice Ireland, 2019). The typical rate for a single adult claiming a non-contributory welfare payment stands at €203 per week. This figure is substantially below the weekly 'at risk of poverty' threshold and so suggests that a reliance on welfare as a primary strand of income almost guarantees a relatively marginal existence. Social liminality in the context of welfare is a somewhat more intangible concept, yet even here there has been some work of note. In the literature, Boland and Griffin (2015a) have addressed the idea of liminality directly in the context of the jobseeker. Drawing on a set of interviews, they show that through being a jobseeker and therefore experiencing the requirement to continually seek work, an artificial liminality is created, and this is characterised by uncertainty, self-questioning and tedium. I effectively take this up here and move it beyond just jobseekers to include other groups of welfare recipients. I also offer a further analysis by taking account of the nature of the relationship between the marginal and the liminal, which, I suggest, are intimately related. Before beginning, I wish to acknowledge and thereby pre-empt two important rejoinders. First, I note that while I am using the idea of liminality in a social context to describe a set of largely very negative experiences, it has elsewhere been used and seen as something much more positive.[1] I also acknowledge that it is a concept that has been used across an array of social scientific areas very effectively (see Warner and Gabe [2004] and Simich et al [2009] for further examples of the concept in use). If there is any novelty in the way the concept is presented here, it lies in the assertion that marginality and social liminality are intimately intertwined to the point of being symbiotic. Marginality is often experienced first, with the effects of leading a consistently marginal existence ultimately leading to social liminality. Nevertheless, it is not suggested that this is necessarily a linear progression, as experiences of social liminality may be frequent but fleeting or may be present consistently; this is wholly dependent on each individual. I also wish to show how marginality and social liminality are themselves affected by a number of distinct experience types and social conditions. For this reason, I introduce Patricia here first and present her experiences as a case study before drawing on the experiences of other participants.

Articulating a marginal and socially liminal existence: what does it mean to exist in this 'space'?

As with work of a qualitative nature carried out in the UK (Garthwaite, 2015a, 2016; Patrick, 2017), the stark reality of what it can mean to eke out an existence when social welfare or benefits are your primary source of income was explicitly evident in the findings of this study in a variety of ways. For example, in an excerpt that articulates and addresses many of the key aspects of marginality and social liminality, Patricia notes that: "… I feel like that my next cheque, will you say, is in the hands of these people. They can press a button and it's up to them whether I get money or not, you know. And you really feel that, like. You really, really do."

The "these people" that Patricia refers to are the administrators of social welfare. When I interviewed Patricia, she was receiving JA while also trying to gain qualification as a social worker. In the period prior to starting study and in the periods in between college years, she was often unemployed, and, as a result, entitled to make a claim for JA. Patricia was deeply affected by her experiences and her story speaks particularly strongly to the marginal and socially liminal nature of being reliant on welfare. In the previous excerpt, she talks about the level of control she feels welfare administrators had over her life. This is particularly apparent in her perception of their ability to conceivably cut her off with the 'touch of a button'. In interview,

Patricia also spoke about a family history of receiving welfare in a way she felt delineated her and her family from the rest of society, positioning them on the edge, excluded and disadvantaged:

> 'I've grown up with parents on Disability or Widow's.[2] And as I said, you do feel like you're on the edge of society. You're not involved. You're not involved with like work. You're not involved – like little things. Like, say, getting involved with the local camogie.[3] If you don't have the money, if you don't have that extra bit of money to get involved with activities outside of school, straight away you feel that exclusion. And usually people who are on social welfare can't afford those extra things, you know, like joining clubs, joining activities, you know.'

This excerpt sums up the nature of what it means to experience being on the margins, materially and otherwise, while also experiencing social liminality. It speaks to the inherently liminal and marginal nature of the 'welfare space'. Being on the "edge", a word Patricia herself chooses, seems to speak to a sense of place and conjures the notion of existing on the margins or of being close to being outside. Much of this is characterised by an inability to afford to take part in society through simple things like joining a club or taking part in social activities. An absence from the labour market also compounds feelings of being outside or 'in-between'. In her later, more personal experiences, Patricia also clearly articulated a marginal and socially liminal existence in relation to what she felt was the intrusive nature of welfare in her life to the point where the language she uses suggests it began to permeate much of her everyday existence:

> '… sending me letters – why didn't I turn up for this course? Why didn't I turn up for this course? You didn't attend this course – as if I am legally obliged to go to these courses, you know. And I was just, like, would these people ever F-off…. Like to be in that vortex all the time … like I always say it, it's like having a tag on your foot. You are constantly at the mercy of those people.'

Patricia describes being "at the mercy" of welfare scheme administrators. It is clear from the language used that a reliance on welfare can mean being in a difficult and uncomfortable space, with Patricia specifically referring to it as a "vortex". She also talks about feeling as though she had a "tag" on her foot, suggesting a sense of latent criminalisation or problematisation accompanying welfare recipiency. Having recognised this marginal and liminal space in which she had lived both as a child and as an adult, Patricia's primary goal is to escape from it; to strive for something different, to shed the skin of exclusion and to leave the welfare space:

'I suppose growing up on social welfare it's always kind of like you want, would you say, a slice of normality. You know, you want to be part of society on a different level. You know, you want to have the career, you want to have the qualifications, you want to be out working. You know, like there is that huge sense of, you know, I want something better.'

The language Patricia uses here clearly speaks to a socially liminal and marginal existence and clearly denotes a sense of place. She talks of wanting to be "part of society on a different level", the implication being that many aspects of life, at the level of welfare recipient, are somewhat less than the ideal; life is lived somewhere 'in-between', and, again, not in a place where there is comfort or where a person would willingly stay. In fact, the language used by Patricia speaks explicitly to a desire to escape. She also talks about wanting "a slice of normality", which speaks to living in a space that is somewhere less than what might be perceived as 'normal' and so denotes the idea of the 'social demotion' that accompanies being in receipt of welfare.

In presenting how Patricia articulates marginality and social liminality, it is arguably clear that marginality and disadvantage are more visceral or physical and therefore immediately recognisable; conversely, social liminality is somewhat more intangible – it is as much about social space as it is about physical space. As previously suggested, when seen in this way, marginality and social liminality are separate, yet, arguably, symbiotic entities in the sense that continual marginality, cumulative disadvantage and exclusion feed a sense of liminality, a sense of being 'in-between'. Having used excerpts from Patricia's interview as a case study to give a sense of how a marginal and socially liminal existence is articulated by those in receipt of welfare, and before moving on to consider the experiences of other participants, it is possible to point to a number of specific factors that coalesce to contribute these experiences. These are:

- poverty, material disadvantage and instability;
- a loss of autonomy and control;
- the inability to take part in society;
- experiencing social demotion.

I address each of these in the following section. In doing so, I begin to draw in the experiences of the other participants.

Poverty, material disadvantage and instability

Examples of how people experience a marginal and socially liminal existence could easily be drawn from across the dataset and they are related to a variety of issues. Key among these, perhaps unsurprisingly, is poverty and material disadvantage. In the first instance, a reliance on welfare can mean a thoroughly marginal existence and one often defined by living week to week or even day to day. This is mentioned by Lisa, a long-term recipient of JA, who, at the time of interview, continued to receive the payment at a reduced rate due to taking up part-time employment:

> '... so you learn to kind of ignore the bills, because if you let that into your brain it's going to eat away at you and build up serious stress. So you just go like that – right, I'll get to that bill when I have it. They can't get it until I have it. So you have that kind of mentality of living. It's kind of very weekly, very daily kind of sense of living.'

This financial instability described by Lisa was strongly echoed across the participant group. Jane, a long-term recipient of OPFP with two children who, at the time of interview, had recently transitioned on to JST, gives several examples that demonstrate the instability and material disadvantage that can accompany and contribute to feelings of being in a marginal and liminal space. First, in the context of unstable housing, she says:

> '... so it's just unstable and I don't know when – you know, you have a two-year contract but what after that? What if the landlord wants to raise it up? And we would love – I would love – to have my own home. You know, that is my goal for the future. And so, yeah, I do feel like that's not a great place to be.'

Second, Jane talks of not being able to afford basic things compared with those who are not in receipt of welfare and whom she perceives as being 'better off':

> 'I'm poorer than them. And, you know, there's times where, like, when it comes to the children's schoolbooks – you know, once a year you've to buy schoolbooks – it's nothing for them, you know, to get the schoolbooks, whereas I'm weeks beforehand in a sweat trying to put away €20 a week to get up – so, yeah, materially I feel less than and I feel that's not great.'

Here we see the reality of a marginal existence described by Jane in stark detail: the uncertainty of tenure, the stress of stretching to afford basic things like schoolbooks and the sense of being 'poor'. It is also possible to get a sense of the social liminality that Jane has experienced through the acknowledgement of a sense of place. Jane talks about aspects of her life with language that clearly transmits a sense of place, somewhere that is "not a great place to be". She also talks about how her experiences make her feel "less than", evoking a sense of social demotion. This has a deep effect on her and, like Patricia, having conceptualised the space she is in this way, her goal is to ultimately exit or escape: "So as of now still on social welfare with the goal of getting off social welfare ... my goal is to come off it, so clearly it's not something I like."

The sense of wanting to exit the welfare space, usually at some undisclosed or undefined point in the future, was something that emerged strongly for almost all of the participants. Again, this was usually articulated in the sense of material disadvantage and the longing for something better, and this is something that people experiencing poverty and hardship commonly describe (Lister, 2021). However, it also denotes the notion of space or place in the context of welfare, not as a destination but rather as an impermanent space, as somewhere it would be better to be away from, a place that is somehow 'in-between' where a person perceives others to be, and where they ultimately wish to be themselves.

A loss of autonomy and control

A further key feature of marginality and social liminality is found in the ceding of autonomy and control that comes with receiving welfare. Martin is a jobseeker who was, technically speaking, long-term unemployed[4] at the time of interview. He had been deeply affected by his experiences of the welfare system and this was apparent, not only in what he said in his interview, but in his demeanour before, during and after it. He informed me that he was very reluctant to come forward and had only done so as he felt he wanted and needed to share his experiences. Martin was also one of the people I spoke to who continued to make contact long after the time of interview. However, he needed numerous reassurances as to the confidentially of the interview process, clearly worried that he would be 'punished' were it to become known he had spoken to me.[5] As described by Patricia earlier, this spoke to the nature of control and power that Martin perceived, rightly or wrongly, the social welfare authorities had over him. How he went on to articulate these experiences illustrates a clear sense of social liminality through a lack of autonomy and control:

'There's definitely a watch. You're definitely under surveillance. Well, not that I can prove, but that's what I felt, that you're – you know, like, for example, last summer I knew not to go near town during the day because they were kind of looking for anyone who was kind of, you know, unemployed, hanging around town, maybe is up to no good.... So they've instant access to your information. Or who's he? You know, and there's obviously information shared between the police and between the Department of Social Protection.'

Whether accurate or not, Martin was clearly deeply affected, ultimately feeling criminalised and under surveillance for being in receipt of welfare, to the point of altering his behaviour and avoiding certain places at certain times. This clearly took a toll on his sense of self as well as his sense of place:

'There could be times where I could say it to myself, you know, I'm not trying hard enough, why is this happening to me? That kind of self-scrutiny or self-doubt that, you know, maybe you're not doing something right. There'd be constant questioning of myself … there'd always be that critical analysis I'd have in my head, you know, from time to time that I'd say, you know, how long is this going to go on for? I don't want to be in this situation, you know.'

Martin is clearly describing being in a space in which he is deeply unhappy and one from which he wishes to escape, going so far as to blame himself for not being able to. Lisa echoes Martin's sense of the pervasiveness of welfare scrutiny into all aspects of a recipient's life:

'It's not a pleasant, encouraging space that kind of helps you to develop into a fully functioning human being, like, you know. It's definitely not – you know, and the constant, you know, the contact that's requested, you know, for people that have issues, like, it's almost like a full job trying – you know, a full-time job trying to keep up with the paperwork demands and requests and get this, get that. And [it] takes weeks to get these paper trails going, you know, and delays in payments and then – you know, you can never – you can't pay your bills on time. So it does become very dominant, like, in terms of how you live your life.'

It is clear from what Lisa says that she views welfare recipiency with a sense of place and space. She talks about it as not being a "pleasant, encouraging space", and also points out that being reliant on welfare can quickly become the dominant theme in a recipient's life, becoming like a "full-time job", accompanied by constant requests for contact. In this respect, what both Martin and Lisa articulate, and what was also clear across the sample in general, is highly suggestive of what Boland and Griffin (2016) have termed the 'ungenerous gift' of welfare in their own study, which contained a sample of participants made up of those receiving JB and JA. The notion of an 'ungenerous gift' is the suggestion that in order to receive the welfare to which a person may be entitled, they first need to give authority to officials in the DSP to monitor and effectively police major aspects of their lives. Both here, and in the work of Boland and Griffin (2016), entering a space where a ceding of control and a loss of autonomy as a result of a reliance on welfare is the norm, is starkly illustrated. This arguably feeds into a sense of social liminality for welfare recipients. Boland and Griffin's (2015a) work on the artificial liminality created in part by the unceasing administrative burden of being a welfare recipient and the toll this takes is also relevant here with Lisa, in particular, describing the "full-time" nature of the jobseeker role.

A further factor through which recipients experienced a loss of autonomy and control can be found in the way in which they are often required to open up or lay bare aspects of their private lives to scrutiny. This level of surveillance is something that begins to skirt very closely towards the types of theories we might more readily associate with the criminological literature, evoking the Foucauldian spectre of the panopticon and tallying with Jørgensen's (2018) suggestion that treating welfare recipients in this way accentuates the societal perception of them as being criminal or criminalised. Consequently, they are likely to feel criminalised themselves, rather than simply being and feeling like persons in need of welfare and support. For example, Scarlett, a long-term recipient of OPFP with two children, talks about having to submit bank statements as a part of maintaining her claim and of how this poses a dilemma for her in respect to what might show up in terms of her purchases:

'... that's my private life, I feel. And yes they supplement me – right now they supplement me.... But I feel that you know, I, you know, work within my means and, like, let's say I want to order Just Eat[6] for the kids or I want to get something nice, you know, that's up to me and I would have felt embarrassed if, you know, that was on my six months' bank account.'

This was common for a number of participants but particularly for those receiving OPFP where a necessity to submit bank statements seems to be more prominent in practice. Jane makes a similar observation: "If I have something that I spent, sometimes you look at it – you know if you went to McDonald's and you put it on your debit card or something and you're like oh, that doesn't look good, you know!"

Grace, who is also a long-term recipient of OPFP with one child and who is talking here in the context of a night out, has also experienced something very similar:

'I mean, like I'll put it this way: I'd look at it and I'd say are they going to think now that I spent – you'd be, like, ooh, I forgot that when I went out that night. I used my card in the Crane Lane[7] and I bought – you know, you can see the kind of four – well, you obviously can't see exactly what I bought, but like the four or six Euros or the four glasses of wine or whatever.'

It is clear from how Scarlett, Jane and Grace have described their separate experiences that opening up elements of what would perhaps normally be deemed as the private details of a person's life to scrutiny by anonymous welfare officials contributes to the sense of ceding personal autonomy and control. It is, in effect, a submission to and for judgement, and, while the criteria for that judgement may not, in actuality, be based on the nature of items purchased, it nevertheless denotes that welfare recipients exist in a socially liminal space where the rules for the receipt of assistance are imbued with the sense of surveillance and are stringently enforced. Undoubtedly, the experiences described here overlap with and fall under the category of welfare conditionality and so speak to the effect that welfare conditionality can have. This will be explored more fully in Chapter 4.

The inability to take part in society

In describing a marginal and socially liminal existence, Patricia spoke about not being able to take part in society at a basic level and this was something that affected all respondents in different ways. For example, Martin describes the exclusion and marginality he experienced due to being unable to get involved in social activities and of gradually withdrawing into a socially liminal space as a result:

> 'Well, obviously, if you wanted to do a certain sport and because there was a cost involved in doing a certain sport, obviously, you know, you would have that barrier ... so I've found myself withdrawing more from wanting to interact socially, definitely, which I find very troubling because I'd really like to get involved in, you know, social activities.... Well, very reclusive. That tends to be the angle that will come into my brain. Maybe I should just separate myself from people.'

Martin talks at first about the inability to take part in social activities as a result of being unable to afford to do so and so this denotes economic marginality. Following this, however, he talks about a purposeful withdrawal from society, a separating of himself from people. Again, the inability to meaningfully take part in social activity was common across the group. For example, Gail, a long-term recipient of DA, talks about becoming detached due to the pressure and financial reality of relying on welfare as a primary strand of income:

> 'So you become extremely detached from reality and society and, as you say, lots of public events or interests or whatever you don't go to because you haven't got the money. And when it comes down to kids you have other parents saying, "Oh, I'll take them all to the cinema

and I'll take them all to the Monkey Maze[8] and I'll take them" – and you're going, "Hmm, I couldn't even take my own daughter never mind my own daughter and four other children." It's very, very difficult.'

The language used by Gail speaks at first to the reality of living on a limited income and simply not having the money to take part in social activities. She also describes a social pressure that arises in the inability to reciprocate when it comes to things like children's activities. Ultimately, she suggests, this results in a detachment "from reality and society". Again, what is arguably clear from both Martin and Gail is that the marginal feeds into and ultimately becomes an aspect of the liminal, a social separation, at first borne out of necessity but often becoming intentional later on.

While what I have presented so far denotes an explicit and very tangible inability to take an active part in particular aspects of society, there can also be more subtlety in what it means to be unable to take part in society. Aside from the inability to take part in the social, there are other, less obvious perhaps, but still impactful aspects of not being able to take part. One such example is not being able to take part in leading what could be construed to be a 'good life':

'I would be really conscious of my kids' health, like, when my kids were younger, and I really had to let an awful lot of that go because I could not afford to buy the nice healthy stuff. Some weeks I could have afforded to buy the beans and nuggets and the shitty stuff, you know, and I hated that. I really hated that.'

Here, Scarlett talks about an inability to provide what she perceives as being a good diet for her children. Again, this clearly indicates the financial and economic marginality inherent in a reliance on welfare and the lack of options that this entails; yet it also speaks to a sense of place, a place where providing a good diet for one's children is distinctly out of reach. This inability to take part through a lack of options was also something that was strongly articulated by Graham, a recipient of JA, who was long-term unemployed at the time of interview: "… it's like this: I had no money, so I had no credit on my phone, so I can't ring these arseholes. You see, it's like this now: poverty is about the lack of options, not about the lack of money, you know what I mean?"

Graham explicitly characterises poverty as a "lack of options". In terms of context, in the given excerpt, Graham is talking about an inability to contact the DSP to cancel an appointment. As a result of this, he claims, his payment was stopped: "They stopped my payment…. So I was not getting paid for nearly three months, because I missed the first appointment."

What is clear, from both Scarlett and Graham, is that an inability to take part can be characterised by more than simply being unable to afford to engage in social activities. Being in a social space where a person is reliant on social welfare as a primary strand of income can ultimately be limiting in many ways, some more obvious than others. Of course, in the first instance this strongly suggests economic marginality and material disadvantage; however, it also denotes social liminality in the sense of being in a place where options are limited and where things can appear to be forever out of reach. While this is presented here in the context of receiving welfare as a primary strand of income, an income on which people must try to survive, it also resonates with much of the literature on experiences of poverty in general (Lister, 2021).

Experiencing social demotion

A further aspect of how participants described experiences of the marginal and the socially liminal can be found in their sense of being socially demoted as a result of seeking to realise their entitlement. In general, experiences of the claims process and the subsequent need to maintain a claim were negative for those interviewed, sometimes overtly so. Furthermore, in the context of marginality and social liminality, there were clear elements of social demotion in many of the participants' experiences that are also extremely relevant here. For example, Alan, a periodic recipient of JA and BTEA, perceived his experiences of making and maintaining his claim extremely negatively and with clear overtones of social demotion:

> 'I always felt like I had done something terribly wrong when I was interacting with these people. Like there was always this guise of suspicion over me, like, what does he want? I hated, I dreaded going in there, you know. Because even though I knew I hadn't done anything wrong I always felt like I had, you know. I always felt guilty of something.'

The experiences that Alan describes here are not those of a citizen entering a social welfare office and being positively assisted to avail of his rights at a time of need; rather, there is a sense of being judged or suspected, to the point where it becomes an experience that Alan dreads repeating. Ultimately, this treatment suggests to Alan that he is not wanted there, and that support would only be grudgingly given, which is, in turn, reflective of a liberal welfare regime and the way in which allowance or assistance-type payments are designed, being based on need within defined parameters rather than on rights: "… so that was this very signal to me like we don't want you, you know, we're not interested in supporting you even, you know, when you need it".

Again, this was a common experience across the participant group. Scarlett, in the context of making an initial claim, makes a series of observations that are very close to those made by Alan: "It's like they're taking you to be someone who wants to, like – I don't know how to say it. I think they take everybody as a fraud until proven otherwise to be totally honest.... It makes me feel like you're being investigated."

Patricia makes a similar observation:

'... like, the minute you went in there you could feel, like, the animosity coming from the people that work behind the counter. Like it felt like everyone that walked in the door was a fraudster, you know what I mean? It's like we were all out to commit some sort of fraud against the state and, you know, they made you feel every bit of it.'

The language used by all three to describe their separate experiences is inherently negative. Alan talks about feeling as though he had done something "terribly wrong" and both Scarlett and Patricia use the word "fraud". Nowhere in these experiences is idea of a welfare state, or welfare commons (Jensen and Tyler, 2015; Boland and Griffin, 2016; Whelan, 2021b), based on inherent rights; rather, the tone is one of suspicion and the message seems clear: seeking welfare is wrong and doing so can result in a much-reduced social status. The way in which each describes being treated or perceived also evokes the notion that the administrators of welfare and the way in which welfare is administered can itself have a stigmatising effect. (Baumberg, 2014, 2016; Boland and Griffin, 2015a, 2016; Patrick, 2017; Welfare Conditionality, 2019). Clearly then, this marks a social delineation that suggests that to enter the world of the welfare recipient is to enter a new, ultimately marginal and liminal, social space.

More on marginality and social liminality

The concepts of marginality and social liminality are, on their own, significant aspects of what is presented here and therefore hard to fully grasp. Poverty and material disadvantage, ultimately resulting in marginality, are ongoing issues in the context of welfare recipiency in multiple jurisdictions. This is not new, and therefore it was no surprise to find the presence of such experiences writ large across the data. What is perhaps new here is the idea that marginality and social liminality seem to begin to function in tandem, sometimes immediately, sometimes over the longer term. As people experience more and more marginality, they can find themselves drawn deeper and deeper into a socially liminal space, a space that offers little comfort and in fact can have a devastating effect on the self-esteem of those who occupy it. This effect is also common in work emanating from the UK (Garthwaite, 2016; Patrick, 2017). It is also worth mentioning that there is more potentially contributing to social liminality than the key factors described so far. Absence from the labour market has been a huge factor for many of the respondents, with prolonged absences significantly contributing to poor mental health and low self-esteem and, again, this mirrors research conducted in the UK (Garthwaite, 2016; Patrick 2017). However, a more fulsome account of this will be given in Chapter 3. Social liminality is also evoked in the geography of welfare recipiency and the welfare state, in long queues, in waiting rooms, in Intreo offices and local social welfare offices, and in post offices up and down the country. Olive, a former JB and JA claimant who was, at the time of interview, in the process of transitioning on to a Tús scheme, summed up this phenomenon in a way that gives a real sense of the spaces that welfare recipients are sometimes forced to occupy:

'So if I just went in to say, "Right, I've got to drop in this form, I've got to drop in this letter", there could be a hundred – not exaggerating – about a hundred people ahead of me. So you were standing out. It was a very public, sometimes a very damp sort of wait, and it was very daunting.'

These experiences, as described by Olive, are of a modern welfare infrastructure, and yet parallels with the past persist. For example, Spicker (1984: 7), in addressing the functionality of the poor law, noted that those who sought relief under the poor law were effectively: '… the objects of a policy intended to deter them from seeking help and mark them off from the normal members of society'.

This 'marking off' denotes space in the psychosocial sense, a social demotion. Place in historical instances was visibly and physically delineated by virtue of the fact that recipients often had to physically enter the confines of a workhouse, denoting a firm and apparent spatial separation (Powell, 1992; 2017; Dukelow and Considine, 2017). This spatial separation was physical, real and geographically bounded. Recipients had to 'go to' and 'enter' a designated space and stay there in order that they might be relieved. Therefore, the marginalisation and the accompanying liminality was a thoroughly physical and visceral delineation, something that occupied physical space and could be pointed to, observed, and even touched. In this respect, there is arguably a dialogue that encapsulates, at a conceptual and partly experiential level, an overlap between the empirical material presented here and historical practices and, though we may have moved a long way from the days of the poor laws, certain logics, particularly the logic of socially demoting those in need of assistance, seemingly persist (Whelan, 2021b).

In concluding this chapter on marginality and social liminality, it is argued that, together in particular, they are a very real feature of the experiences of welfare recipients at various levels. Ultimately, I have aimed to show that living a marginal existence and doing so while occupying a socially liminal space makes up a very real element of what it means to receive welfare and is itself made up of a number of features, namely:

- poverty, material disadvantage and instability;
- a loss of autonomy and control;
- the inability to take part in society;
- experiencing social demotion.

Many of the people I spoke to, the people whose voices have been introduced in this chapter, will, at different times, have experienced all four. The data presented here are, of course, limited to a specific geographical location. Yet they do tally with data from other jurisdictions[9] in many ways, which in turn reflects what McIntosh and Wright (2019) along with Wright and Patrick (2019) have referred to and what I have referred to here as 'shared typical' aspects of lived experiences in the context of welfare recipiency that go beyond and across local or jurisdictional boundaries. In the next chapter, I turn my attention to further 'shared typical' aspects of lived experiences in the context of welfare by demonstrating how the work ethic has an impact on those receiving welfare.

3

The effect of the work ethic

Having looked at how being a welfare recipient can mean occupying a marginal and socially liminal space, I now explore some of the factors that permeate experiences in this space. In this respect, this chapter looks at the role that work and the work ethic have in shaping the experiences of welfare recipients by drawing on evidential data. While, again, focusing here on a distinct set of empirical materials, I nevertheless continue to suggest that the 'shared typical' (McIntosh and Wright, 2019; Wright and Patrick, 2019) nature of the data means that the experiences confronted here may have much in common with experiences in other jurisdictions, particularly where similar (liberal) welfare regimes persist. Before presenting the empirical materials, I first 'set out my stall' by describing what I mean by the work ethic, my conception thereof being somewhat novel, albeit extrapolated in previous work (Whelan, 2020b). Effectively, when I talk about the work ethic, I mean a social phenomenon that is created by the continuous linking of paid formal employment to feelings, experiences and inherent ideas of self-value and self-worth. This type of thinking also includes and incorporates a tendency towards the 'valorisation' of work, and overwork, alongside the 'cult' of work that seems to dominate popular and political discourses surrounding what it means to be of value and to be valued, in modern Western societies at least (Frayne, 2015, 2019; Sage, 2019; Whelan, 2020b; Boland and Griffin, 2021). Conversely, being in receipt of social welfare, of various types, is considered almost as the antithesis of being in work and is therefore seen as a deeply shameful social position. I have referred to this elsewhere (Whelan, 2020b: 4) in the following terms:

> The act of performing work is presented as being 'the thing itself' the work ethic, on the other hand, is the social fetishisation of work which resultingly sees the performance of formal work as valorised, glorified and dominant in popular and political discourses that encapsulate what it means to be of value and to be valued. Building on this, it is also proposed that being in receipt of social welfare is considered as the antithesis to being in work and is therefore seen as a deeply shameful and stigmatised social position.

Effectively, then, I suggest that the work ethic is not simply an internal response to the absence or presence of work, but is also '... an objective social force that can be externally enforced or "foisted upon" persons meaning it is not only a purely internal or subjective response to the absence of work' (Whelan, 2020b: 4).

The contradictory nature of the work ethic and how this interacts with and is threaded through welfare regimes is also something that has been suggested by Boland and Griffin (2021: 2), who note that:

> ... there is a contradiction or paradox at the heart of the welfare state.... With one hand it supports the unemployed, yet simultaneously it demands certain things of them, mainly that they seek work, but also attend meetings, undergo assessment, write CVs, work on themselves, retrain, and strive continuously to redeem themselves.

Arguably, such individualising discourses and their effects are couched within the wider ideological discourse of contemporary neoliberalism (Harvey, 2007; Wacquant, 2009). While I may be presenting the work ethic in a particular way, I am not alone in acknowledging its power, and there has been documentation of this phenomenon in both historical (see Spicker, 1984; Powell, 1992) and contemporary literature. Again, Boland and Griffin (2015b, 2016, 2021) and Patrick (2016, 2017) have addressed similar themes from a conceptual and empirical perspective, and the effect of the work ethic has featured in the work of Sage (2019), who, in particular, has focused on the damaging effects of the work ethic on those who find themselves detached from the formal labour market. Frayne (2015) has also entered this conceptual territory in exploring the refusal of work and what this might mean for those who refuse it. More recently, diverse scholarship has explored the close relationship between work, precarity and welfare practices in a variety of jurisdictions and contexts (see Prendergast, 2020; Torsvik et al, 2021; Boland and Griffin, 2021; Hansen and Nielson, 2021; Im and Komp-Leukkunen, 2021; Kissová, 2021; Molander and Tirsvik, 2021; Redman and Fletcher, 2021 for just some examples). It is from these scholarly contributions that this chapter takes its lead, with a view to building on this work while also preserving the uniqueness of the specific research context.

Where does the work ethic come from? Formative experiences in familial settings

First, it is important to look at how participants articulated the importance of work in the context of formal paid employment, along with where participants first become exposed to, and first experience, the power of the work ethic. In this respect, there is a strong body of evidence within the data and across the different payment types, which demonstrates the importance that participants attach to work in the form of formal paid employment, and this is something that is often first introduced in familial circumstances. Frank, a long-term recipient of DA, talks first about what working has meant to him throughout his life:

'It was just an amazing life I had. I thought I was the luckiest man in the world. I had a job and I could do the things that *I* wanted to do. If I wanted to go out and have a meal I could go out and have a meal. I'd be paying my own way. Nobody was paying for me.' [Emphasis in original.]

In this excerpt, Frank talks about the importance of formal paid employment in the context of the life and opportunities he felt it had provided him, allowing him to feel lucky and granting him the ability to pay his own way. However, this sense of the importance of work and of paying your own way was not accidental, and was instilled in Frank from a young age. When asked where his sense of work ethic came from, Frank spoke passionately about his mother:

'My mother. Without a doubt my mother. She worked all her life. She die[d] at 51 but she worked so hard and she worked for half of nothing, but she always taught us, you know, you go out and you make your own living, you don't depend on other people to help you.'

The language Frank uses here in relation to the values to which his mother introduced him is very strong. The cornerstone of this value position devolves on the notion that "you don't depend on other people" and that "you go out and you make your own living". Inherent in this is the suggestion that not doing so – that is, by not working and making your "own living" – you are doing something shameful. Frank, in particular, spoke very strongly on the importance of work. As someone who had 'worked all his life', in predominantly hard physical occupations, he found himself in need of assistance in the form of DA after having a serious accident at work that ultimately left him unable to work. This was devastating for Frank, who seems to have carried the values he learned in his formative years and from his mother into his adult life, thus clearly linking a sense of his own intrinsic worth and well-being to being in formal paid employment. As a result, he found the thought of receiving social welfare extremely difficult:

'Didn't want to accept it. I mean to say, when you work from 13 right up to here, nearly in your fifties, you don't want to accept the fact that you can't work anymore. You don't want to accept the fact that you have to live on social welfare … other people are paying for to keep you.'

And, while undoubtedly one of the most emotive voices of those interviewed with respect to work, Frank was not alone in articulating the importance of work to self-worth and well-being. Here, Trish, a long-term recipient of JA, talks about the importance of work in the context of making job applications:

> 'I want to be working. I'm a good worker. I'm a hard worker. It's just a change in the career. And I'm after getting a few rejection letters. That kind of sets me back. But that's normal, you know. Of course it's normal. But I'm going to push through it. I know I will. It's just getting there.'

Trish talks about being a "good worker", a "hard worker", and of wanting to work, clearly demonstrating the value she places on formal paid employment. She also rationalises her current unemployment by articulating it as part of a change of career or something to "push through" as part of the act of "getting there", which again conjures that sense of liminality discussed earlier.

How people come to be 'out of work' in respect to being estranged from paid formal employment is also something that is apparent from the data. These stories are rich and varied and demonstrate the complexity of life, something that arguably gets lost when we reduce our descriptions of people to 'unemployed' or jobseeker. Frank, as we saw earlier, found himself unable to work because of a serious accident. Trish left work to care for her partner, who was experiencing significant mental health difficulties and was in need of continuous care. Although, given the circumstances, she may in fact have been eligible to receive Carer's Allowance,[1] she insisted that she didn't want to pursue this avenue for various reasons. In the first instance, she felt that caring for her partner was just something she should and would do out of a sense of duty and love. However, aside from this, she did not want to become too distant or too estranged from the labour market, choosing to remain a jobseeker with a view to ultimately returning to work. Again, as was the case with Frank, this sense of a work ethic and the importance of making your own way was instilled in Trish from a young age in a familial setting:

> 'My dad worked hard all of his life. He was never down in the Social Welfare looking for whatever, you know. So he did try to teach us not to go to the Social Welfare but it was there for us if we needed it, you know … but I was never on the one career. I did everything and anything, you know, to make money, hence my dad's instillment in me, you know.'

The language used by Trish to describe her father and the values he tried to impart overlaps with that of Frank in how he described his mother and her values. In Trish's case, she talks of her father, who, she says "worked hard all his life" and never sought help or social assistance, even suggesting that he tried to teach her and her siblings "not to go to the Social Welfare", an act that at once valorises work and demonises social assistance. Again, the message inherent in the valorisation and impartation of values such as these is that to not work is something shameful. By definition, therefore, to seek social assistance galvanises this sense of shame (Whelan, 2020b), shame itself being a painful burden to bear (Fischer, 2018), as demonstrated by both Trish and Frank. For Trish, this internal conflict around what it means to be working versus what it means to be receiving social assistance was imbued with further complexity in that she described living in a disadvantaged area where she perceives there to be a 'cultural normalcy' around receiving social assistance: "Obviously in the Northside[2] you run to get your dole to help out. I helped out my dad. You know, my brothers did it." Nevertheless, this apparent acceptance of receiving social assistance as a standard life experience was overshadowed by the strong values that Trish's father imparted, namely that work was good and that receiving social assistance or 'the dole' was something to be avoided.

This experience of work being held up as being virtuous by family members was common across the participant group. As can be seen with Frank, a DA claimant, the effects of this were felt across the different payment types and not just by those who were, as might be expected, in receipt of jobseeker-type payments. Though we are looking here at a texture of social life that encapsulates the sociology of sociality, it is nevertheless worth remembering that the targeting of groups beyond jobseekers for re-entry to the workforce does exist in formal policy (see GOI, 2012, 2013, 2015, 2016, 2021) in a way that arguably conjures the historical notion of 'setting the poor on work' (Powell, 1992; Whelan, 2021b). Scarlett, an OPFP claimant, made similar remarks to those of both Frank and Trish:

'I know that lots of people are brought up to work hard, I suppose, and lots of people – times ago, you know, no one wanted to ask for help and [it was] looked down upon to ask for help.... Well, like, I reckon – I was brought up to work hard, so, you know, I was working from 13, you know, and I wanted a job and I like working, you know.'

Again, the language used here demonstrates the values of hard work and of working hard being imparted in formative settings. Scarlett talks about being "brought up to work hard", of working from a young age and of liking work. This latter point is particularly interesting, and it should be borne in mind that the purpose in presenting these findings is not to 'attack' work as a viable, valuable and potentially enjoyable human activity. Rather, it is to illustrate the potentially damaging effects and efficacious nature of the 'work ethic', specifically as it relates to formal paid employment. The performance of work is presented here as being the 'thing in itself'; the social scaffolding that grows up around work is what has been named here as the work ethic and relates in particular to paid formal employment (Whelan, 2020b). In this respect, it is notable that in all instances where people described needing or wanting to work for reasons relating to self-esteem, self-efficacy and identity, they spoke in the main about formal paid employment. In general, charitable, voluntary or informal work did not appear to hold the same level of prominence for participants, and, as illustrated in the examples given so far, much of the prominence of formal paid employment seems to stem from formative experiences and the subsequent expectations they engender about what it means to be 'good'. For example, Mary, a young JA claimant[3] at the time of interview who found herself unable to work due to severe social anxiety and who was fully unemployed at the time of interview, talks about her parents' reaction to finding out that she was out of work and had applied to receive social assistance:

'… they were very much, like, the kind of, like, oh, you know, we've worked all our lives and, like, you know, we've never been on social welfare, and all this kind of stuff. And, you know, they were like basically just not happy about it, just saying, look, you know, like you're on this now and stuff like that and, like, you know, basically they felt like, oh, well, like, how hard is it, like, to get a job nearly, like, you know.'

Again, the language is strikingly similar to the other examples discussed except that, in this case, rather than experiencing the impartation of strong work-related values in a formative setting, Mary speaks about experiencing what it means to contravene these values as an adult child. There is, first, the valorisation of work, both obvious and inherent in a turn of phrase such as "we've worked all our lives", and this is coupled with the shame imbued in the very notion of receiving social assistance through the words, "we've never been on social welfare" (Whelan, 2020b). There is also a strong sense of a fear of the 'other' on the part of Mary's parents that seems to stem from their unhappiness at the thought of their daughter entering a space she should not, according to their values. Mary was deeply affected by her parents' response to her need to seek social assistance, with relations between them, particularly between her and her mother, ultimately becoming strained:

'So I guess that was very difficult, like, then when I kind of got that feedback. So I suppose then overall I kind of felt, you know, very kind of, like, down about being on it then because I felt it was kind of stigmatised then straight away. And even, like, when I thought, oh my God, like, well, if this is what my own parents are thinking, like, what are, like, you know, everybody else, you know, kind of thinking about it?… That was very hard, yeah. I think from that time, like, like I'd say my relationship even probably with my mum kind of dropped a bit, we'll say.'

Mary talks openly about feeling stigmatised by her parents' reaction, questioning what they must be thinking of her and ultimately feeling that the relationship between her and her mother has been somewhat damaged as a result of her being out of work and in receipt of social assistance. Mary also clearly picks up this sense of being 'othered' by her parents, wondering what they and others must think of her now that she is out of work and reliant on a welfare payment. This sense of othering and of being othered is quite strong across the participant group and will be returned to later. Consistent with the work of Baumberg (2016) and Patrick, (2017), alongside feeling othered, Mary also clearly experiences stigmatisation here in that it is clear she feels and has experienced being devalued by others because of her reliance on a social welfare payment. This seeps into a sense of personal stigma as Mary questions her own identity. Taken together, these excerpts arguably offer a stark window into the potential effects of the work ethic on individuals who find themselves unable to work, regardless of the reason or reasons for unemployment.

Broader social discourses

As well as experiencing how values surrounding the work ethic can be strongly imparted in close familial settings, many of the participants experienced the power of the work ethic in broader, more social, domains, outside of the immediate family. In this way, the work ethic can be seen to act as a social or societal mechanism experienced in different spaces and in different ways. This suggests that even if people are not exposed to a strong set of values valorising work and demonising social assistance early on or in a formative period, they may still become exposed to and affected by them in later stages of life. For example, in interview, Jane expressed the idea that she grew up in an area and in a household where there was an acceptance around the idea of engaging with the social welfare system and where there certainly appears to have been little or no censure attached to doing so in times of unemployment. In the exchange described by Jane below, she mentions how she first becomes aware of a different view on the part of others. It is a slightly complex (perhaps messy) excerpt, but is nevertheless worth sharing as it captures the social texture of the work ethic very well:

'I remember speaking to one friend of mine who I had just met who was from Douglas and, you know, very middle-class and she never went on the dole even when she was unemployed. You know, she would just keep looking for a job – "Oh, I'll have to get a part-time job." Now, I remember my mum explaining to me later, well, she probably has the means – her parents have the means to give her money, you know … all the time, whereas I don't, so yes, you go and you sign on the dole while you're waiting for a job. But more than that I remember her having a reaction when I said I was signing on the dole…. I remember her saying, like, "Why?" She couldn't understand. "Why don't you just look for a job?" And her thing was really go out and look for a job immediately whereas I did have a kind of lackadaisical attitude of, well, I'll sign on the dole *while* I'm doing it, you know.'

Jane describes engaging with the social welfare system in what could be suggested to be a perfectly reasonable, rational and correct way during a period of unemployment. Interestingly, however, she does describe herself as having a "lackadaisical attitude" towards seeking to claim welfare. It is unclear whether or not Jane feels this about her attitude now after much exposure to the work ethic and so is, in a sense, looking back, or if she felt it about herself at the time the incident she describes took place. Going on the available context, the former seems much more likely. It is also clear from her description that engaging with welfare was something that was not discouraged or condemned in any way in a close familial setting. Nevertheless, Jane becomes exposed to the work ethic later through contact and conversations with people outside of her immediate circle. In the exchange she describes, stigmatisation and a type of othering can be seen to occur, mirroring experiences documented in other work (Patrick, 2016, 2017) and that may therefore be seen as 'shared typical' (McIntosh and Wright, 2019; Wright and Patrick, 2019). The other party appears to be very 'taken aback' by the idea of engaging with social welfare, even at times of unemployment, and can't understand why Jane doesn't "just look for a job". This exchange, and perhaps others like it, had an effect on Jane and as a result changed her outlook in relation to the work ethic despite the fact that she may not have had access to same levels of social and economic capital as others (Crossley, 2017). Nevertheless, because of this, and albeit primarily reliant on a welfare payment, Jane describes how she endeavours always to remain at least partly employed as a way of demonstrating a good work ethic, which is something she has come to see as important: "I would just say I feel better about myself when I have a part-time job … it's just not being completely dependent. I suppose it shows you're not completely dependent on social welfare and it also shows you have a work ethic."

Jane talks about feeling better about herself when she has a part-time job. She links this to ideas about dependency, but she also directly references having a work ethic. Inherent in this excerpt too are overtones of social deservingness (Whelan, 2021b). It can also be suggested that Jane has illustrated the concept of personal stigma (Baumberg, 2016; Patrick, 2017) here, in that having a part-time job appears to offset, to a degree, any negative views she may have of herself as someone in receipt of a welfare payment.

The social reinforcement of the work ethic, experienced by Jane, was also something that many other of the participants experienced in direct contact with people outside of their immediate circle. For example, Martin talks about the negativity that goes with revealing being out of work and reliant on welfare:

'From my perspective I've experienced there to be a stigma involved in mentioning that you're in any way accessing the welfare system – for whatever reason – if it's disability, death in the family. No matter what the reason is, it's still viewed in the same perspective that, you know, that person – you know, we're all working and paying for this guy.... I've experienced it first-hand on the forklift course, I've experienced it looking for positions for jobs. Once you mention that you're unemployed or that you've been out of work for so many months, so many years, they're just – you know, immediately the conversation changes.'

Martin directly references the imposition of a stigma and links this to both receiving social welfare and to being unemployed thus demonstrating the 'toxic symbiosis' of worklessness and welfare receipt (Whelan, 2020b). He suggests that there is a stigma attached to a reliance on social assistance regardless of the reason and that this is then further exacerbated, in a social setting, by mentioning an absence from formal paid employment. He also evokes Baumberg's (2016) concept of stigmatisation in the sense of how he feels he is viewed by other people. Inherent in this excerpt are ideas around social reciprocity, but there is also clear evidence of the societal reinforcement of the work ethic, mediated, on the one hand, via a sense of shame or stigma around receiving welfare and on the other by an overt negativity surrounding unemployment. Below, Clive, a recipient of JA who has been unemployed for a period of approximately ten years, talks about experiencing similar exchanges in a social setting:

'I've had it now, for example, with a friend of mine over the way. Just a thing he said about people that are on the dole, you know what I mean, that they should get off their asses and get work.... That, you know, people will say, "Ah, these bums, they never worked a day in their life, they don't want to work, why should they, they're on social welfare", you know.'

Clive describes an exchange with a friend that is replete with familiar tropes. Again, the two-sided attack based on the dual nature of a reliance on social welfare and an absence from the labour market are to the fore in this exchange (Whelan, 2020b). Clive's friend feels that unemployed people who are receiving social welfare should "get off their asses and get work". Clive, as someone who is experiencing both welfare receipt and unemployment, does in fact 'belong' to the category about which his friend is speaking. In this sense, Clive is experiencing the societal reinforcement of the work ethic, and, while he may not be in a position to do anything about it in terms of acquiescing to his friend's latent demands, he cannot but be affected by it. As it happens, Clive appeared to be a person of some resilience and was able to reject the labels inherent in the societal reinforcement of the work ethic. Here, for example, he resists the narrative that people purposely choose a life reliant on welfare:

> 'I don't think that is true at all. I mean, who in their right – like there's very few. Maybe there's a very few people that are of that mentality but I don't think it's prevalent. It's not the majority. Most people don't want to do that.'

However, not everyone will negotiate the effects of the work ethic and other stigmatising labels in the way that Clive appears to be able. For those who cannot, not only do they experience stigmatisation by virtue of how they feel they are perceived by others, but they are also likely to experience some degree of personal stigma based on a negative perception of self (Baumberg, 2016; Patrick, 2016, 2017).

So far, we have seen the importance that many of the participants attach to work. We have also seen how participants can first become exposed to the work ethic, which is often, though not always, imparted in close familial settings through a strongly articulated value position. We have seen that this can often then be reinforced at a social level outside of what might constitute an immediate circle. Aside from these powerful exposures to the work ethic, participants were also often aware of yet broader reinforcement in the form of popular and political discourses that also tend to valorise work and denigrate welfare 'dependency'. Redman and Fletcher (2021: 2) have noted this practice in the upper echelons of political discourse in Britain: 'The Prime Minister, David Cameron (2011), declared that social security provision had fuelled a surge in irresponsible behaviour and (under-)class cultural values including voluntary unemployment and an entitlement mentality.'

In Ireland, a recent example of how this semantic negativity surrounding welfare can manifest at a high political level is to be found in the Welfare Cheats Cheat us All[4] campaign of 2017. This was a political campaign, spearheaded by the then Minister for Social Protection, Leo Varadker TD, and ostensibly launched to combat 'welfare fraud', which was overtly suggested to be ubiquitous. The terminology used was suggestive and hostile. In an arguably brash and obvious ideological move, the word welfare was situated alongside the word cheat, a move that some in positions of power have since admitted as regrettable, the connotations being obvious (Ó Cionnaith, 2017). Notably, the campaign was run during a Fine Gael[5] leadership race, and, by virtue of his winning said race, the aforementioned Leo Varadker TD went on to become Taoiseach before taking up the role of Tánaiste after a change in government. As this campaign was in full flow, as ads appeared on billboards and on radio stations, the welfare state chugged on. People, including many of those interviewed for this study, quietly went on receiving welfare payments, made the journey to 'sign on', to collect payments in the post office, to attempt to establish new entitlements, to continue to maintain existing ones and so on. This raises questions about what the experiences of those receiving welfare must be like in a country where politicians in the top echelons of the Irish political apparatus blithely politicise and stigmatise its receipt. If the Welfare Cheats campaign is a macro example of the status of contemporary discourses in this space in the Irish context, and one that is often replicated in popular media (Boland and Griffin, 2015a, 2016; Whelan, 2020b), then what must the micro interactions that make up the lives of welfare recipients be like? Suffice to say that many of the participants were aware of the politically driven Welfare Cheats Cheat us All campaign of 2017 as being, or at the very least having the effect of, a politically expedient framing device for a 'common-sense' welfare consensus. In the following excerpt, Grace acknowledges the tone of the campaign: "Well, you know, Leo[6] was out for blood for social welfare fraud a couple of – a year ago."

Grace uses very strong language to illustrate her impression of the tone and central concern of the campaign. Clive also referenced the campaign directly, again paying particular attention to the spirit in which it was run:

'I mean, with the Taoiseach saying that, you know, your Taoiseach telling you, like, the only interest they have, like, is people that get out of bed in the morning.... I mean, God Almighty, what kind of a profoundly stupid thing for a person, you know, to say.'

Clive refers directly here to a phrase that, at one point, appeared to be a staple for the current administration, and the Minister for Employment Affairs and Social Protection at that time in particular, in the form of "people that get out of bed in the morning". Albeit clearly devoid of nuance, the inherent suggestion here seems to be the valorisation of work along with the denigration of 'idleness'.

Popular media is another space in which the work ethic seems to be continually reinforced and by which some participants were directly affected:

'… news stuff, especially, yeah, like tabloid newspapers will often target welfare recipients as again I would say the scapegoat of an issue and they'll blow up figures and say it's this whole – it's a crisis, you know. Like it's this big sensational kind of thing that they're draining the economy or whatever.'

In this excerpt, Alan talks about the effect of media such as tabloid newspapers, which, he suggests, give disproportionate coverage to welfare recipients, creating moral panic in the tradition of Cohen (2011) and effectively scapegoating them. Mary echoes much of this point in the context of radio programming:

'I suppose I've heard so many conversations on the radio and different, like, you know, conversations that people would have had on the talk shows and things like that and it just kind of seems to be the same thing and those kind of words are coming up all the time and, like, it just nearly kind of associates with yourself then. You kind of think, oh, like, am I actually that person? Like am I actually like a lazy person? You know, things like that. So you kind of, you know, you feel like kind of ashamed nearly that you're on it [welfare benefits].'

Mary uses language that clearly demonstrates how deeply affective and effective the reinforcement of the work ethic, along with the denigration of welfare recipiency, can be at this level. She finds herself questioning her personhood, asking herself whether or not she is lazy, and ends up with confused feelings that are tinged with shame and personal stigma (Baumberg, 2016; Patrick, 2017). Alongside this broader societal reinforcement of the work ethic in the context of popular media such as tabloid newspapers, television and radio, many of the participants experienced a type of social or moral policing on various online platforms. For example, Grace talks about reading the comments that often follow an online article in which there has been reference to unemployment and the receipt of social welfare. She too finds herself questioning her own personhood as a result:

'Yeah, so there might be an article and there might be a man and he's not working or whatever, or a woman who has a child and she's not working, or she is working and – whatever – somebody gets a bit of social welfare.… There's just [a] little clause in one of the sentences in the big long article. And then in comments it's, "Oh, social welfare", you know, people are just tearing somebody to shreds over the fact that they get social welfare. And I suppose that affects me because I'm thinking they're all thinking that – they all would think that about me.'

Trish describes similar experiences in the context of Facebook and the reaction there to an increase in the basic rate of social welfare following a government budget announcement:

'Well, you know, someone on Facebook sometimes about the social welfare saying that extra fiver was coming in March. It's just all the comments underneath.… It's hatred, you know, the things people say. It's really – because you don't know someone's circumstances, first of all, you know. These are just keyboard warriors. I don't know what I'm trying to say. It's just like negative across the board, you know.'

Both of these two excerpts demonstrate the societal reinforcement, in the online space, of the work ethic along with a widespread assumption that receiving social welfare or assistance is inherently 'bad'. Some of the participants who had these experiences tried to resist and even to counteract this social narrative, but arguably to little effect:

'… it gives me the sense that I don't have a voice then, because I think here's a false – (a) the media are presenting a false representation of an issue, (b) a large group of the population are writing negative comments about this issue down here, and (c) I'm now trying to present facts and information that I think might be able to change people's attitudes and minds and again show the nuance of a situation, you know, and I'm more or less told I'm a fool, you know. So that's a very frustrating situation for somebody who's been there, you know, to be in.'

Here Alan describes making attempts to introduce what he sees as facts that may influence and inform people. Ultimately, however, he is left frustrated by the experience. It is difficult to know why Alan feels the need to offer this resistance. Ultimately it suggests that he rejects the labels associated with 'worklessness' and welfare recipiency. Nevertheless, the fact that he feels the need to resist these labels publicly, in fora where there appears to be little to gain, suggests that he feels at least somewhat personally stigmatised by their propagation. However, it should be noted also that it is equally possible that he engages in activity such as this as an act of politics or citizenship from below.

Types of work

So far, the focus has been on where and when the work ethic is introduced for and experienced by participants. The wider societal reinforcement of the work ethic in various spaces has also been explored. It has also been shown that, for some, narratives surrounding work and the work ethic are often intimately bound up in ideas around 'making your own way', the antithesis to which appears to be a reliance on social welfare that is generally seen as 'bad' or even deviant or immoral (Whelan, 2020b; Boland and Griffin, 2021). This raises a question about what in fact can be said to constitute work. As briefly mentioned earlier, types of work are also important, with charitable, voluntary or informal work failing to hold the same prominence as formal paid employment. For example, when it was pointed out to Frank that there are ways of contributing to society other than through formal paid employment, he replied:

'Yes, but the reason I'm focusing on the labour market is I want to be able to have the times that I had where I can put a bit of money away. I want to be there to get things for my children. And that's the most important thing to me, to get something, to find something out there. And I am trying. I am looking.'

Here, Frank addresses the reality of material disadvantage that can come with a reliance on welfare as a primary income strand, the marginal, which we introduced earlier. He talks about wanting to be able to put "money away" and to buy things for his children, and these are clearly extremely valid reasons for wanting to work. He finishes by saying finding formal paid employment is the "most important thing" for him and that he is continually trying in this respect. Nevertheless, Frank did, at other points, acknowledge that he has gained a sense of purpose and efficacy from more informal contributions to society, through volunteering with organisations such as the National Learning Network[7] and the Scouts, and through just generally helping out neighbours:

'Through the National Learning Network we went through a lot of different voluntary areas. We had them coming to talks. Over the year we had people coming down talking to us about what was out there that we could do. I helped with several things over the years. I did a lot of help with the Scouts one time. I did a lot of help with the elderly, which I still do off my back, not because someone – there's two women that every week now in weather like this now I take them down shopping, bring them back home. If it's too wet they give me the money to go shopping, I bring back the list, how much it costs, say there you go. That gives me – when I'm doing that I feel good.'

Other participants seemed to view charitable or voluntary work as something to be engaged in with a view to being in a better position to take up formal employment should the opportunity arise. This might also be viewed as having much in common with the socially liminal nature of a reliance on welfare as discussed in the previous chapter.

Martin clearly articulates the importance of 'charity' work: "So you have to be kind of in a job even if it's only part-time, you know, doing charity work or something. That seems to be a lot … eas[ier] to get into a position than [just] being in the welfare system." However, in this example, he does so in the context of using it to better his prospects of gaining formal paid employment, something he feels he has less chance of attaining through a reliance on welfare alone. This suggests that charitable work holds a lesser position than that of formal paid employment. Nevertheless, some participants, such as Lisa, were better able to derive a sense of value and identity from chartable or voluntary work:

> 'I've done voluntary work since I was about 12, like. I always try and give something back. So that's how I kind of equate getting that payment is that I'm always involved in voluntary work, like, you know…. Well, it's self-worth, you know. And it's also society giving you worth as well. Like, you know, it's you're validated, I suppose.'

Lisa articulates voluntary work as a key component of her identity. However, she also uses her engagement in voluntary work as a mode of rationalisation for receiving welfare, suggesting that she does, in actuality, see some difference between voluntary work and more formal employment. However, she ultimately talks about self-worth and of feeling validated, suggesting that for some people, there is an inherent worth in non-formal work that can offset at least some of the negativity that a non-adherence to the formal work ethic can engender.

Aside from charitable or voluntary work, many people work informally in a variety of ways such as through caring for adult loved ones or children in the home and, arguably, this is a further area of the world of work that is not seen to be as 'real' as formal paid employment. Of course, there is a long tradition of academic and activist literature that addresses this very point, particularly from the feminist perspective, much of which is outside the scope of this book (see Toupin [2018] for an excellent overview). Nevertheless, it has, for some participants at least, functioned as a space into which the effects of the work ethic have crept and so should be addressed briefly. The way in which the work ethic manifests itself here appears to be through the falseness of assumed idleness, that is, the idea that a person who is *not* in paid formal employment and who *is* in receipt of welfare must, by default, be idle. For example, Trish, who it will be remembered was unemployed due to a need to care for her partner, talks about the general perceptions of another family member who it appears assumes continuous idleness on the part of Trish and so is less than pleased when Trish is unwilling or unable to help out: "[I]t's how she would view me, you know. Or she could ask me to do something, I'd always say yeah. But, say, the one time I couldn't she was, 'Sure, you're not doing anything anyway.'"

And in the following excerpt, Trevor, a long-term recipient of DA who suffers from severe bipolar disorder, talks directly about what he sees as the assumption of idleness, and, indeed, laziness, on the part of those who are in work with regard to how they view people receiving welfare:

'I think people just assume that people who receive benefits are just freeloaders and they're not giving anything back, you know. And, you know, that is a stereotype and it's extremely judgemental but sadly that's just the way the world is. If, you know, one part of society feels like they're working really hard to get money and then they see another part of society getting free money, they're immediately just going to attach the stigma to that, you know, which is wholly unfair because you notice that a lot of the people who are receiving the money are, you know, on the majority in need of it for some reason, whether it's a social reason, psychological reason, physical reason, or, you know, any.'

During his time on DA, Trevor had 'worked' in the context of completing a master's degree and subsequently a PhD. Nevertheless, it is clear in how he articulates what he sees as the general perception of welfare recipients in society that he feels that this kind of 'work' or contribution is not seen as valid and that, needs aside, people who receive benefits are perceived as getting 'something for nothing', despite what they may or may not have achieved during their period of receipt.

So far, this chapter has addressed the effects of the work ethic on participants in receipt of social welfare by focusing on family, community and social factors in the introduction, enforcement and reinforcement of the work ethic. However, the work ethic is also something that many of the participants in this study experienced as being 'built in' to all aspects and stages of the welfare system itself and so it is to this particular area of experience that attention now turns.

The enforcement of the work ethic by the welfare system

A strong emphasis on the work ethic and on finding work is something that many of the participants experienced during their interactions with administrators in the welfare system. As might be expected, this tended to be strongest for, and most frequently encountered by, those receiving jobseeker payments. In Ireland, as demonstrated in Chapter 2, there has undoubtedly been a strong turn towards activation as a broad instrument of social policy in the period since the global financial collapse (Boland and

Griffin, 2016; Dukelow and Considine, 2017; Whelan, 2021b; McGann and Murphy, 2021). However, the emphasis on finding work has arguably become even more formalised and apparent in the Irish welfare system in recent years through the introduction of 'job-matching' entities such as Turas Nua and Seetec to whom jobseekers are now often referred after a period of approximately 12 months of continuous unemployment. Despite this, the emphasis on finding work begins immediately for those claiming a jobseeker payment, with claimants being expected to be keenly aware of their responsibilities in order to receive their payment from the outset. These responsibilities include:

- being available for work;
- being fit for work;
- genuinely seeking work;
- unable to find work.

Jobseekers must also commit to engaging with Intreo's employment advice and training referral services. They are also advised that if they fail to honour this commitment, it will lead to a reduction or withdrawal of their jobseeker's payment. A visit to any local or regional Intreo office will show posters and proffer literature, generously dispersed throughout, that make plain these responsibilities. It is clear then that the emphasis for welfare claimants, and jobseekers in particular, is strongly on work from the beginning of their interaction with the welfare system. It is, of course, possible to conceive of the responsibilities attached to the receipt of a jobseeker's payment as aspects of conditionality and this is something that will be visited in detail in Chapter 4. For now, however, the way in which an emphasis on work is 'built into' the receipt of social assistance is the key concern.

In the following excerpt, Alan describes an experience that clearly demonstrates the emphasis that is placed on the work ethic and on finding work by welfare administrators:

> 'Yeah, so you're kind of regularly filling out forms saying you've applied for jobs in this place on this day and, you know, whatever. Every time I interacted with someone in the office they'd ask me, "How often are you applying?" One day I kind of wasn't being particularly mindful and I just said that I – I think she said, "When did you last look?" And I said, "I looked the day before yesterday." And this was early in the morning, you know. And she said, "Why didn't you look yesterday?" And it was this immediate kind of, like, you're wasting our time here.'

Alan describes the regularity with which he was expected to look or apply for jobs. He also describes the negative reaction he encountered having been perceived to not be applying enough. At this point, Alan was still engaged directly with Intreo and had not been referred to a job-matching service. Patricia echoes Alan's point in relation to frequency, describing the high level of postal contact she received relating to making job applications: "… [w]hat was really annoying me when I came home was the fact that I kept getting sent out a letter every few weeks just to say that I had to prove what jobs I had applied for." Again, it is clear here that the emphasis is very much on the work ethic and on finding work.

This need to constantly be on the lookout for work and to be ready to prove oneself in this respect was something that affected many of the participants. Here, Olive describes the rigorous steps she took to both find work and to keep proof of her jobseeking activities on hand should it be required:

'It was all work. And there was a big folder. I remember the green folder where I put all the ads from the papers or the ad from the internet and the job and the application, whether it was application form or CV, and then there was the reply back. So they all were kept and they were all put in date order, I suppose so that when that letter might come then I'd have my proof on hand.'

The efforts undertaken by Olive clearly show how an emphasis on the work ethic is contained within the Irish social welfare system and how this filters into the lives of welfare recipients, affecting them deeply and dictating their activities, to an extent at least, in a process of 'reformation' (Boland and Griffin, 2021). Boland and Griffin (2015a; 2015b; 2016; 2021) have also acknowledged something similar in their work with Irish jobseekers and on the sociology of unemployment. In conceptualising jobseeker-type payments as constituting 'ungenerous gifts', they raise questions about the conceptualisation of the recipients themselves, who, they argue, are reconstituted, through a model of responsibilisation, as no longer simply being passively unemployed but rather as active jobseekers who must be reformed (Boland and Griffin, 2021). The inherent suggestion in this is that those in receipt of jobseeker-type payments take on the role of constantly being expected to search for work and that this is stringently enforced and reinforced by the welfare system. This has certainly proved to be the case for many of the participants in this study. Olive in particular is interesting in this respect as much of the period to which her data refers constitutes the late 2008 onwards, a period in which Ireland reached record levels unemployment and during which there was a clear and apparent shortage of labour market opportunities (Dukelow and Considine, 2017; McGann and Murphy, 2021). In this respect, it could be argued that the emphasis placed by government departments on seeking employment in what, at the time, was a fundamentally broken labour market was in actuality more indicative of the policy response to the Irish crisis that was as noted earlier, characterised by a rapid and severe turn to austerity.

Along with receiving correspondence through the post, welfare recipients and, again, jobseekers in particular, are often expected to meet face to face with an assigned Intreo officer where the emphasis again seems to be primarily on work and jobseeking activities. Below, Peter, a long-term recipient of JA who has had experience of both Intreo and Turas Nua, describes his experiences of meeting with an Intreo officer over a six-month period:

> 'Well, I went in I talked to him about myself and about work and what work I'd like to do, and that was fine. Then I had to call down to him every two weeks and prove that I was looking for work. And I wasn't finding any work. That just basically was it. And I was there for six months....'

Although these meetings were apparently benign, it is clear that there was an emphasis on work and on finding work. After a six-month period had elapsed, Peter was referred to Turas Nua. This personal or caseworker approach was something experienced by many of the participants, usually involving face-to-face meetings with an emphasis on work. Below, Mary describes her experience, which clearly overlap with Peter's:

> 'I, like, have a caseworker, kind of a specific fella that I go to on I wouldn't say a very regular basis. It's kind of like intermittently really that I would go to him, and he's just kind of there to – basically, you know, you have a personal progression plan and he'll go through all that kind of stuff with you. And he kind of, you know, will be there to give – you know, if he sees any jobs online, you know, he'll give them to you, or any courses that he thinks might be, you know, good for you then he will kind of recommend them to you and stuff like that.'

Again, the emphasis in these meetings is very much consistent with reinforcing the work ethic. Mary has a "personal progression plan" and jobs and suitable courses are recommended at the meetings. While the tone of these frequent meetings as described by both Peter and Mary may on the surface appear to be largely formulaic and mundane, the data show that in actuality these, as well as other general contacts from the DSP, could be highly stressful occasions for many of the participants and had the potential to engender upset, nervousness and even fear, as described by Mary: "I suppose the nerves came when, like, I'd get a letter to say you have a meeting to see how you're getting on and all this kind of stuff. So I guess it was very – like, it's very nerve-wracking."

It should also be noted that attendance at meetings such as these is mandatory, falling under the 'committing to engage with Intreo's employment advice and training referral services' aspect of receiving jobseeker-type payments, with recipients facing a potential sanction for non-engagement. Here, Patricia describes how this was made plain by the Intreo officer:

"... like, she kept reinstating [restating] it: 'It's mandatory that you're here. It's mandatory that you're here. You have to comply.' And then I had to sit down and fill out a contract and in the contract you have to say what your goals are.'

If the reinforcement of the work ethic is built into the Intreo system as it relates to jobseeker-type payments, this appears to become even more pronounced when claimants are referred to to private service providers such as Turas Nua, something over which claimants have no control. This is not surprising as entities such as Turas Nua and Seetec function specifically to move people from the live register and into formal paid, preferably full-time, employment and profit from doing so.[8] Many of the participants in this study have had experiences such as these, specifically with Turas Nua, which operates primarily in the southern region of Ireland, thus covering Cork city, suburbs and townlands. In the first instance, the modus operandi of Turas Nua appears to very much mirror that of the Intreo service. Here, Peter describes in detail his initial introduction to Turas Nua:

'I went down into Turas Nua. You've an interview. There's about 15, 16 people in the group and they go through their introductions and how they're going to help you find work and this, that and the other. And then you get assessed with one person and she's meant to help you find work. And you report to her every week, maybe two weeks, and if you don't turn up your social welfare will be docked. So I says, "Grand, fine." I turned up. You give your CV and she puts it up on the computer.... They were just telling us that there's great opportunities in Cork and this, that and the other, and there's work out there for everybody and we'll all find work for ye. And I went, "Grand."'

It is clear from Peter's description that the work ethic is strongly reinforced from the very initial stages. Again, this is not altogether surprising, given the mandate of entities such as Turas Nua that operate on the basis of a 'payment by results' contract that must dictate their strategy in part at least. However, this is then coupled with an explicit threat in the form of sanctions for non-engagement. Present also in the experience described by Peter is the language of responsibilisation: recipients are clearly told that there are "great opportunities" and that there is "work out there for everybody". Use of language such as this is arguably imbued with the latent suggestion of failure on the part of those referred to Turas Nua, a failure to seize the "great opportunities" and to avail of a seeming abundance of work. It is arguable that this type of opening gambit can be explained, in part at least, by what many participants experienced as the enforcement of an 'any work, any job' policy on the part of Turas Nua and this is consistent with much of the literature (Collins and Murphy, 2016; Boland, 2018; Boland and Griffin, 2018, 2021). Staying with Peter, who was very animated when describing the following exchange, this was something he certainly experienced very strongly:

> "'Why aren't you applying for this job? What aren't you applying for that job?" I said, "I don't want to do that job and I don't want to do that job." "But you have to find work." I said, "I'm looking for work." I says, "Why are you doing this job?" "Because I like it." "And that's why I'm going to look for them job, because I like them." I says, "I'm not applying for a call centre and I'm not being sent to a call centre." I said, "I won't do that work."'

In the end, in what could perhaps be considered to be an act of disguised compliance (Ferguson, 2011), Peter describes feeling that he was really just going through the motions:

> 'Yeah, it's get work, get work. "Where's your emails?" I said, "There's my emails." "Why aren't you applying for this job? There's a job there, there's a job there." I said, "I'm not qualified for that." I said, "I'm not doing telesales. I don't like it, I'm not doing it." I was just applying for jobs I knew that I wasn't going to get to keep her happy.'

The emphasis on the part of Turas Nua in what Peter describes is not only on finding suitable or 'job-matched' work, but also on 'any work', regardless of the wishes of the claimant. Peter resists this at first, but in the end finds himself applying for jobs he feels he has little chance of getting in order to match the expectations being set down for him. Other participants, such as Martin, also described the heavy emphasis on constant applications: "I was given a job sheet. The job sheet had 17 to 20 jobs to be applying for. So I just felt like it's an empty sheet, it needs to be filled. But then when you're filling it every two weeks that's a lot of jobs...." Here, Martin describes applying for anywhere between 17 and 20 jobs on a fortnightly basis. Without wishing to labour the point, this is of course to be expected to a degree, given the context. Nevertheless, it still represents an incredibly strong emphasis on the work ethic as the basis for how legitimate social assistance is granted and received.

A further aspect of how the work ethic, and, in particular, the emphasis on 'any work, any job' is explicitly articulated in this context, comes in the form of an apparent lack of a 'sight of the individual' or individual approach on the part of Turas Nua that seems to run contrary to the very notion of 'job matching'. Many of the participants who had contact with Turas Nua experienced this. Trish certainly experienced this, and, as a result, ultimately found her engagement with Turas Nua to not only have been expensive but ultimately to have been a waste of time:

'I was with them a year and, to be honest, I was going in every week and we were doing the same thing every week. "We'll work on your CV now this week." I was, like, "I've a perfect CV." I wanted help in other aspects, you know. They didn't help me, you know.… I felt I was wasting money going down there, first of all, on buses, money I didn't have, you know, to go down there. It was repetitive and I felt no one was listening to me, you know.'

In interview, Trish explained that she had wanted to do a forklift course with a view to finding employment. However, she felt that Turas Nua was very resistant to this, insisting that this would not be an avenue through which she would be likely to find work. Graham, echoing Trish, also felt that the service was not specifically matched to his needs:

'Right, now, they gave me a highly coloured CV, right. I couldn't recognise myself from the description, right. And your man took me through how to kind of send an email, right. But, sure, I mean, it's like this: what fucking use is it to me? Because no one I know actually sends email.'

Again, it can be inferred here that this lack of an individual approach, coupled with an 'any work, any job' culture, suggests a rigid reinforcement of the work ethic as something that was strongly experienced by participants who had contact with Turas Nua. Graham also finds himself disempowered and disadvantaged here by an expectation that jobseekers will have access to and actively use particular types of technology. Ultimately, experiences with Turas Nua were negative across this particular participant group. Some participants were able to resist this approach and the feelings it engendered more than others. In one such moment of resistance, Patricia, who was very animated in recalling the following exchange, manages to aptly sum up the general sense of Turas Nua and the feelings it tended to engender for the participants in this study:

'"Ye actually make me feel like I should have a tag on my foot." I said, "The communication here", I said, "everything", I said, "is just –", I said, "Everything is wrong about this." I said, "The whole thing is wrong."… Like you had people in front of you – a say there was, like, maybe a 60-year-old woman. She had a limp. She was sitting right in front of me being interviewed and I could hear her whole history, her whole employment history, someone asking her, "Oh, you're only working three days a week, why aren't you working five days a week?" I could hear anything that was going on right in front of me…. It was like a job concentration camp.'

In the next chapter, I continue with the task of documenting the experiences of those I interviewed and in doing so move from what may be described as a deeply rooted sociological phenomenon in the form of the work ethic to an area where the instruments of social policy drive a particular type of sociological experience. Having presented an abundance of empirical materials on the work ethic as it has been conceived here, I suggest that it is something that occupies a powerful and multi-layered social space. The data drawn on here suggest that introductions to the work ethic, and the values that valorise work, often, though not always, begin in intimate familial settings. These values are then further reinforced in the wider circles through which people ultimately traverse and even more widely reinforced and disseminated through political and popular discourses with respect to welfare framing (Jensen and Tyler, 2015; Patrick, 2016; Devereux and Power, 2019). This analysis suggests that the work ethic operates at the level of multiple social strata, meaning that although a person or persons may not be exposed to the work ethic in certain contexts, they may very well be in others. The work ethic is particularly powerful in the welfare space due to the fact that, operating alongside the common-sense notion that work is 'good', is the idea that receiving social assistance is 'bad'. This leads to the demonisation of welfare recipiency, with welfare recipiency ultimately operating as somewhat of a code or proxy for 'laziness' or being 'workshy' and thus the very antithesis of what it means to be working and 'good' (Whelan, 2020b). The work ethic also forms a major part of the structure of the Irish welfare system through which it is threaded and made explicit in both policy and practice. Welfare recipients receiving jobseeker-type payments are particularly susceptible to being exposed to this, meaning that they experience claims stigma, at least in part, as a result of the emphasis on employment for those in receipt of social assistance. The work ethic also feeds into various types of social stigma. For example, many of the participants experienced stigmatisation both in direct contact with other persons and in various online fora, at least partly as a result of their status as unemployed and almost certainly because welfare receipt and worklessness operate, as mentioned, as two sides of the same coin. Othering and fear of the other is also something that informs how those who find themselves out of work are perceived by the employed members of their families, communities and societies. Undoubtedly closely related, and in particular to the latter part of this chapter, is the question of how welfare recipients experience welfare conditionality and what effect this has. This is addressed in the next chapter.

4

Welfare conditionality

In this chapter, I present materials that show how different types of welfare conditionalities have been experienced by those who took part in this study. In this respect, I intend to look at the processes of formal welfare conditionality, although I do attempt to nuance this in my analysis as I have done elsewhere (Whelan, 2020a). In Chapter 5, I introduce empirical materials that evidence something less formal, something less tangible than welfare conditionality or at least more implicit than explicit. There I introduce how welfare recipients attempt to maintain compliance and engage in impression management practices. I flag this here on the basis that both sets of phenomena are very intimately related. However, it makes sense to first introduce the formal and explicit ways in which separate aspects of the same sets of experiences are acquitted before moving on to evidence how even that which appears simple on the surface is, in fact, psychosocially complex. Before moving on to present the empirical materials that make up the bulk of this chapter, however, I first briefly discuss the concept and practice of welfare conditionality.

I have argued elsewhere that conditionality has arguably always been part of formalised welfare regimes dating at least as far back as the poor laws and the condition of less eligibility (Whelan, 2020a). Others have also acknowledged the historical embeddedness of the conditional nature of welfare receipt, though it may once have been called 'poor relief' (Powell, 1992, 2017; Watts and Fitzpatrick, 2018). In this book, it is experiences of the modern processes of welfare conditionality that we are concerned with, and it is generally accepted that there has been a more pronounced turn towards welfare conditionality in the latter part of the 20th and beginning of the 21st centuries. Indeed, welfare conditionality is an area that has attracted and continues to attract international research interest (see Soss et al, 2011; Collins and Murphy, 2016; Dywer, 2016; Millar and Crosse, 2018; Watts and Fitzpatrick, 2018; Hansen, 2019; McCashin, 2019; Redman, 2019, 2021; Gaffney and Millar, 2020; Murphy, 2020; Whelan 2020a; Boland and Griffin, 2021; Dukelow, 2021; Finn, 2021; McGann, 2021; McGann and Murphy, 2021; Redman and Fletcher, 2021 for just some examples). Watts and Fitzpatrick (2018) have referred to this turn as the broadening and deepening of welfare conditionality, particularly in Western democracies, a process that has been characterised by increasing severity and sanction. The geographical distinction made here is important. This is because the welfare conditionality of the Global North, and of the liberal welfare regimes of the Anglosphere world in particular, can be very different from the welfare conditionality of the Global South. In the case of the latter, conditional cash transfers can often have behavioural conditions attached to them as a form of incentive for things such as school attendance or engagement with health services (Watts and Fitzpatrick, 2018). Conversely, in the more 'advanced' or 'developed' welfare regimes of the Global North, the techniques of welfare conditionality are more likely to be characterised by things such as strict and predetermined behavioural criteria, monitoring and verification, practices around deservingness or entitlement and sanctions for non-compliance (Watts and Fitzpatrick, 2018; Whelan, 2020a). The sanctioning and censure of welfare recipients by the state through the processes of conditionality arguably evokes a sense of latent criminalisation, certainly evoking ideas of deviance and operating almost like a 'secret penal system' (Wright et al, 2019). This secret penal system is then aimed at groups such as the unemployed, young people, those who are sick or disabled, low-income families and one-parent families (Wright et al, 2019). These groups of people make up the 'subjects of conditionality' (Watts and Fitzpatrick, 2018), becoming 'ideological conductors' who form the basis for policy choices (Wacquant, 2009; Tyler, 2013), or folk devils whose portrayal in popular media helps to mould public opinion (Cohen, 2011; Jensen and Tyler, 2015). Like ideas around the work ethic discussed in the previous chapter, ideas encapsulated within the processes of welfare conditionality bear the hallmarks of the broader neoliberal project in the form of a bundle of blunt dichotomous notions such as dependency and self-reliance, idleness and industriousness, givers and takers, strivers and skivers. Of course, together these ideas also inform an underclass narrative which is itself grounded in the work of Mead (1992. 1986) Murray (1984, 1990, 1994) and others (see Selbourne, 1994; Etzioni, 1997) while also being espoused at the level of politics (Devereux and Power, 2019; Redman and Fletcher, 2021).

Having suggested something about how welfare conditionality is perceived, practised and discoursed in the liberal welfare regimes of the Anglosphere, it is important to offer a definition, contested though this is likely to be, of welfare conditionality as it is used here. In their work on the levels and levers of conditionality as a possible method for measuring changes within welfare states, Clasen and Clegg (2007) offer the three-pronged framework of category, circumstance and conduct, each of which makes up a facet of conditionality. Category is, of course, the primary condition for receipt of a particular welfare payment, and it may mean young, older, unemployed, disabled, parenting alone and so on. Category, while simple to understand, is nevertheless important as it denotes a payment for some pre-determined person or group and not a payment for everyone, so, for example, a person below retirement age will not be entitled to receive an old-age pension.

Circumstance is closely related to eligibility and as such, circumstances are multifaceted. Financial circumstances may come to light through the process of means testing and this may permit or prevent partial or full entitlement. Social insurance contributions or employment status may be a factor in deciding entitlement. Finally, conduct refers to the specified patterns of behaviour required of welfare recipients in order to maintain entitlement. I take these concepts up for use in my analysis. While I draw on all three dimensions continually throughout this chapter, it is this latter strand of Clasen and Clegg's (2007) framework that is of primary concern here. In this respect, it is useful to broaden this out, and the following definition drawn from the longitudinal Welfare Conditionality[1] project's final findings report (Welfare Conditionality, 2019: 8) provides a useful starting point: 'Welfare conditionality links eligibility for collectively provided welfare benefits and services to recipients' specified compulsory responsibilities or particular patterns of behaviour. It has been a key element of welfare state reform in many nations since the mid-1990s.'

Here, as with Clasen and Clegg's (2007) conduct parameter of welfare conditionality, the basis for legitimate receipt is linked to specified responsibilities and patterns of behaviour. Effectively, and because we are concerned with lived experiences, this is how I use welfare conditionality here. However, when presenting empirical materials, I build on this in two ways, first, by showing that many aspects of welfare conditionality, though they are often not thought of as such, can make up the bulk of conditional activities. These, I argue, can constitute the mundane reality of life as a welfare recipient. They constitute the drudgery, the oft-repeated, and the inane, and these aspects of welfare conditionality have been documented by Watts and Fitzpatrick (2018) and by the author elsewhere (Whelan, 2020a). Second, there are also, arguably, 'hidden' or at least less well-known areas of conditionality that may only become apparent when the boundaries they set down are contravened. They are not hidden in the sense of the information being unavailable, but may 'appear hidden' in that the information may only be revealed when asked for. It is to this, much broader conception of conditionality, which the findings presented here refer. In this respect, I draw both on direct and obvious examples of welfare conditionality as more subtle or hidden examples. I start by presenting material that illustrates the initial claims process – what I have termed here 'submitting for judgement'.

Experiences across payment types: submitting for judgement

Conditionality is something that has affected all participants in this study across the different payment groups, the specificity of which is reliant on payment type. In respect to DA and IB, the primary condition for receipt of these payment types is that the recipient is unable to work due to injury, illness or disease. In the case of IB, this payment is directly linked to social insurance contributions and paid on a time-limited basis. In the case of DA, applicants must submit to a means test and must satisfy a habitual residence condition (HRC). Aside from this, applicants are expected to be able to substantiate their injury, illness or disease and are required to submit reports from their own general practitioner (GP) and other relevant medical or clinical practitioners, all of which are then subject to review by a state-appointed medical assessor. A physical assessment or assessments can also form part of the overall assessment process. This process was something that Frank experienced when he first applied to receive assistance:

> 'I've had to prove that I was genuine – you know, that's how I felt. I had to get notes off my GPs. I had to get notes off of the specialist. I go to the pain clinic, I had to get notes off of him stating, yeah, this man is attending me because of his back, this is what's wrong, this is the part of his back that's giving trouble. It's like you constantly have to do it.'

Here Frank talks about feeling the need to prove that he was genuine, and this was something experienced by many of the participants across the different payment types. Essentially, Frank describes building up a body of evidence in order to prove his worthiness, to offer evidence of his circumstances (Clasen and Clegg, 2007). This suggests that while welfare conditionality is often conceptualised as the steps recipients take in order to continue receiving a payment, it is also an aspect of qualifying to receive a payment in the first place. It is a process that, in the first instance, is tempered with the veil of judgment before latterly becoming much more about monitoring, surveillance and a strict adherence to predetermined conditions. Ultimately, and apparently despite the evidence provided by his GP and others, Frank had to submit to a medical assessment, a process he found particularly difficult:

> 'I was scared going in because I knew I was going to come out in more pain than when I went in. He'd get your leg, he'd put it up, he pinned it back, and you'd be in tears. And I say, "Doc, you have to stop." And there's one stage I had to get off the couch and I wouldn't let [him] touch me and I walked out. I couldn't. Like the pain the man put me in I spent a couple of days sleeping on the ground, on a hard ground, because I couldn't go to bed with my back.'

This was something that Frank described experiencing on more than one occasion. In the first instance, it seems unnecessarily intrusive and invasive, given that Frank had already, by that point, provided documentary evidence attesting to his prevailing medical condition from several qualified medical practitioners. Nevertheless, this was part of Frank's process of making a successful claim to receive DA. When asked why he felt he had been examined in the way that he had, Frank was certain as to the purpose: "The purpose was to prove to who[m]ever the powers be that I'm a genuine person and he's [the assessor's] just there to try everything just to make sure that I was genuine, that I wasn't pulling a fast one."

It is clear from what Franks says here that he viewed the assessment process, at least in part, as a submission to and for judgement. Again, this also chimes with much of Clasen and Clegg's (2007) framework in that this part of Frank's experience seems to form part of an assessment of category; Frank must show that he is, in fact, unable to work due to injury. Moreover, Frank talks about proving that he is a "genuine" person, someone who is worthy of assistance, which speaks to conduct (Clasen and Clegg, 2007). This submission to judgement is something that has been addressed elsewhere. Jayanetti (2018, np), writing in the context of the UK welfare system, has labelled this 'punishment beatings by public demand', conceptualising access to welfare entitlements as 'a set of institutional trials to determine whether individuals are sufficiently morally worthy to receive benefits' (np) and suggesting that in order to receive assistance (np):

> … every individual must prove that he or she is worthy of public money, that they have done everything imaginable to avoid needing benefits and nothing to put themselves in their situation. Every aspect of their life and mindset is rendered fair game for scrutiny.

The concept of 'punishment beatings by public demand' also suggests that while the mechanisms of conditionality are structurally bounded, in that they are administered and carried out within a welfare system, they are nonetheless guided and influenced by public perception and discourse in the form of the welfare framing consensus (Jensen and Tyler, 2015; Boland and Griffin, 2016; Patrick, 2016; 2017; Watts and Fitzpatrick, 2018; Whelan, 2020a). This was something that was certainly evident in the Welfare Conditionality (2019: 4) findings, which showed that a majority of respondents, many of whom were themselves subject to aspects of conditionality were inclined to: '… commonly endorse the broad principle of welfare conditionality and there was widespread support for policies that promote responsible behaviour'.

It can be argued that the experiences described by Frank meet the description of 'punishment beatings by public demand' given earlier, with the scrutiny he underwent going so far as to move beyond the symbolic violence talked about by Pinker (1970) in the context of welfare to include the actual infliction of pain. Also inherent in Jayanetti's (2018) argument is the concept of deservingness, which will be explored in Chapter 6.

This submission to judgement, or set of trials, though it may have manifested differently in different cases, was something experienced across payment groups as part of the qualifying process. Below, Martin describes the process in the context of JA:

'I found it to be very rigorous, especially having to undergo it several times over non-stop, one after the other after the other. Detailed bank accounts – six months' banks accounts. It can be very demanding as to what information you have to – for example, my parents had to … undergo testing as to what school they went to in 1934 and things like that. I found it to be very, very rigorous as to what information they needed.'

In respect of jobseeker-type payments, qualification for JB is directly linked to social insurance contributions and is time-limited. The overarching conditions that must be met in order to qualify for JB and JA are predominantly centred on work and include being available for and actively seeking employment. Claimants must also not have left paid employment directly before making a claim, as doing disqualifies them from receipt for up to 12 weeks, during which time they may be entitled to receive SWA. Aside from the basic requirements, it is also necessary to undergo means testing and to meet an HRC. While perhaps not as visceral or physically intrusive in nature as the medical assessment undergone by Frank, what Martin describes here nevertheless seems to border on forensic, a type of bureaucratic trial. He describes finding the process to be "very rigorous" and again this speaks to the high level of scrutiny that claimants must undergo in order to establish worthiness. It is also clear that there is a struggle on Martin's part to gather the necessary information. This, in turn, raises questions about the necessity to submit certain types of information. In particular, Martin describes his parents needing to provide information as to what school they attended in 1934. Whether this was wholly accurate or not on Martin's part, it does raise the question of just what types of information are necessary in the context of meeting an immediate need. Despite this, Martin suggests that the penalty for not submitting the correct required information was as serious as potentially having a claim dismissed: "There were these letters that used to come in and there was 'provide this information' – 'or the claim would be dismissed'."

Graham also describes a forensic level of scrutiny or bureaucratic trial in the context of re-establishing a claim, a process he too felt was overly cumbersome and at least partly unnecessary: "I had to fill in about ten fucking forms. Now, this is all information they already have, right. Nothing is going to change at my time of life … oh, here, fill that in. I mean, they're computerised."

Again, Graham's experience speaks to submitting to forensic scrutiny via the need to provide copious amounts of information in order to establish his worthiness, that is, to establish the veracity of his particular circumstances (Clasen and Clegg, 2007). He is clearly also left feeling that much of what he is required to provide is unnecessary as the information is already available to welfare administrators, an assertion that, whether wholly accurate or not with respect to the specificity of processes, is nevertheless not without credence or basis given that service user data is increasingly managed and stored electronically. In the following, Olive echoes both Martin's and Graham's experiences:

'It was very much you have to have everything perfect. If they want a letter phrased in a particular way from your employer, if they wanted something, then if it wasn't exactly right there'd be a bit of a pause or a bit of hesitancy to say, well, when is that starting, or when are you starting that, or – you know, everything was questioned, everything was I wouldn't say aggressive but it was suspicious.'

Olive describes needing to have everything in perfect order when submitting information. She also describes having to do so under the veil of suspicion if not quite aggression and this again appears to be an element of circumstance: the category must be right, the circumstances must be established (Clasen and Clegg, 2007).

In an example of what could perhaps be considered one of the more hidden, or at least less explicit, aspects of welfare conditionality discussed at the beginning of this chapter, Peter describes the reaction by welfare administrators to the revelation that he was going on holiday, something he had arranged and paid for prior to becoming unemployed:

'… at the same time now I signed on the Social I was going on holidays. And your one says – I said, "I'm going on my holidays." And she said, "What are you doing down here looking for money?" I said, "Excuse me, I'm not down here looking for money." I said, "I'm entitled to my social welfare." She says, "No, you're not entitled to social welfare," she says to me.… I said, "Okay, well, look, I've a holiday paid for." I says, "I paid for it while I was working." "Grand, away you go." "I'm going off to Alaska." "Oh, you've money to go to Alaska and you're down here looking for money off us."'

There is a very clear tone of judgement in this exchange as it is described by Peter. The inherent suggestion appears to relate to circumstance; Peter should not be trying to establish a claim to a social welfare payment while at the same time planning to go on holiday, despite the fact that this arrangement was made and paid for prior to his becoming unemployed. He is also made starkly aware that he is "not entitled to social welfare" as a matter of right; rather, he may or may not be after detailed scrutiny, thus evoking the liberal nature of the Irish welfare regime. While this exchange speaks mainly to an aspect of 'scrutiny under suspicion' (Whelan, 2020a), the formalised conditionality attached to the reality of going on holiday while attempting to establish a claim to social welfare was also made plain:

> 'That's what she said to me. And I'm going – I said, "It's paid for."
> I said, "I was working. I paid for a holiday." I said, "I'm entitled to go
> on the holiday." And she said, "Okay, when you go on holidays," she
> says, you've to bring back my boarding flight and show them and my
> hotels, the hotel I stayed, and show them. And I went, "Why do I have
> to show you that?" "That's what you have to show us."'

Here the formal, and arguably more deeply hidden, nature of welfare conditionality is laid bare. Peter can go on holiday, but in doing so he needs to provide documentation to attest to this. When he asks why this is the case, he is simply told that that is what is required.

This experience of 'scrutiny under suspicion' was common for many of the participants across payment groups. For example, here Grace describes a similar level of scrutiny in the context of applying for OPFP:

> '… there was a lot of questions, but then also the other side of which is
> why are you not getting maintenance? Where is he? What's his name?
> How do we know you're telling the truth? All this kind of stuff. And
> you're just, like, I don't know, I barely know the fella!… So they'd ask
> me to and you'd have to send in a form, or, you know, you'd have to fill
> it out, and maybe your rental agreement, all that kind of stuff again.…
> Bank statements, everything. So you do feel like you've no privacy, like.'

In Grace's case, much of the initial focus appears to be on the question of child maintenance payments, something that was difficult for Grace given her personal circumstances. She also details the familiar process of filling out forms and submitting documentation. Again, there is an inherent thread of submitting for judgement and scrutiny here, the undergoing of 'institutional trials' (Jayanetti, 2018). The general conditions that must be met in order to establish a claim to OPFP include being aged under 66, being the parent, step-parent, adoptive parent or legal guardian of a child or children under the age(s) of seven and being the main carer for the child or children. Aside from this, however, claimants must demonstrate the appropriate circumstances; namely, they must submit to means testing, must meet an HRC and must not be cohabiting with a partner or spouse. Scarlett describes a similar experience when making her application for OPFP: "I remember I needed an awful lot of stuff for it, which I found it hard to gather. So there's lots of stuff that you need for it. Everything is looked into. You almost feel like you're being investigated." Again, echoing the experiences of Grace, the tone described by Scarlett is one of scrutiny under suspicion and, along with needing to provide "an awful lot of stuff", she specifically references feeling as if she is being investigated.

So far, this chapter has described the nature of the welfare conditionality experienced by participants in the process of establishing a claim, and this has, in the main, devolved on establishing appropriate circumstances, thus mirroring a key component of Clasen and Clegg's (2007) framework. It is argued here that this involves a submission for judgement and the undergoing of 'scrutiny under suspicion' in what could be considered a set of 'institutional trials' (Jayanetti, 2018). However, this represents only the beginning of the conditionality process. As claimants work to maintain their entitlement, they are subject to continued conditionality that shifts form, becoming much more about monitoring, surveillance and a strict adherence to predetermined conditions alongside aspects of the mundane, habitual and expected. These experiences speak much more to Clasen and Clegg's (2007) conduct component of welfare conditionality and to the subsequent definition of conditionality offered earlier in this chapter by drawing on the Welfare Conditionality (2019) project. Elsewhere (Whelan, 2021b), I have referred to this as the 'where you must go and what you must do' component of welfare conditionality. It is to these aspects of welfare conditionality that attention now turns.

What happens now? Where you must go and what you must do

Having submitted for judgement, undergone a set of bureaucratic or institutional trials and been subject to scrutiny under suspicion, successful applicants now enter a new phase of welfare conditionality, one that is characterised by ongoing scrutiny and continuous monitoring. Jane describes this level of monitoring as 'constant':

'... you have constant reviews, you know, where they send out these review sheets, and I think – because I have Rent Allowance as well you've two reviews. So you've the review from your One-Parent Family, but then you've your review from your Rent Allowance as well.'

When asked what kinds of information were required during these reviews, Jane replied:

"They're asking about do you get maintenance, if so, how much, if not, why not? They're asking you about your tenancy, how much rent you pay, your bank statements, if you're working or if you're studying." It is clear from what Jane says here that the level of scrutiny undergone at the time of establishing a claim does not 'drop off' or 'relax' once that claim has been established; rather, it persists in much the same format. This was common across the participant group and across payment types. Staying with OPFP recipients, Scarlett talks specifically about the continuing feeling of being investigated in the context of maintaining a claim: "You have to maintain it, yeah. And again there's still the investigation feel, constantly having to send in six months' bank accounts." Again, the key word used by Scarlett is "constantly" and she goes on to paint a picture of what this constancy comprises, echoing Jane's experience of the process: "Constantly. You know anything changes and I need to source forms, I need to go to the city, get form, tell them everything. Everything about my life needs to be known."

A common focus of review for the OPFP participants in this study was the continuous need to provide up-to-date bank statements. This is arguably an intensive level of scrutiny and one that many of these participants found difficult to deal with, as Scarlett describes:

'… I feel that, you know, I, you know, work within my means and, like, let's say I want to order Just Eat[2] for the kids or I want to get something nice, you know, that's up to me and I would have felt embarrassed if, you know, that was on my six months' bank account. But I suppose that's me.…'

This excerpt was used in Chapter 2 to illustrate the concept of social demotion; however, it works equally well when illustrating the monitoring and the adherence to predetermined conditions that accompany the legitimate receipt of OPFP. Scarlett talks about feeling embarrassed about the nature of some of her purchases, which she knows will inevitably be viewed by those administering her review. Grace has faced similar embarrassment and has sought to adjust her behaviour as a result:

'… it's made me a little bit more conscious about what I use my card for. And, like, I know that sounds a little bit ridiculous but, like, I do purposely kind of say I'll only use my cards for the groceries, petrol, and then if I want to go out I will only use cash.…'

Grace is clearly conscious of the nature of her purchases and of how she perceives they will look, meaning that she is clearly affected by the review process that forms part of the conditions for maintaining her entitlement. She may still "go out", but she is affected enough that, in doing so, she will only take cash. This was also an issue for Jane:

'... if I have something that I spent, sometimes you look at it – you know, if you went to McDonald's and you put it on your debit card or something and you're, like, oh, that doesn't look good, you know!... I'd be very aware of, like, well, yeah, that doesn't look great ... so I can kind of get rid of that part.'

Jane talks about purposely tailoring her bank statements to remove what she sees as problematic purchases, perhaps purchases that she feels somebody receiving welfare should not be making. Inherent in the behaviour described by both Grace and Jane are ideas about maintaining compliance and engaging in impression management, both classic strategies of social behaviour in the tradition of Goffman (1990a). This is something that is revisited in Chapter 5. In the context of welfare conditionality, these behaviours speak to an aspect of conduct as given by Clasen and Clegg (2007), albeit the conduct exhibited in these cases may, in actuality, be more 'softly perceived' by Scarlett, Grace and Jane than rigidly required of them.

The level of continuing scrutiny having established a claim was not in any way limited to those receiving OPFP, but was generally the experience across the payment groups, and living under this type of continuous scrutiny as a form of specific and required conduct was something that many of the participants clearly found very stressful. Clive describes a sense of needing to work to maintain a claim, particularly due to a fear of having a payment stopped: "All the time it's kind of awkward to keep the claim because you can at any stage lose it if you're not careful. So you have to be careful if you want to keep claiming anything from the social welfare system."

This reality of being suddenly cut off, and without explanation, was something that some of the participants did in fact experience. Alan, who was having difficulty receiving correspondence due to changes in address, describes experiencing this on more than one occasion:

'They don't contact you by phone or anything else. They just cut me off every time. So I might not know for a week or two because I'll just go into deficit on my account.... There's no communication other than the letter that they've sent to my home.'

Alan, who was estranged from his immediate family due to difficult personal circumstances, was unable to access post at his family home. This meant that any correspondence sent there was unlikely to reach him. The result of this was that he was cut off from payment on numerous occasions leaving him in the position of having to re-establish his claim. This process of cutting off payment when conditions are deemed not to have been met seems to function as a 'sanction without warning' within the Irish welfare system, which, while perhaps not describable as being wholly 'hidden' can nevertheless result in an unexpected and sudden cessation of payment. Equally, the very fact that an expectation of timely responses to correspondence holds the potential for this particular outcome to occur denotes a less explicit and more 'expected' form of welfare conditionality in the context of conduct (Clasen and Clegg, 2007).

Trevor was also someone who experienced the effects of this. At one point when receiving DA, Trevor took up an opportunity to pursue a PhD, which, as it involved travelling to Belfast during the week, meant living, at least part of the time, in another jurisdiction. Again, this contravened one of the arguably less explicit areas of conditionality as it relates to DA and Trevor found himself cut off before subsequently becoming embroiled in a bureaucratic dispute in which he fought to have his claim reinstated. Below, he talks about the experience of his payment being stopped:

'She pressed stop very quickly, yeah, I think as soon as she realised that I was not in quote, unquote "Ireland", which is a point of contention for me personally, but, look, we won't go down there. But quote, unquote, I wasn't in "Ireland", I wasn't in the State. Yeah, she pressed stop immediately and there was no kind of talking to her.'

Subsequently, on discovering where the line was in terms of the conduct conditionality that existed around his particular situation, Trevor managed to take the steps necessary to re-establish his claim and complete his studies:

'... so when you move to a new jurisdiction there are certain rules that have to be met and I think it entails a letter from your psychiatrist saying that they recommend you do the course, if you're going to college, and then a letter I think from a university stating that you're not working.... I think they didn't have much to stand on really because my psychiatrist backed it up, the university backed it up, and it was pretty obvious that, you know, I wasn't lying to anyone. This was what I was doing and the Disability Benefit was affording it.'

While the outcome was ultimately successful for Trevor, this was a period he described as very stressful and his experiences highlight the potential impact of some of the less explicit aspects of welfare conditionality. Trevor subsequently decided to manage impressions differently in future contacts with welfare administrators, essentially holding back certain information for fear of being cut off: "... well, I mean, look, I don't know. I think it's sad. It would be nice if it was a lot more open and transparent for everyone really and there wasn't always the kind of impending fear that they might cut you off."

Wait just a minute, Mr Postman

A further aspect of how continuing scrutiny was experienced as stressful and difficult for many of the participants, and one that once again shows the very real effects of the encroachment of the welfare system into the lives of those who interact with it, was something as simple as receiving correspondence by post. Of course, an aspect of the ongoing scrutiny incorporated into the overall structure of conditionality necessitates a degree of communication between the administrators of welfare and the recipients thereof. Indeed, it is perhaps so expected as to appear mundane. It was noted by many of the participants in this study that such correspondence appeared, at times, to border on the frequency of constant. With this in mind, receiving correspondence from the DSP was something that many of the participants in this study really appeared to dread, with some participants even having a visibly stressful reaction to the topic during interview. When articulating her experiences of receiving correspondence by post, Jane describes a viscerally powerful reaction that gives a real sense of just how impactful this facet of welfare conditionality can be: "I get a pain in my stomach…. Stress straight away…. I get a pain in my stomach when I'm opening it…. It's just always, you know, a review or something's wrong or 'Come in,' you know."

And, far from isolated, this was common for many of the participants and across payment groups. Here, for example, Trish makes a strikingly similar observation: "I dread. My heart goes. I see the envelope and I'm, like, oh God, what do they want now, you know?… I get the sweats, you know. What do they want now?" And here, Grace describes something similar: "I'd say it's *quite* stressful, especially for somebody like me. I get anxious over the smallest things. The small things panic me. And getting another letter in the door, it freaks me out."

It is clear from these accounts that receiving the continuous correspondence that goes along with being monitored and procedurally contacted as a welfare recipient can be an intensely stressful experience, and this can arguably be conceptualised as one of the more hidden or less obvious aspects of welfare conditionality, at least in the sense that it is not commonly perceived as such. It is a factor of circumstance, as given by Clasen and Clegg (2007), in that it appears to be about the continuous process of establishing and then re-establishing legitimate circumstances. Yet, it also creeps into conduct, as recipients are naturally expected to acknowledge correspondence while complying with what is asked of them. Not doing so, as we have seen earlier, can even lead to benefits being cut off. Not only then does welfare conditionality denote conditions for how welfare recipients are expected to behave, but the administration of this conditionality ultimately 'conditions' those under its authority to react in certain ways. As shown earlier, hidden or less apparent conditionalities, when revealed, can effectively 'condition' recipients to engage in maintaining the visage of compliance through impression management; more than this, however, it can also induce fear, stress and anxiety.

A further aspect of one of the more mundane, less explicit, and arguably normatively expected, aspects of conditionality that had a deep effect on many of the participants and that can be characterised as conduct-related, was the need to engage in particular 'welfare activities' in open public spaces. This is explored in the next section.

The public face of welfare recipiency under 'expected' conditions

For a welfare recipient to successfully realise an entitlement they cannot simply stay at home, and apply over the phone or online. Making a successful claim involves a degree of physical activity. It necessitates a claimant to enter the physical geography of the welfare state, to queue in obvious proximity to other members of the public, to liaise, in person, with welfare administrators, and to be interviewed, often with little privacy – essentially, to dedicate oneself to the goal of establishing, or not as the case may be, an entitlement based on predetermined criteria. Much empirical work demonstrates that this is the case across multiple jurisdictions (Hays, 2003; Boland and Griffin, 2015a; Patrick, 2017; Watts and Fitzpatrick, 2018). Once this has been successfully achieved, recipients must continue to enter the physical geography of the welfare state, to sign on, to collect payments, to hand in medical certificates, to further liaise with welfare administrators and so on. This will have been a reality, and at the time of interview continued to be so, for most of the participants in this study, and was an aspect of 'expected' welfare conditionality with which many of the participants struggled a great deal. Harley, an IB recipient who had suffered a serious mental breakdown leading to her reliance on the payment, describes struggling with this aspect of managing her claim in the context of collecting her payment at the local post office:

'… it's that haunting moment sometimes walking into the post office and people knowing what you're doing, yeah.… The post office will always be a problem.… I think generally the women in there are just very … it's almost as soon as you take out that card, it's like, you know, they don't look at you as much. And I don't know if that's the way

I look but I go, "Have a nice day. I hope you have a great time. Thank you so much." You know, I would be pleasant mannered and stuff but it always seems like there's, you know, literally as well as physically, there's a block in between us, like, there's some type of friction.'

Harley clearly struggles with this aspect of managing her claim. She describes entering the post office as a "haunting moment" and suggests that it will always be a problem. She also describes perceiving a change in how she is received once she produces her social welfare card, thus revealing or 'spoiling' her identity (Goffman, 1990a). Whether or not this is the case, what it does denote is the difficulty with which Harley experiences this aspect of mundane or 'expected' conditionality. This public face of claiming, at the post office in particular, was something that many of the participants struggled with. Jennifer, a long-term recipient of OPFP, describes something similar to Harley's experience:

'I think it's a bit, yeah, degrading, like, to meet neighbours in your local post office and all this when you're collecting – everyone knows you're collecting your money. Like, that would bother me.... I suppose because it's the local post office. Like, you're always going to meet someone. And then you have, like, your card and you're going along. I think everyone knows what you're there for, and I just think that some people can be very judgemental.'

Here, Jennifer conjures a sense of social shame. She specifically refers to using the local post office as "degrading". Again, she refers to producing her social welfare card as though an act of revelation, effectively marking her as a welfare recipient and making her purposes plain to other members of the public. Again, this speaks to elements of Goffman's (1990a) classical conception of stigma, specifically the notion of possessing a 'discreditable' stigma, that is, one that is not immediately obvious and can be hidden up to a point. Of course, the bearer of such a stigma can engage in 'passing', but an act such as producing a social welfare card during the public process of collecting a payment undoes the pretence and reveals that which the bearer finds "degrading" and would rather keep hidden. James, a long-term recipient of DA with significant mental health issues, also found collecting his payment at the post office difficult to negotiate at times, and links this specifically to the work ethic along with his own sense own sense of internal ethics:

'Well, I used to feel very uncomfortable about doing it, you know.... I suppose I felt that I was wrong to take it when I should be looking for work more sincerely or something like that.... Out looking for it more. More actively I suppose I should say, you know.... I suppose it's just my ethics, you know.'

Grace describes facing particular issues around how she looks, and how others perceive her, when collecting her payment at the post office:

'... there's almost a sense of guilt when you have a new pair of shoes or you have gotten your hair done. And that shouldn't be the case.... I suppose it's just the way it is. But I feel like you would be kind of like, oh, where did she get the money for this? And you go into the post office and you're collecting your money they're like, oh, you know, you got your hair done, or whatever, like.'

Grace echoes the experiences of Harley and Jennifer. There is an element of social shame, as well as a concern about how she feels she might be perceived, and this appears to devolve on ideas around public judgement, deservingness and what constitutes legitimate expenditure for a welfare recipient. Scarlett found the public face of receiving welfare difficult too, and, as a single parent, this was exacerbated when her children were younger and had had to accompany her when she collected her payment:

'I found that embarrassing because I would have been going in with my baby in the pram as a young mother. Yeah, I would have found that embarrassing. I think now that I'm older I wouldn't have found that as embarrassing, but at the time I did.'

Scarlett at least seems to have been able to move beyond the embarrassment she experienced as a younger mother. Nevertheless, it was something she found difficult at the time. Aside from the post office, privacy within the spaces that constitute the geography of the welfare state was something that many of the participants also struggled with, as Lisa articulates:

'I mean, the spaces themselves are not conducive to privacy or confidentiality. You know, there's no sort of design plan or thought gone it in according to what it is that's going on, you know.... You're clearly on display, like, you know. And if you know who the people are then you know what the person is in talking about. So again no privacy even when there's kind of voice privacy, shall we say. But, yeah, I mean, maybe that's part of the design.'

Lisa describes a fundamental lack of privacy and likens this too, in effect, being "on display". Interestingly, she also questions whether the infrastructural design might not be intentional in this respect. This question of design is interesting as it was something that several of the participants mentioned in respect to the public element of making and maintaining a claim. For example, Olive questions the essential purpose for which a building, in this case a local social welfare office, was designed: "This building wasn't designed for what it's supposed to do because it can't even contain the people that are supposed to be engaging with it. Maybe they've never been that busy since it was built, I don't know."

Olive had been accessing the buildings concerned since the late 2008s, a time that coincided with the Great Recession. Undoubtedly, there would have been an influx of people in need of social assistance at that time, brought on by the rapid and severe downturn in the Irish economy, and it could be argued that many of the buildings in use at that time were almost certainly not designed with recessionary numbers in mind, previous recessions notwithstanding. Nevertheless, what Olive goes on to describe certainly speaks to the potentially stigmatising nature of interacting with and within the physical geography of the welfare state, a necessary condition and an aspect of necessary conduct (Clasen and Clegg, 2007) when making and maintaining a claim:

'… could they not open, like, 15 or 20 minutes early when they see there's a queue and at least let people stand – even if they're not at their desks, if the blinds are down – could people just not stand in from the weather and from the rain and just be afforded some little bit of space?'

Olive describes the indignity of standing in the rain waiting for welfare offices to open, the building unable to cope with the influx of people and the staff apparently not willing or able to ameliorate the situation. As frustrated as Olive may have been, she nevertheless displays a degree of acceptance and understanding of the necessity of her situation. Other participants in the study have no such compunction and are clear about what they feel the public face of making and maintaining a claim ultimately represents:

'We have our dignity, yeah? And I think dignity is a thing you must protect in people if sometimes they can't protect it themselves…. And it's very undignifying, that. You know, the very fact the way it's set up. You've to go down to the dole office. You must go down and sign, you know…. You must go there. It's almost as though it's designed to take away people's dignity.'

Here, Clive sums up the concept of hidden, less explicit or 'expected' welfare conditionality, and the effect it can have. He questions the way the system is set up. Ultimately, he concludes that in order to make or maintain your claim you *must* go where you are directed; it is a condition of receipt and one that arguably has a deep effect on human dignity.

In conclusion, this chapter has shown that, for the participants who took part in this study, the initial process of making a claim constitutes a submission to judgement, the undergoing of a set of 'institutional trials' and, at the very least, a submission to 'scrutiny under suspicion'. This analysis is in line with the framework offered by Clasen and Clegg (2007) in that once category has been decided, the process of establishing the circumstances for legitimate receipt then follows and indeed continues beyond the successful establishment of a claim. There is also much empirical evidence, referenced throughout this chapter, that demonstrates the 'shared typical' (McIntosh and Wright, 2019; Wright and Patrick, 2019) nature of these experiences, meaning that what has been presented here is likely to be replicated within other jurisdictions where similar processes are to be found. It has also been shown that welfare conditionality begins at the point of making a claim, with claimants being expected to meet specific and predetermined conditions in order to successfully realise their entitlement. Following this, and on successfully realising their claim, recipients are subjected to further conditionality that takes the forms of ongoing monitoring, assessment, surveillance and a strict adherence to predetermined conditions. These, in the main, are behavioural or conduct conditionalities (Clasen and Clegg, 2007). Importantly, the chapter has also shown that welfare conditionality can function over a number of levels, from the explicit to the expected and even to less obvious or 'hidden'. In the case of hidden conditionalities, recipients often only become aware of requirements as a result of infringing or contravening the boundaries of a particular condition unknowingly. Expected conditionality essentially makes up the nuts and bolts of welfare recipiency; it is where recipients must go and what they must do in order to successfully realise and ultimately maintain a claim (Whelan, 2021b). As well as recipients being expected to enter the geography of the welfare state, the boundaries of conditionality often also extend into the homes of recipients through necessary correspondence. These are all areas that the participants here have struggled with to varying degrees. It is argued here that, taken in tandem, these aspects of conditionality, comprising the submission to judgement, the engendering of fear and the degradation of public welfare activities, have a deep effect on the welfare recipients who experience them. As has been shown in part here, this, in turn, can lead to a practice of maintaining compliance through impression management – two areas that are intimately bound and that form the basis of the next chapter.

5

Maintaining compliance and engaging in impression management

Impression management as a concept is certainly something that is strongly associated with the classical work of Goffman (1990a) in the context of social stigma and is perhaps most associated with his notion of 'passing' as it applies to those with a discreditable stigma. It is also something I have discussed in the context of welfare recipiency elsewhere (Whelan, 2021a). The various 'masks' people wear in presenting themselves in multiple contexts was a key concern for Goffman and something he explored much more fully in earlier work (1990b). For clarity, impression management is the process into which people enter in order to hide, or at least manage, the 'spoiled' or stigmatised aspect of their social identity. The data drawn on here show that many of those interviewed regularly engaged in this process in a welfare context in order to 'maintain compliance'. I argue that this was manifestly twofold with respect to the fact that many of those interviewed found it necessary to apply these techniques to at least two aspects of their lives. First, many of the participants gave descriptions of engaging in impression management in their general day-to-day interactions in order to maintain compliance with what it means to be a 'good citizen' in the eyes of others and this notion of goodness is strongly tied to ideas around reciprocity and deservingness, discussed in Chapter 6. Complying with notions of goodness essentially involved managing that part of their identity associated with welfare recipiency by hiding it or by attempting to lessen its impact. This, in turn, shows not only that many of the participants have an awareness, or a perception, that the part of their identity associated with welfare recipiency is 'bad' or 'shameful', or that it may be viewed as such, but that they take steps to ensure it is managed or kept hidden altogether, evoking the concepts of both personal stigma and stigmatisation (Baumberg, 2016; Patrick, 2017). It is argued here then that these very acts, this continuous process of impression management, undertaken in order to maintain compliance with notions about 'goodness' or 'good' citizenship, is a significant part of the contemporary welfare experience. Similar themes can be found in other literature. Patrick (2017), for example, has explored ideas around 'citizenship from below'. Notions of 'good' and responsible citizenship are also likely to inform judgements of welfare administrators at the street level (Lipsky, 2010 [1980]; Brodkin, 2012; Torsvik et al, 2021; Ratzmann, 2021). Moreover, research has shown that the way in which categories of persons such as 'the unemployed' are generally viewed resonates with notions of citizenship, whether 'good' or 'bad', as well as with perceived levels of deservingness, although this may be jurisdictionally specific (Nielsen, 2021). The relationship between citizenship and welfare has roots stretching back to early social policy (Marshall and Bottomore, 1992) and has also been explored extensively in more contemporary entries (Dwyer, 2000, 2016). With respect to notions of the 'good citizen' specifically, the concepts of personal stigma and stigmatisation are also very apparent in the data. For clarity, following the work of Baumberg (2016) and also Patrick (2017), who has mobilised these concepts in her own work, they can be defined briefly as follows:

- **personal stigma:** a person's own sense that claiming benefits conveys a devalued identity;
- **stigmatisation:** the perception that others will devalue your identity as a result of claiming benefits.

By exploring the data, I demonstrate how these ideas are borne out in lived experience and how they form one part of the rationale for the practice of impression management.

Alongside engaging in impression management as part of a process of signalling 'goodness' in general, many participants also described engaging in impression management in contacts with the administrators of welfare in multiple contexts such as in person, through correspondence or through direct action or omission. This type of impression management is different from that which has previously been described because it serves a different purpose – in this case, the purpose of preserving what it means to be a 'good welfare recipient' in the eyes of those tasked with administering claims. Participants often achieve this through compliance with welfare conditionality but also through careful management of their own information. Part of this drive to conform or comply certainly bears analysis, which suggests it may be the result of the successful application of neoliberal governmentality. These acts of self-regulation or self-governance do undoubtedly have much in common with ideas around the internalisation of discourses and the successful integration of technologies of the self (Foucault, 1988; Wacquant, 2009). However, the analysis presented here pulls in a different direction to suggest that something else is also happening. In so doing, the data show that compliance mediated through impression management, in many of these instances, is much more likely to be 'disguised compliance', or 'partial non-compliance', that is, the impression, in full or in part, of compliance given in the stead of actual compliance. The concept of disguised compliance is not new and has been explored in literature concerning the social professions, most notably, social work. Ferguson (2011), for example, uses the concept of disguised compliance in his analysis of how parents encountered in child protection settings very often stage-manage the social worker's visit by presenting themselves and their environment in what they perceive to be a favourable way in order to 'cloak' what may be seen as problematic. More recently and directly concerned with a welfare setting, the work of Finn (2021) in the Irish context and Redman (2021) in the UK have uncovered similar practices. Through 42 interviews with jobseekers, Finn's (2021) study demonstrates a welfare system that eschews individuality and offers only 'superficial engagement', resulting in claimants producing what he terms as a 'performance of feigned compliance', a practice not unlike the disguised compliance documented by this author here and previously elsewhere (Whelan, 2021a). In the UK, Redman (2021) draws on longitudinal interviews with 15 young men and demonstrates how claimants can act to subvert policy and prioritise their own needs and interests in the context of trying to survive in a welfare system that is increasingly hostile and demanding. As will be seen, evidence of similar practices was uncovered here, with participants often appearing compliant where they are not through careful management of appearances and information. Partial non-compliance then is taken directly from the data and conceptualised as being somewhat different to disguised compliance. It is presented as being the acts or actions that nominally compliant welfare recipients display in order to hide what they see as problematic aspects of their information and behaviour. These types of compliances, then, quite apart from technologies of the self, are much more an aspect of survival. They are about surviving in a welfare space that is discoursed in a language of scarcity (Patrick, 2017; Boland and Griffin, 2021; Redman, 2021) and employing the necessary techniques to do so. Again, it is argued here that engaging in this continual process of impression management in order to foster a vision of compliance, forms a major part of the contemporary welfare experience in a way that is likely to be a 'shared typical' (McIntosh and Wright, 2019; Wright and Patrick, 2019) component of experiences within welfare states that are broadly similar. In both types of impression management, there are aspects of performance, the performance of the 'good citizen' in the case of the first area explored and the performance of the 'good welfare recipient' in what is explored further on. I start here by looking at how welfare recipients manage the welfare component of their identity in their day-to-day lives.

Managing impressions in day-to-day life: complying with notions of 'goodness'

As noted in the introduction to this chapter, many of the participants interviewed often felt the need to manage the part of their identity associated with welfare recipiency, and this took on various forms. In the first instance, it was often as straightforward as simply lying, whether directly or by omission. For others, it meant making attempts to 'skirt' around this particular area of their lives by framing it in a particular way. For most, it included aspects of both. Here, for example, when asked whether he would ever bring up unprompted the fact that he was receiving welfare, Martin talks about attempting to avoid entering into conversations about this particular aspect of his life when meeting people who may not necessarily know that he is receiving welfare: "Not unless I was questioned or unless it came up in conversation I wouldn't divulge ... I'd try and avoid it or change the subject." At times when conversations such as these persisted, Martin was prepared to answer in such a way as to allow him to continue to manage this aspect of his identity: "I'd say I'm an engineer in a certain industry.... I'm an engineer in a certain industry. That's the usual response I give."

When asked why he felt the need to manage conversations in this way, Martin was unequivocal: "Just from my perspective that's what I feel I need to do because I just feel that if you divulge anything involv[ing] the social welfare system, it's just, like, viewed very negatively."

What Martin describes here in the first instance is, arguably, recognisable as straightforward impression management in the tradition of Goffman (1990a; 1990b) with latent aspects of the performative (Butler, 1988). However, when probed further as to the reasons why he feels the need to engage in this social strategy, the concept of maintaining compliance with an image of the 'good' citizen reveals itself. Social welfare is 'viewed very negatively'; associating oneself with this is to associate with, and, in part, take on, this negativity, so Martin chooses where possible not to divulge his reliance on welfare. This practice was very common across the participant group and across payment types, with the vast majority of interviewees suggesting that they would not divulge their reliance on welfare if possible and with reasons similar to those given by Martin, reasons that are tinged with 'performing' good citizenship (Butler, 1988; Goffman, 1990b). Trish talks at first about lying in respect of her reliance on social welfare: "I've lied to people once or twice that I was working when I wasn't working, just sometimes not to mention the social welfare part."

Similar to Martin, Trish markedly prefers not to mention social welfare if possible, going so far as to lie. Again, similar to Martin, where conversations such as these persist, she has a strategy in place to manage impressions: "Well, I'd always say I'm a childminder. And they'd say, 'Are you working at the moment?' I could navigate around sometimes. Sometimes I was working.... But the time I wasn't I'd lie. I'd basically lie. Just say, 'Yeah, I'm working....'"

Again, when asked why she felt the need to manage impressions in this way, Trish was equally unequivocal: "Social welfare equals negativity."

As with Martin, the concept of maintaining compliance with an image of the 'good' citizen reveals itself here. Trish declares that "Social welfare equals negativity"; associating oneself with this is to associate with, and, in part, take on, this negativity.

Open versus closed strategies

Both Trish and Martin were recipients of JA at the time of interview and, accordingly, as shown in Chapter 3, were more likely to be aware of and affected by the pervasiveness of the work ethic. This may, in turn, have fed into how and why they managed aspects of their identities. However, given that participants on other payment types were as likely to respond in the same way, the phenomenon of maintaining compliance with notions of good citizenship through impression management seems to be more malleable and ubiquitous. For example, Harley, who, as indicated earlier, was in receipt of IB at the time of interview, at times engaged in much the same strategy: "I know that I'm not working, but my hobby would be modelling all the time. So if people are, like, 'What are you doing?' I would say, 'Modelling.'" Harley described suffering a severe mental breakdown shortly before the time of interview and, by her own admission, was not in a position to work. Nevertheless, at times she clearly felt the need to manage the part of her identity associated with receiving welfare. At first, it might appear that this could have as much to do with not wanting to reveal personal information, as it related to her mental health, but this, in fact, was something that Harley described speaking about quite freely when deploying a more open impression management strategy. Essentially, she suggested that when she conflated the two, she found it easier to talk about an absence from the workforce and a reliance on welfare, effectively suggesting that her poor mental health had the effect of legitimising her welfare recipiency:

> 'So I informed people that I would be on social welfare if it ever came up in conversation and they kind of – they all were really good. They were, like, "Oh, are you working?" I would say, "No, I'm not at the moment, I'm sick." Like, oh, yeah. And I said, "I'm on social welfare." And everyone took it really well. You know, people are nosey just by nature and they were like, "Oh, what's that for?" I said I just had basically a mental breakdown. And I think everyone was really understanding. It depends, you know – the most important question, I think, is "Why?" When people find out and I answer why, they understand it a bit more ... it kind of makes sense. I deserve something.'

Here, Harley describes taking a more open, less cautious, approach to general impression management. She suggests that people, in general, understand her specific need to receive social assistance. Strikingly, she also enters into a discourse surrounding deservedness and this, again, not uncommon phenomenon in the context of welfare recipiency, is discussed in Chapter 6. Importantly, what Harley also shows is that engaging in impression management as a way of maintaining social compliance is a reality across payment types. The sometimes-open approach taken by Harley was certainly less common among participants. Jennifer, for example, is categorical about taking the opposite approach. When asked whether, in a social context, she would ever openly volunteer the information that she was in receipt of welfare, specifically OPFP, her response was unequivocal: "Oh, no. God, no, never … I guess I'd be a little bit embarrassed or I would think that that person would think less of me, you know … I wouldn't be volunteering the information."

Jennifer evokes both personal stigma and stigmatisation here (Baumberg, 2016; Patrick, 2017) as she describes the potential to feel embarrassed or socially demoted as her primary reasons for not sharing the fact that she is in receipt of welfare. However, it is also true to say that a more open approach to impression management does not always work and can in fact have more overtly negative consequences. In another example, Frank, who, as previously discussed, was receiving DA at the time of interview, describes a journey in engaging in impression management. Frank described previously having a bad experience of encountering stigmatisation for divulging his status as a welfare recipient to a member of the public on a bus journey:

'We were talking one day on a bus and he was asking me what was I doing and I said, "Well, at the moment I'm on social welfare because I had an accident." He said, "Oh, yeah, that's thieving the country, stealing from the country." And that brought me to another level down.… He said that to my face and he got up and he walked on to another seat.'

This person was unknown to Frank and, from what Frank describes, made no distinction as to 'deservingness' based on Frank's circumstances. As a result of this interaction, Frank became much more tactful about managing his information, choosing thereafter to hold back rather than divulge:

'Wouldn't say anything about what I do. If they said they work at something – "What do you do?" – I'd say, "Oh, this and that." That's what I say because I'd be afraid to open my mouth in case they'd be the same way.… I'd leave that bit out now.… When you get an experience like that you think that everybody's the same.'

This experience was also something that directly affected Frank's ability or desire to engage in social activities:

'I don't get involved in social activities.… It is because of that. It's because you don't know what people are going to say and you're thinking the worst. And it might never happen again – it could have been just that once – but you're always thinking, "I'm not going to get involved in this; I'm not going to get involved with that."'

Withdrawing from the social in the way Frank has described here was also something that affected many of the other participants. It can also be noted that much of what has been extrapolated here links strongly with the concepts of social liminality and marginality discussed in Chapter 2.

The effect of impression management: withdrawing from the social

The reluctance to engage in social activities due to ongoing issues around impression management was something that affected many of the participants across payment types. As well as linking this to social liminality, it is also possible to suggest that it is tied to notions of the good and good citizenship. In the previous example involving Frank, we see that his bona fides as an active and reciprocal member of society was called into question in a social context, and other work (Patrick, 2017, Nielsen, 2021) shows that people do hold on strongly to the views Frank describes encountering. As a result of being unable or unwilling to 'perform' good citizenship, Frank removes himself from social situations. Other participants undertook similar 'journeys'. Below, Alan talks about how, at first, his impression management strategy in relation to welfare recipiency was quite open. However, after what he describes as numerous negative encounters, this changed:

'… initially, I suppose, I was a bit more green and I didn't mind; I would be more open and honest. But I would just continuously have negative encounters and, you know, later on you might experience – I just thought I'd always try and steer the conversation in a different direction. I would avoid and dodge the question. It's just not something I really wanted to get into with people, you know.'

Essentially, Alan found himself facing hostility and struggling to manage social situations as a result:

'I found that I would tell someone, "Look, I'm unemployed at the moment." And I would say it innocently, you know, and then I would immediately get a sense of judgment, you know. There was an awful lot of negativity surrounding, like, "Oh, why are you unemployed?" Some people would be very invasive.… You know, it just felt like I'd done something wrong, you know. It was almost personal for them.'

And, not unlike Frank, as a result of this overt hostility, invasiveness and stigmatisation, Alan found himself suffering considerable personal stigma and ultimately withdrawing from social situations rather than engage in continued impression management:

'The result of that, like, is I personally started to see myself very negatively, definitely. You know, and I would find that I wanted to socialise less because I didn't want to have to kind of negotiate these conversations, you know – because it's something people ask you an awful lot, like – "What are you doing?"'

Clearly both Alan and Frank find the performative dynamic of impression management difficult, eschewing the need to engage in it by withdrawing from the social. This was something that affected Olive similarly and ultimately led to her adjusting her behaviour as an avoidance strategy:

'I was tired of people asking me what are you doing now, where are you going now, what are you going to do, what happened? You know, constant questions – which were fine initially but I suppose when you got asked them every single time it got a bit boring. So there'd be a reluctance, there'd be a big reluctance then began to develop to partake in those kind of events or began to mean that when the thing was over I'd be gone home. I wouldn't be standing around chatting to you or anything, I'd be just, "Right, that's it."'

The way in which Frank and Alan, in particular, describe their separate experiences suggests that, for each of them, their first instinct is to be honest and open. However, negative experiences that called their citizenship into question, cumulative in the case of what Alan describes, caused them both to reconsider this strategy. In the first instance, they evade or omit; however, their respective experiences also suggest that one form of impression management can essentially consist of avoiding altogether the situations in which this is necessary, and this was also true for Olive. Taking the experiences of Harley, Frank, Alan and Olive together, it appears that an open, less cautious, impression management strategy can work, in part, for some. For others, however, its effects are hard felt and ultimately deleterious. This, in turn, speaks to the importance of context.

Welfare recipiency: a general trend towards keeping it hidden, and the importance of context

While impression management is clearly complex and while some of the participants tended towards a more open strategy of performance, they were very much the exceptions. The dominant tendency among those interviewed was to keep the area of their lives relating to welfare recipiency managed or hidden altogether. Nevertheless, this is not to suggest that impression management constitutes an either/or, bilateral choice between being open or closed about sharing information; rather, for many of those interviewed, it was context-specific and multiple factors came into play. Here, for example, Trevor describes thinking carefully about when he might choose to divulge his reliance on a welfare payment: "I don't want to talk about it to everyone. So I would be careful about who I choose to talk to that about and also at what stage of my relationship I would talk about that."

For Trevor, taking these types of decisions were made doubly complex due to the nature of his disability, essentially meaning that to divulge his receipt of DA necessarily also meant divulging his ongoing struggle with bipolar disorder. Trevor, therefore, shows an awareness of the potential for social stigma to occur, something that has been well documented in the contexts of both illness and mental health and welfare recipiency (Garthwaite, 2015a, 2015b; Baumberg 2016; Patrick, 2017; Tyler, 2020). For Trish, making decisions about just what to divulge tended to devolve on her sense of the person to whom she was speaking and whether or not she is likely to be negatively judged: "It's like when I meet someone I can kind of read what they're like first of all. You know, they could have had a different background to me. Sometimes they're snobby, you know. Sometimes they're okay."

Here, Trish arguably displays a degree of class consciousness (see Milner, 2019 for a discussion of the same), specifically attaching importance to a person's background, and this ultimately tempers her decision-making process when choosing just what to divulge about her personal circumstances. Scarlett also displays a similar tendency. At first, like others, she tries to avoid conversation in the general area of welfare recipiency: "… I would try not to. I wouldn't very openly say that…. If it comes up in conversation I will say it but I wouldn't feel particularly – I'm not proud of that, you know."

Here, as with others, Scarlett references a sense of overt negativity surrounding a reliance on welfare recipiency, something contrary to 'goodness', specifically referring to her sense of pride. As is also the case with other participants, she is prepared to guide conversations to reflect other aspects of her identity, specifically choosing to refer to the part-time work she had recently taken up at the time of interview: "Well, I'm okay now because I work. So I would say I work and I wouldn't really say anything about generally. Before, I would have just said, 'Oh, I'm just a mummy,' you know."

Scarlett describes using an impression management technique that essentially consists of accentuating the 'positive' and omitting the 'negative' as she sees it. Like Trish, Scarlett is also keenly aware of context and of whom she perceives she is speaking to:

'I suppose it depends on where I am. But I'd feel I'd be judged for that or looked down on or someone might question my abilities as a parent or my abilities as a person in general ... it depends again who I'm with and my perception of them, you know, and whether I feel that they would judge me for that or not.'

Like Trish, Scarlett is conscious of who she is talking to and what their perception of her might be. She tailors her 'performance' accordingly and refers specifically to the possibility of being 'judged', 'looked down on' or to having her abilities as a parent or as a person questioned. Again, this speaks to an overt negativity surrounding welfare recipiency, the potential for personal stigma and stigmatisation (Baumberg, 2016; Patrick, 2017) and the careful management of information that arises as a result. As with many others, Scarlett engages a strategy of accentuating what she views as the positive aspects of her identity over those she perceives as negative or less favourable, and this was a very common impression management strategy for many of the participants. Olive describes doing something similar: "I was working part-time and that was always the thing that was emphasised in talking to people."

This is turn demonstrates the value placed on paid formal employment and the difficulty people encounter when an absence from the labour market becomes conflated with welfare receipt (Whelan, 2020a). In a further interesting example of an impression management strategy of this type, Jane describes deliberately including information about her attendance at college in conversations unprompted: "... you know, even if they don't ask I might sneak it in there – you know, 'When I go to college later,' you know, or 'I have an essay to do' or something. So then they know and it's a conversation starter."

Jane describes engaging in a strategy of mentioning her college attendance in a deliberate attempt to accentuate that particular aspect of her identity, in effect, distancing herself from welfare recipiency. This tendency to accentuate the positive, particularly in relation to education, which is generally viewed as something 'good', was a common strategy for those who had or formerly had links to an educative setting. Lisa, describes something similar: "So I think when I was a student, say, on the Back to Education, I felt a bit more comfortable because I was doing something or seen to be doing something." Gail, a long-term recipient of DA with long-term and serious mental health and mental illness difficulties, deployed a similar social strategy: "Well, normally I'm doing something, to be honest. Either I'm in college, like last year, I'm looking after my daughter, which is a full-time job, or I'm doing some kind of part-time work. I try my best to be busy ... I talk about the positives."

Gail is talking about how she would describe herself to someone she is meeting for the first time. She, like Lisa, Jane and Scarlett before her, talks about accentuating the 'positives', something she references directly. It is perhaps not surprising that people, in general, would talk about those aspects of their lives that they view as positive; after all, being in education, or part-time work or working in the home is just as big a part of a person's life as is receiving welfare. However, what is key here, from the point of view of how welfare recipients engage in impression management strategies, is the deliberate avoidance of mentioning or discussing welfare recipiency. This, in and of itself, denotes a perception of the overt negativity surrounding the receipt of welfare on the part of those receiving it, meaning that for those in receipt of welfare, just how much of their personal information they are willing to divulge, if or when they choose to do so, is largely dependent on context. This awareness of context, though different for each person, was, nevertheless, very common across the participant group and across payment types. In a final example of just how impactful this process can be, Mary describes how she weighs up social situations and how she ultimately makes decisions around what to divulge:

> 'Like, I think, probably depending on the person, I think. So, like, if I was kind of chatting away with them and I felt quite comfortable with them, then I would probably bring it up if, kind of, I was asked, you know, like "Oh, what do you?" or whatever. But, like, I suppose if I probably wasn't very comfortable with the person, then I probably would be a bit like no, I don't want to kind of mention it. Or if I kind of did *have* to mention it, then I probably would feel quite awkward maybe mentioning it, yeah.'

So far, this chapter has concentrated on how the welfare recipients interviewed for this study engage in impression management in their day-to-day lives. It has shown that, across the strategies used, there is a general tendency to attempt to try to avoid the negativity associated with welfare recipiency in order to maintain compliance with what it means to be a 'good' person or citizen in the eyes of others. This, in turn, evokes Baumberg's (2016) concepts of personal stigma and stigmatisation. However, as outlined in the introduction to this chapter, the participants interviewed here also engage in similar tactics when interacting with the administrators of welfare, and it is to this area that we now turn.

Impression management and maintaining compliance when engaging with welfare administrators

Maintaining compliance with what it means to be a 'good' welfare recipient often tends to devolve on the fundamental aspects of welfare conditionality discussed in Chapter 4. The subtleties of behaviour driven by the internalisation of discourses is also an area that may bear fruit in terms of an analysis. However, the interview data also show that many participants engage in a degree of impression management when engaging with the administrators of welfare and that they do so in order to foster a positive image of a 'good' client or welfare recipient in a bid to continually justify access to what are constituted as scarce resources. To a certain extent, this phenomenon can be described as a type of 'disguised compliance'. As mentioned earlier in this chapter, disguised compliance is a concept of familiar use within the broad spectrum of literature surrounding the social professions such as social work, to which Ferguson (2011), in particular, has made a notable contribution. I take this analysis up here and apply it in the context of lived experiences of welfare recipiency. For clarity, 'disguised compliance' essentially amounts to the 'stage management' of information, actions and materials in order to give an impression of 'full compliance'. Use of the term 'full compliance' is important here too, as it distinguishes between being fully non-compliant and being only partially so. Many of those interviewed here will have been compliant with almost all of the various aspects of what is required to successfully manage a welfare entitlement; they may only be non-compliant in a minor way or ways. Thus, I move beyond disguised compliance and introduce the concept of partial non-compliance. There may also be very good reasons why the interviewees behave in the way that they do. The welfare space is projected in a language of scarcity as being resource-limited, something that claimants and recipients are made to feel in every part of their welfare trajectory. In this respect, impression management that fosters the image of the 'good' welfare recipient is very much about survival and the need to 'keep a hold' of what are much-needed resources. However, it must be noted that impression management is complex and does not always relate to disguised compliance or even partial non-compliance. Sometimes, the reasons for impression management appear to be as simple as recipients putting across to welfare administrators what they feel is a positive image of themselves in the hope of favourable treatment or of being 'left alone'. It must also be acknowledged that particular aspects of disguised compliance or non-compliance, interpreted sympathetically by the researcher, may be seen entirely differently depending on who is doing the looking. It could equally be asserted that particular acts of partial non-compliance, such as the withholding of financial information, are a type of welfare fraud, and this is how such acts would likely be viewed by welfare administrators were they to subsequently come to light. Yet even here partial non-compliance is not the 'feckless' or 'deviant' act it is often purported to be (Runswick-Cole and Goodley, 2015; Wincup and Monaghan, 2016, Patrick and Reeves, 2021).

Fostering the image of the 'good' welfare recipient

Putting across a positive image to welfare administrators as a mode of impression management differed for many of the participants. For example, Jane links forming a favourable impression to work and to the work ethic:

> 'I feel better about myself when I have a part-time job. And I feel like when I'm on the phone to the social welfare people that if I can say, well, I am working … alongside rearing my two children by myself, I feel a bit better about that – and I feel it's received better.'

Here Jane states plainly that by virtue of working part-time she feels she will be better received by welfare administrators and that this eases her communication with them. This was a point she reiterated several times during the interview: "I feel that social welfare can't really say much to me if I'm always showing that I'm working a bit."

Earlier, in Chapter 3, it was shown that the work ethic is writ large when it comes to welfare within administrative contexts. The fact that recipients would feel the need to accentuate work with respect to how they communicate with welfare officials therefore makes contextual sense. This is not to suggest that Jane only engages in part-time employment in order to manage impressions with the administrators of welfare, as her reasons for working and for wanting to work are undoubtedly complex and varied; rather, it suggests that, for Jane, being able to point to the fact that she is employed part-time forms a useful part of an overall impression management strategy. Aside from this, however, Jane also engaged in more overt impression management in terms of managing specific aspects of her information. As discussed previously, many of the participants, Jane included, struggled with sharing financial information, such as bank statements, particularly in respect to what they saw as problematic purchases. Returning to consider this same aspect of welfare conditionality, it can be seen that Jane was also careful to manage her information in order to not fully divulge all aspects of her income:

> '… there's been times where I would omit a certain month maybe. Like they might have [asked] for six months and I notice that in that last month there that maybe I got money from the Assistance Fund or something like that – and I just won't put in that last month and I'll say, well, if they get back to me and insist upon it I will, but otherwise I'm just putting in five months and see what they say.'

Here Jane can be seen to be engaging in careful, surreptitious, impression management, specifically in respect to her finances. Inherent in this excerpt also are the concepts of disguised compliance and partial non-compliance; Jane appears to be complying with the conditions for legitimate receipt, but in reality, this is not the case, and she tailors her information in the hope that it will go unnoticed (disguised compliance). Nevertheless, while Jane may be attempting to control what information she includes, she is not being fully non-compliant; she does, after all, submit the majority of what is requested and, so, in this sense, may be characterised as being only partially non-compliant. Aside then from the act itself, Jane's motive for the described omission is arguably understandable and entirely sensible: "... because my fear, you know, is that they would take it off me in a different way and then what was the point of me getting it?"

This type of impression management strategy speaks to ideas around survival and making the best of available resources in the welfare space. In doing so, it leads directly to another reason why many of the participants engage in impression management strategies such as this: fear of negative consequences.

Managing impressions due to a fear of the consequences

Earlier Jane talked about her not unreasonable fear that she would lose the benefit of extra income should she reveal it and this practice of managing information in order to 'avoid' potential negative consequences was common across the participant group and across payment types. For example, Martin, who was personally, deeply affected by negative experiences with welfare administrators, is unequivocal about guarding his information much more selectively than perhaps he had at first: "... from learning how the system operates I'd be probably more evasive than I've been ... I'd be probably more reluctant ... to communicate to the office. It'll be just, 'Hello', 'Thank you.'" Martin specifically describes being 'evasive', communicating only what he absolutely needs to while remaining cautious or even reticent to say or do anything more than give the standard colloquial greetings required. This reluctance to divulge or to be open based on previous bad experiences along with the perception that to do so may, in turn, initiate further aggravation was also something Trevor described. In the following excerpt, Trevor describes making tentative inquiries in the context of what might happen to his payment should he decide to pursue a master's degree. In describing a telephone conversation with administrators from the DSP DA section, he talks about specifically withholding information relating to his personal circumstances on the basis that it would or could make life difficult for him:

'I phoned them they didn't know the answer, and I knew that because they didn't know the answer that ... it would mean a big investigation to find out what that answer was, like.... It would mean an investigation that I probably wouldn't win just because of the technicalities and there probably wouldn't have been the empathy to the situation and there probably wouldn't have been the kind of almost common sense applied to the situation because it would be black and white. And so, yeah, I just wasn't willing to go down that road. And I think from my knowledge of other people who've been in similar situations they would probably agree. And that's sad, because I think – well, I mean, look, I don't know. I think it's sad. It would be nice if it was a lot more open and transparent for everyone really and there wasn't always the kind of impending fear that they might cut you off.'

Trevor describes deliberately withholding information regarding his personal circumstances as he feels that not to do so would likely result in a difficult outcome. His current personal circumstances may not fully comply with his receipt of DA, but, regardless, he is not inclined to fully investigate whether this is the case. It is clear from both Martin and Trevor that this form of impression management, which largely consists of impression management through the non-disclosure of information, is indicative of the necessity to foster survival techniques in the welfare space. In the cases of Martin and Trevor specifically, it is clear from their separate descriptions that they have had negative experiences due to full disclosure in the past and that this has tempered their approach to information sharing and, ultimately, to impression management. This in turn suggests that impression management, as a strategy to be used when engaging with welfare administrators, can be as much about non-disclosure or withholding as it can about overtly fostering the image of a 'good' welfare recipient. This withholding of information in order to not be exposed to potential negative consequences was something that did cause some participants to take decisions that were, arguably, detrimental to their overall well-being. For example, at the time of interview, Mary was suffering from serious and diagnosed social anxiety, but this was something she chose not to disclose as she was afraid of the consequences, a fact she revealed when asked if she had told her Intreo officer about her diagnosis:

'No, I haven't, and probably the reason why is because I'm probably nervous that I don't know what would happen. I don't know if I would be taken off the Jobseeker's or if, you know, there would be some consequences from it. And I suppose it's always a thought in my head that, like, it's something that probably should be brought up, but there's always the fear that like oh, I'll be taken off it and, you know, I kind of don't know what'll happen then after that in a way.'

Mary, who originally found herself unable to work due to this anxiety, could potentially be a candidate for DA, a successful claim for which would remove the need for continual job searching in the short to medium term.

Nevertheless, and despite being at least vaguely aware of the prospect of receiving a different payment, she chooses to keep this aspect of her personal circumstances hidden, afraid of what the consequences might be should she reveal it. As a result, she is expected to engage in a continual hunt for employment, something with which she struggles:

> 'Like, I do get very anxious. Because the whole job-hunting experience is anxious for me anyway, but then the experience of nearly knowing someone is kind of looking over your shoulder all the time kind of makes it even more kind of anxiety-ridden then because you're trying to kind of, you know, just, you know, focus on one thing but then you're, like, worried that, like, oh, I'm not doing enough.'

Mary's experience shows that engaging in impression management with welfare administrators is a complex phenomenon and is not necessarily always undertaken to the betterment of those who engage in it. For many of the participants, engaging in impression management in this way can also mean not speaking up in the presence of welfare administrators even in instances where they feel they should. Again, this speaks to a degree of maintaining compliance with what it means to be a 'good' welfare recipient as well as to a fear of consequences. For example, Trish, speaking specifically in the context of her interaction with Turas Nua, describes her reluctance to speak up in a situation where she otherwise might have done so:

> 'I never spoke up for myself to any of them, saying, look, you're asking me to do the same crap every week; can you please help me.... Because I didn't want the dole on my back. If I tell them – say I told them I had a problem with them. They're getting straight on to the social welfare and my payment is being cut when I can't have that. I was afraid basically, you know.'

Here, it is arguably clear that Trish perhaps wanted to speak up; she certainly held strong opinions unvoiced. Nevertheless, she chose to remain silent, 'afraid' of the consequences should she voice her opinion. Again, this speaks to deploying an impression management strategy that maintains compliance with being a 'good' welfare recipient and that fosters survival in the welfare space. Interestingly, while Trish describes demonstrating a necessary degree of self-control in order to manage impressions and maintain compliance, she was also one of the few participants to fully divulge, without reticence, instances of disguised compliance by working 'under the table', while receiving JA:

> 'To be honest I always thought I'd have an extra bit of money in my pocket. I kind of look at it from that angle. But I'd always be watching

over my back…. I have done that for a few years, I would admit that. You know, I think everyone has. But you're never comfortable because you know you're doing something wrong. And it just takes one person to rat you out.'

While Trish freely admits to engaging in an act of disguised compliance by working illicitly, it is also clear that this is something she was uncomfortable doing, describing it as "doing something wrong". This shows that while engaging in aspects of disguised compliance may be a reality for some welfare recipients, it is not the 'immoral' or 'feckless' process that it is often portrayed to be as part of a common-sense framing of welfare recipiency (Jensen and Tyler, 2015). Trish did not enter lightly into arrangements such as she described, but did so in order to gain 'an extra bit of money' and was clearly conflicted in doing so. Ultimately, she suggests she would be happier to work full-time and within the system, with the ultimate aim of no longer having to engage with the social welfare system: "I'd rather full-time than be part-time, you know, because sometimes I think it's not worth it to be part-time and drawing [benefits]. Again you're still dealing with the Social Welfare, you know. I just don't want to be dealing with them." Trish finishes by talking about getting to a place where she no longer needs to 'deal' with the administrators of social welfare. Given the complex permutations involved in doing so for Trish and the other participants of this study, it seems a completely understandable desire.

In conclusion, this chapter has shown that many of the participants engage in impression management in various contexts. First, many of the participants engage in impression management in the interactions that make up their day-to-day lives. This may take the form of lying or omission, or it may involve accentuating the positive aspects of their identities, such as work or education, while simultaneously relegating those aspects of their lives that they view as negative, namely a reliance on welfare. Because of the negativity associated with welfare recipiency, it has been argued that these acts of impression management constitute an attempt to maintain social compliance by projecting the perceived or preconceived image of the 'good' citizen. Alongside this, it has been shown that many of the participants engage in impression management in their interactions with welfare administrators. The reasons for this are varied and consist of attempting to maintain compliance by projecting the image of a 'good' welfare recipient, as well as managing information due to a fear of potential negative consequences. The chapter has also described instances of disguised compliance and of partial non-compliance and, again, the reasons for these are varied. Engaging in these types of behaviours requires engaging in continual and complex psychological and social activities, the reality of which must undoubtedly affect a person's sense of self. Overall, it is argued here that engagement in the continual processes of impression management and maintaining compliance forms a major part of the lived experiences of welfare recipiency. It is also argued here that these are likely to have a 'shared typical' (McIntosh and Wright, 2019; Wright and Patrick, 2019) dimension, meaning that the knowledge offered here potentially extends to other, similar, welfare regimes. The next chapter addresses the question of deservingness in the context of welfare recipiency, and how the effects of this are prone to manifest through the practice of othering and self-justification, coupled with feelings of shame around the norm of reciprocity.

Deservingness: othering, self-justification and the norm of reciprocity

When it comes to human welfare, debates surrounding deservedness or deservingness, who should get what and what they should have to do in order to get it, have arguably been omnipresent, taking in discourses surrounding sturdy beggars, the able-bodied and impotent poor, the deserving versus the undeserving, up to and including formalisation via the workhouse test and its direct descendant the means test (Beresford, 2016; Dukelow and Considine, 2017; Glennerster, 2017; Powell, 1992; Whelan, 2021b). This type of thinking has become firmly entrenched and enmeshed in the fabric of societies, in the liberal welfare states of the Anglosphere world at least, and has affected the participants interviewed for this study. Consequently, it is something to which many of the participants have given voice. As well as voicing awareness and opinions as they relate to deservedness, many of the participants have tended to deal with the question of their own deservedness in a particular way and using particular strategies. Essentially, this has devolved on a tendency to engage in the 'othering' of other welfare recipients, which is then coupled with a tendency to justify their own recipiency. As will be seen, this is clearly a complex psychological and sociological area for the participants interviewed here. Engaging in the othering of other welfare recipients denotes a value position that may be out of sync with or contradictory to the personal circumstances of those engaged in othering, hence the subsequent need for distancing or self-justification. It is a practice that clearly forms part of the contemporary welfare experience and, as such, there is a cognate literature (see Shildrick and MacDonald, 2013; Bratton, 2015; Garthwaite, 2016; Pemberton et al, 2016; Patrick, 2016, 2017; Welfare Conditionality, 2019) that documents this, thus illustrating the 'shared typical' nature of these phenomena. On the basis that othering is a practice that forms part of the contemporary welfare experience, the question of why this is so still remains, that is, why do welfare recipients engage in the othering of other welfare recipients? Patrick (2016, 2017), has addressed this directly and has conceptualised engagement in these practices as a form of 'citizenship from below'. Essentially, she suggests that claimants reappropriating negative assessments of benefit claimants for use against others in a similar position may indicate a broader acceptance of the welfare framing consensus in the UK. She also argues that othering among welfare recipients can be understood in the light of what are seen as scarce resources, with individuals essentially competing by emphasising the deservingness of their own entitlement while simultaneously undermining that of others. This, in turn, suggests that othering forms the basis of attempting to survive in a welfare space that is constituted in a language of scarcity, and this is certainly congruent with and therefore indicative of a 'shared typical' aspect what Patrick (2016, 2017) has shown and what is presented here. Looking further afield, Bratton (2015), writing in Canada, has articulated the practice of othering as a complex cultural phenomenon, showing how many of the 24 participants in his study on welfare discourses, persons who were themselves receiving welfare, held negative views of others on welfare. Many of Bratton's (2015) respondents also made arguments suggesting that they accepted the culturally bounded stereotypes that exist around welfare recipiency in the Global North while also buying into the 'taxpayer as victim' narrative, a narrative that is prominent in the data presented further on. This worthy/ unworthy–self/other dichotomy as a cultural phenomenon, as suggested by Bratton (2015), does have a place within literature of this type going much further back (see Kingfisher, 1996; McCormack, 2002; Hays, 2003). This work also suggests that othering strategies on the part of welfare recipients are at least partly generated within the norms of reciprocity, with those failing to reciprocate potentially bearing significant social costs as a result, and that this is strongly tied into questions of deservingness. It is in this grasping for deservingness and legitimacy that the tactic of discrediting other recipients, as a way of preserving one's own identity, is forged. Closely linked to this is the emotion of shame, which may be said to be socially constructed and co-produced by being a combination of negative self-assessment made in light of the expectations and assessments of others, real or imagined (Chase and Walker, 2013). Attempts to combat this sense of shame, therefore, may also result in the tactic of othering and also self-distancing. Whatever the psychosocial impetus behind othering in a welfare context, what remains clear is that it is undoubtedly very real and that certain groups, namely immigrants, those with substance misuse issues, 'fraudulent' disability benefit claimants and those with no previous employment experience, tend to repeatedly come in for negative assessment in this respect (Runswick-Cole and Goodley, 2015; Wincup and Monaghan, 2016; Patrick, 2017; Patrick and Reeves, 2021). Many of the participants in Patrick's (2017) work, for example, commented on the familiar tropes of the immigrant family that seems to get everything, or the person on a disability payment who is not really disabled, and, when taken in light of the ostensibly scarce resources thesis, it is easy and maybe even understandable to see how such commentary emerges among welfare recipients. As will be seen, many of the participants interviewed for this study engaged in similar practices.

As noted, closely related to views surrounding deservingness is the question of social reciprocity. Reciprocity is certainly a concept that has been addressed at length in the context of social policy and welfare recipiency, perhaps most notably by Titmuss (1968, 1974, 1987, 1997), who tackled head on the concept of altruism in social and health policy and, like much of his work, emphasised his preference for the values of public service over private or commercial forms of care. In making his case, Titmuss (1997) pointed to blood banks as the perfect example of social altruism at work, arguing that, as no discernible benefit was likely to accrue to those prepared to donate blood – there was no payment in cash or in kind and donors were extremely unlikely to ever knowingly meet those who had benefitted from their donation – blood banks represented a perfect form of social altruism based on a norm of beneficence and social reciprocity. In effect, this argument suggests that this is something people are inclined to do as part of the human condition, that the express need to 'pay it forward' is something that people, under the correct conditions, feel strongly. More recent work (Parsell and Clarke, 2020) has revisited these ideas in calling for a reciprocal model in the context of charity. Although the concept and the 'doing' of welfare has undoubtedly become more fractious since the post-war period in which Titmuss (1997) wrote, the effect of social reciprocity is arguably still incredibly powerful. Taking up Titmuss's (1997) idea, what is of concern here is the question of what happens to people when opportunities to engage in socially altruistic activities are limited or altogether unavailable; how, in effect, people experience being the beneficiary of the 'altruism' of others, when they have no opportunity to reciprocate. Many of the participants here were aware of the 'norm of reciprocity', which, as welfare recipients, they felt they had 'failed' or were unable to live up to. For many, receiving welfare was constructed as 'taking while not giving' and this was something that they struggled with in the context of their own deservedness. Many of the participants in characterising welfare recipiency as 'taking while not giving' were in effect engaging in a process of questioning their own deservedness and, in so doing, showing the extent of the potential for considerable personal stigma (Baumberg, 2016; Patrick, 2017; Parsell and Clarke, 2020).

Taking these ideas forward, the following paragraphs suggest that, in the first instance, welfare recipients are deeply affected by the question of deservedness in a general sense and by their own deservedness in particular. As a way of combatting this, therefore, many participants tend to engage in othering coupled with self-justification. Ultimately, however, this practice encapsulates a contradictory value position, leaving those who engage in it attempting to do a 'psychological double-step' to condemn the very act that they themselves are 'guilty' of committing.

A consciousness of the question of deservedness

Beginning by exploring the question of general deservedness, this was a social theme that many of the participants appeared to recognise. For example, Martin suggests that some payments are seen as more deserving than others:

'I definitely think there's less of a stigma with accessing disability payments than there would be Jobseeker's. Jobseeker's you're kind of view[ed] as being oh, you're this no-good guy who's, you know, not willing to work or not wanting to work or that kind of perspective.'

Martin, echoing the ancient debate (Whelan, 2021b), suggests that less stigma tends to attach to the receipt of disability-type payments. He also suggests that those in receipt of jobseeker-type payments are more likely to be seen as responsible for their own 'dependency'. This is a point that is also echoed by Gail: "I think probably people who are on Jobseeker's get a worse time than anyone else."

Gail, in particular, is interesting in that, as will be shown further on, she demonstrates that having an awareness of the debate surrounding deservedness does not itself prevent recipients from engaging in the practice of othering. Much of the awareness for participants around questions of deservedness tended to stem from what they feel is a general tendency within society to question the legitimacy of welfare recipients. In the following excerpt, Scarlett relates this specifically to her own personal circumstances as a recipient of OPFP:

'... you know, unfortunately what an awful lot of society would feel about young mothers, single mothers claiming from the government. There is a – you know, I don't like say huge, but there is a good proportion of society with a very certain view of that and I would have reflected that onto myself ... it's a bad perception within society, I feel, that people ... in any sort of help or assistance from Social Welfare should not be allowed to indulge in anything. That's actually a very, very common thought of some parts of our society.'

Scarlett addresses this societal perception directly, suggesting that there is a general view that those receiving welfare should not be allowed to "indulge in anything". She also talks about reflecting this perception onto herself, demonstrating the effects of such discourses on experiences of personal stigma in the context of welfare recipiency. These discourses are, of course, deeply embedded not only in the quasi-theological domain, but also in the social and political domain where they have garnered much currency in recent decades (see Murray, 1984, 1990, 1994; Mead, 1986, 1992; Selbourne, 1994; Etzioni, 1997).

In terms of having a general awareness of the question of social perceptions of deservedness, Clive was one of the few participants to have addressed matter directly: "… there is that perception there that there is a deserving poor and a non-deserving poor. And there isn't really." Here Clive talks about the social perception of there being a deserving and an undeserving poor, a position he ultimately feels is false and went on to describe as dangerous. While many of the participants did display a general awareness of the social question of deservedness, most did not address it in as direct a fashion as Clive; rather, it tended to emerge in the practice of othering coupled with self-justification, an issue discussed in more detail in the following section.

Questioning deservedness through the practice of othering and self-justification

When it comes to the practice of othering among the participants of this study, analysis of the data shows that it tended to occur on a continuum, ranging from quite strong and overt in some cases to something far more subtle in others. In almost all cases, the othering tended not to focus on actual groups or individuals who were directly known to the participants, but rather on some perceived group or individual, some 'other' with questionable moral character, who was out there somewhere and engaged in some sort of dishonesty or fraud, or who was perhaps abusing the system. In almost all cases, participants tended to follow up incidences of othering with self-justification, sometimes apologetically so, in order to distance themselves from those being othered.

Overt othering and self-justification: a focus on particular groups

In the following quote, Gail, who has experienced a long absence from the labour market due to significant mental health difficulties, is shown engaging in some, arguably, very strong othering of those experiencing long-term unemployment: "These lazy layabouts, kind of, you know, they're 25 years on Jobseeker's. Even saying 25 years on Jobseeker's! It's called *Jobseeker's*! When I was on Jobseeker's I was actively searching employment." Gail displays very strong views here about those in receipt of jobseeker-type payments. The othering is strong in tone yet light on detail or specifics, targeted at a specific group but arguably in a vague way. She also engages in the process of self-justification by referencing her own experience of receiving a similar payment, during which, she insists, she was actively seeking employment. Gail also goes much further than this, suggesting a system of staged sanctions for those she views as being in receipt of a jobseeker-type payment for unacceptable periods of time:

'I think maybe if you hit ten years then you should have, like, 75 per cent, and then if you hit another five years, you know, you go down to 50 per cent, and then if you hit another five years 25 per cent, and at that stage, I mean, that would be really detrimental to your lifestyle but it would give them an incentive to try.'

She also suggests that those receiving jobseeker-type payments are either not trying hard enough or are less than honest in their attempts to find employment:

'People who say there's no jobs are liars. I shouldn't say liars, but you know what I mean. There are jobs. There are *always* jobs. There are so many businesses and premises and every kind of service looking for people to be human, to do a job and get it done well.'

Alongside suggesting her own ideas for managing jobseekers and jobseeker-type payments, Gail is largely in agreement with the current form of welfare conditionality in this context in a way that mirrors what has been presented in other literature and in other jurisdictions (Bratton, 2015; Patrick, 2016, 2017, Welfare Conditionality, 2019):

'The fact that that system is there, that needs to change, you know, that Jobseeker's, like, they are making sure people are going out and looking for jobs and doing their interviews and handing in their letters and all that. I think that really needs to happen.'

In all of this, Gail has engaged in very verbose and unapologetically strong othering of welfare recipients on a different payment trajectory from her own. She has suggested laziness and dishonesty on the part of jobseekers; she has also shown herself to be largely in agreement with the level of conditionality that surrounds the legitimate receipt of jobseeker-type payments and has even suggested some additional conditions of her own. Clearly, there is a strong sense of a particular value position in what Gail has articulated and there is a strong sense of what constitutes deservedness that goes with this. However, when it comes to her own long-term welfare recipiency and absence from the formal labour market, Gail is quite willing to distance herself from how she portrays others and to engage in self-justification:

'... for me I feel like I'm not really somebody who should take it, but in reality I find it difficult to find the job that can sustain. And

I would be perfectly happy to find a job and let circumstance take me off Disability Allowance, but that's the way it works.'

Here Gail suggests that, were it not for her personal circumstances, she would rather be working and not receiving DA. While what Gail describes here may in fact be true, in the sense of her believing this to be case, it must nevertheless be explored in the context of her very strong remarks about those receiving jobseeker-type payments. Essentially, what Gail does here is to remove fully the responsibility for receiving a welfare payment from herself, effectively suggesting she is a 'victim' of circumstance and of the ways in which things work. Again, this may be accurate and true. The purpose here is not to condemn Gail, either for her views or for her circumstances, but to understand the logic process she undertakes in justifying herself while simultaneously condemning others. In the following excerpt, she distances herself further from those she condemns: "So I wouldn't see myself as oh, she's a jobseeker for the last 15 years. That to me would be embarrassing. The fact that I'm entitled to an allowance that sort of facilitates me working when I can it's not too embarrassing for me." Again, she removes herself from the realm of jobseeking here and suggests that her need for the receipt of welfare is different and perhaps more justified.

Gail was far from the only participant to engage in this type of strong and overt othering and while Gail had engaged specifically in the othering of a payment group different from her own, this practice also tended to happen within payment groups. Below, Peter is very adamant about how he views a portion of other JA recipients:

'Well, there is some people that play the system and they do it very well. And then there's genuine people who need the money, need the help, and are willing to work. And then there's another side of people that do not want to go to work, they're quite happy living off the social welfare, and they never had a job in their life.'

Like Gail, the othering Peter demonstrates here is, on the one hand, quite strong and condemnatory, yet, on the other, it remains vague. He refers to "some people" or to "another side of people", yet these people are somewhat intangible, they are 'out there', somewhere in the distance. However, Peter, like Gail, did articulate strong views on a particular cohort:

'See, the big thing with the welfare was there was a lot of Polish people – not being negative about anybody – there was a lot of Polish people and … they could fly over, sign on, and fly back. And they were getting the social welfare. And then the ash cloud went up. It was only then the Social Welfare copped on. Oh, that money's going there.'

Peter directly references the Polish community in Ireland, suggesting that many of them were engaged in welfare fraud and that this came to light during the necessary halt to air travel that occurred as a result of a volcanic ash cloud disruption in 2010.[1] Peter is engaged in the strong othering of a particular group here. Like Gail, he is also deploying a strategy of self-distancing, and so in effect justifying his own welfare recipiency through this act of singling out a particular group for negative attention. This shows, arguably, a more subtle form of distancing and self-justification, even though Peter was also much more overt in this respect. As was shown earlier, Peter found experiences of welfare conditionality difficult and frustrating, specifically his experiences with Turas Nua. It is through this lens that he perhaps most strongly condemns a portion of his peers while justifying his own recipiency:

'Turas Nua is a waste of time. They're not helping anybody. They're just forcing people to find work that they don't want to do. It might help some people because some people are lazy and they need a push. Maybe that way. But I was always looking for work.'

Here, Peter is unequivocal that, although there may be some "lazy" welfare recipients out there, he is not one of them. Interestingly, this phenomenon of the othering of 'non-Irish' welfare recipients as a means of distancing one's own recipiency from a perceived un-deservedness was not limited to Peter. In the following excerpt, Graham describes, at length, an interaction with a welfare administrator where he overtly engages in a similar tactic, though in a much more forceful manner. He also engages in some extremely strong othering as he recounts the event:

'Like, they start refusing people – like, they're giving it to foreigners, you know. I mean, I remember going over to an interview in the dole, right, and your man says to me, "Oh, we're mad trying to get people back to work." I said, "If you were serious about getting people back to work you'd fuck out all the foreigners."... And your man says to me, "Oh, that's racist."... "It's not racist," I says. "It's not racist if it's true." And, I mean, anyway, it's like this: you need to look up the word "racism". Apartheid is racism, right. Segregation is racism, right. The penal laws were racist, right. They know all about law[s] that are racist, right. But me using the word "black" in a sentence is not racism, you know what I mean? But there is that middle-class bullshit that goes on, you know. You say anything against a foreigner you're racist. There's such a thing as legitimate comment, right.... Now, I did a security course but, I mean, it's like this now: like ageing on 60 I don't want to be fucking wrestling with Romanian gypos[2] or fucking – you don't know what you're going to catch off of these cunts, right.... I mean, it's like this: they're being brought in here and given everything that I had to earn, right. Because I remember saying to one of them, like your man, like the fella now that said to me, "Oh, we're mad trying to get people back to work."... Well, he started I was racist. And I said, "Furthermore," says I, "between you and me and the fictional foreigner whose rights you're so concerned with I'm the only one who actually paid in a shilling."... Everyone on the outside of the glass as far as they're concerned is dole-sucking scum, right, even though the major parasites are inside the glass.'

Here, Graham engages in a long and particularly hateful tirade about how 'non-Irish' or foreign welfare recipients are treated within the Irish welfare system, suggesting that they are treated more favourably than their Irish counterparts and rationalising his deeply problematic views when challenged. Of course, in the context of othering, what Graham engages in here, albeit deeply unpleasant and offensive, is unsurprising and arguably somewhat of a classic strategy. In the UK, Patrick (2017), as noted earlier, has argued that, on the one hand, such tactics are indicative of a wider acceptance of the welfare framing consensus there. On the other, she argues, othering among welfare recipients can perhaps be understood in the light of what are seen as scarce resources, with individuals essentially competing by emphasising the deservingness of their own entitlement while simultaneously undermining that of others. As with maintaining compliance and engaging in impression management, othering then can be about survival in the welfare space and, echoing the work of Patrick (2017) and argued here, is reflective of ideas surrounding deservedness. Graham, like Gail and Peter, is distancing himself and his own deservedness from those he perceives as less deserving, in effect legitimising the basis for his own recipiency. The tropes he employs are trite and familiar, although he appears to hold his views with some conviction and continued to engage in this type of othering for substantial periods of the interview:

'Now, more and more are foreigners drawing welfare. Now, nobody ever talks about foreigners. They talk about the Irish people. Because it's racist to talk about foreigners. No, it's racist to run down the Irish people. Like if you discriminate against anyone based on their ethnic origin, that's racism, and that's what they're doing to the Irish working class. Like because the bar is lower for a foreigner, right. They actually refused to consider Irish-born people returning to this country for welfare, right, but you can come here an AIDS-ridden African, right, they'll house you, clothe you, feed you, educate your children, and pay a hundred grand a year for your retroviral drugs.'

While Graham arguably represents an extreme example of overt othering, the commonalties with Peter and Gail are apparent, nonetheless. There is the othering via the condemnation of another recipient group, and this acts as a distancing mechanism or a form of self-justification as well as being a lens through which to view matters of deservedness. There is also often an explicit attempt at self-justification and, again, this is arguably utilised as a tactic to preserve self-deservedness.

Overt othering and self-justification with less specific focus

Other participants did engage in a form of othering that was still arguably strong and overt, but more general and perhaps less focused on a particular group. For example, when asked if there was a general negative perception of welfare recipients, Trish suggested that there was, but, in doing so, laid the blame squarely at the door of the recipients themselves: "Oh, definitely, definitely, because most of them are lazy gits, you know what I mean."

The language used by Trish here is quite strong, referring to most, if not all, welfare recipients as "lazy gits". She goes on to to suggest that this phenomenon is geographically bounded and speaks directly about a cultural normalcy around welfare receipt:

"Well, I grew up in Northside.[3] Alcoholics everywhere – not everywhere, but you could see the downside of giving people so young this free money in a way – which is what I called it, you know. They never tried to improve. They just got lazy. They were given money and they just sat there, you know. And that happened a lot in the Northside and it's still going on today, you know.'

Here Trish is very specific about what she feels the effect of welfare has been in the area in which she grew up. She paints a bleak picture, describing a culture of dependency, and suggests that a lack of ambition creeps in where people have ongoing access to "free money". Her argument, which is based on her own first-hand experience, is undoubtedly reminiscent of concepts such as the 'underclass' and echoes the claims of the proponents of this type of thinking (Murray, 1990, 1994). Doubling down on her viewpoint, Trish also goes on to distinguish between those she sees as being deserving of support and those whom she feels are not:

'... now, people with disabilities and things like that, you know, even medical – all these people deserve it, you know. And some people actually find it hard. They can't find work, you know. But there's a big high percentage that – a lot of people shouldn't be getting the dole, you know.'

She also makes direct reference to "dole cheats" and suggests they annoy her, despite the fact that she also admitted to engaging in this particular aspect of disguised compliance herself: "I would know of a lot of families where they are signing on and the husband is in a full-time job. They're cheats basically, dole cheats, you know, and they annoy me."

Different from Gail, who singled out those receiving jobseeker-type payments, and also from Peter and Graham, whose focus was specifically on non-Irish welfare recipients, Trish engages in othering using very broad strokes. Many of the actions she condemns she has also freely admitted to performing herself. However, she does take steps to distance herself from the picture she paints: "It wasn't a long-term thing. I was saying I'm just doing this now just to – whenever I was getting the work. And a stepping stone. This is after getting a little bit longer than that, you know, at the moment." Here she describes receiving welfare as being a stepping stone to something else, although she admits she has now been receiving it for longer than she is comfortable doing. She also suggests that her mind-set is ultimately different from that of many of those she has described:

'They get lazy and – you know. I've been in that trap. I know how they feel. But to be on it years and years and years. It's like how can you – are you happy like that, you know, really? Are you so used to it? It's quite sad really, you know.'

At first, Trish shows empathy here, describing having had similar experiences to those she previously so easily condemned. Perhaps inevitably, however, she distances herself, questioning how the people can be happy in long-term receipt and describing it as "quite sad". This practice of self-portrayal as a 'different' or atypical type of welfare recipient was also quite a common form of othering. Here, for example, Jennifer describes seeing what she clearly feels is a 'different', perhaps more nefarious type of, welfare recipient:

'... I suppose outside the post office and that you do see, like, certain types then coming in and collecting in a gang, you know. Like even in Douglas[4] there on a Thursday morning, if you go down and you're doing a few bits, you do see like some people going in and you know that they're just taking it ... they're just taking the mickey, like. And then they're out all weekend just drinking....'

Clearly, Jennifer does not see herself in the same way as the welfare recipients she describes. She describes seeing people in the post office "collecting in a gang". She obviously feels these people are not entirely genuine and suggests that they may be "out all weekend" drinking. Lisa also portrays herself as a very different or atypical welfare recipient, even going so far as to suggest she has received feedback in this respect as a result of her atypical actions:

'Well, like, I remember going into the office down on Washington Street, I was just calling in to, like – I can't remember what stage this was at. It was probably about three years ago. And I was like, "Is there any courses I can do?" And she was like, "We never have people walking through the door asking to do things. We always have to chase them, you know!"… Like, I'm up for anything basically. So, like, any types of courses or learning or whatever it is, you know, I'd happily kind of oblige….'

Later, she goes on to distinguish herself further on the basis of her voluntary work:

'And I think for people it makes a difference if you're at home drinking cans and watching *Judge Judy* than if you're volunteering 20, 30, 40 hours a week somewhere. You know, so I think there's a judgement on what kind of a dolehead are you, like, you know? And so I probably would be classified as a good dolehead!'

Here she suggests that the type of welfare recipient you are can and does make a difference. Like others, she distinguishes between the idle or lazy welfare recipient who may be "at home drinking cans and watching *Judge Judy*" and the 'good', industrious or active welfare recipient. In the process, she engages in the practice of othering and self-justification. As with other participants, Lisa is quite vague and anecdotal when it comes to the objects of her othering, unlike Jennifer, who appeared to have a far more solid idea with respect to othering, citing people she had seen at the post office. What is inherent in each of the exchanges with Trish, Jennifer and Lisa is the spectre of deservedness. Each of them, in different ways, attempts to distance themselves from more problematic portrayals of welfare recipiency, presenting themselves as 'different' or 'atypical'. In doing so, they are each presenting as being deserving and suggesting that others may be less so.

Subtle othering and self-justification based on 'common sense'

The othering practised by Gail, Peter and Graham is described as 'overt' and 'focused' simply on the basis that in each case, specific groups were singled out for negative attention in strong terms. Shown here also was a tendency towards an overt form of othering that was perhaps less focused on particular groups. Others still engaged in othering through the process of presenting themselves as 'different' or 'atypical'. However, for many of the participants, engaging in the practice of othering was far more subtle, often appearing to stem from no more than the simple belief that there are people 'out there' of questionable moral character who are 'cheating' the system – folk devils in the tradition of Cohen (2011). Again, detail was almost always scarce and vague, and this form of othering tended to be based on 'feeling' or on 'common sense', which itself may have its impetus in the welfare-framing consensus (Jensen and Tyler, 2015; Boland and Griffin, 2016; Patrick, 2016, 2017). For example, in the following extract, Harley engages in the practice of othering in a manner that is almost 'throwaway' and certainly far less considered than the examples given previously: "There's some people that genuinely are happy not doing anything, and in a way I'd love to be able to be a part of that, but I could never abuse the system. Like, that's just me." Here, Harley engages in othering by suggesting that there are "some people" out there who are happy "not doing anything" and who may be inclined to "abuse the system", and that she herself could never "be a part of that" despite sometimes being tempted. Harley offers no detail here; she simply suggests that such people exist. She is not necessarily inclined to condemn the behaviour of those she suggests are prepared to abuse the system, but neither is she prepared to fully excuse it. She begins to justify herself by suggesting she would not be happy to deliberately abuse the system. She continues this self-justification by further distinguishing herself:

'I think that when people talk about being on the dole, social welfare, Illness Benefit, people would normally think that you're sitting at home doing nothing. But I have gotten my arse up most days, but because of my mentality or just my mental health that I've gotten up, I've gone out with my friends. Like I've been very proactive with my life.'

Here she distances herself from what she feels are perceptions of laziness or idleness, suggesting that she has been "very proactive" with her life and that this is ultimately down to the type of person she is. There is quite a lot going on here for Harley. She engages in the subtle othering of other welfare recipients, but does so based on a vague, unsubstantiated and arguably 'common-sense' perception of welfare recipients in general (Jensen and Tyler, 2015; Boland and Griffin, 2016; Patrick, 2016, 2017). In doing so, she is keen to distance herself from such perceptions by articulating her own deservedness. This practice of othering, based on a sense of there being some 'other' out there who is prepared to abuse and cheat the system, was very common across the participant group and across payment types. For example, Frank appears to be willing to accept without equivocation that there are people who are cheating the system: "… it's because when you're on something the genuine people – yeah, we know there's people that are not genuine, but the genuine people want to give something back."

Frank suggests that "we know" that there are people out there who are "not genuine", and he distinguishes between those who are genuine and those who are not on the basis of genuine people's supposed desire to "give something back". It could be argued that Frank has engaged in a type of othering here but not in any direct way, rather very generally and based on 'common sense'. James also demonstrated this common-sense acceptance of the 'bad' welfare recipient on being asked whether or not he felt welfare fraud was a prevalent phenomenon in Irish society: "Oh, there must be. Yes, there are really.... Oh, it must be quite common now because – it must be quite common."

And here we see Jennifer, again based on a common-sense perception, make a similar point in the context of those who she suggests are working while receiving welfare: "I do think that some people do take advantage. Not everyone, but I do think there's a lot of people that have partners like working full-time and then they're claiming."

Clive, who undoubtedly came across as the most 'pro-welfare' participant of those interviewed, also makes a claim that people can and do cheat the system and that this has the ultimate effect of making life difficult for those who are more genuinely in need of assistance:

'Yeah, because there are people – I know there are people that are cheating it, because you can cheat it. And a lot of people do cheat it. And that buggers it up. Maybe not a big area again. But then there are people that really do need it and don't get it.'

Finally, in an excerpt that perhaps most fully demonstrates the almost kneejerk process of othering based on 'common-sense' perceptions of welfare recipients, when asked what words tended to occur to her when thinking of those receiving welfare, Jane answered: "I mean, 'lowlife' came into my head there just automatically when you said that.... That's what came up. Yeah, I'm not a lowlife, you know – which is judgmental now from me." Jane quickly volunteers the word 'lowlife' and then follows this by quickly distancing herself from such a description. Encapsulated within this short excerpt is the overarching tendency to other welfare recipients based on 'common sense' perceptions and to then quickly distinguish oneself from such perceptions.

So far, this chapter has focused on the othering and self-justification practised by many participants as a method of distinguishing themselves and both conveying and preserving their own sense of deservedness. It has been shown that this practice has many permutations and can range from the overt to the subtle, can target specific groups and can be based on little more than common-sense perceptions of welfare recipiency. For the remainder of this chapter the focus changes, taking up the work of Titmuss (1997) and others

(Parsell and Clarke, 2020) to illustrate the effects of social reciprocity and how this is also something that causes recipients to struggle and grapple with their own sense of deservedness.

Social reciprocity and questions of deservedness

In the first instance, many of the participants were aware of and affected by social reciprocity in a general sense. For example, Clive talks about how he feels welfare recipients are perceived as a cohort who take from society but offer little:

'Yeah, because you don't want to be perceived by your peers as, you know, a bleed on them or a leech on them or, you know, affecting their life in that sense, because that's probably the way they'll see it. You know, you don't want people to perceive that. You don't want people to think that of you, right.'

He also suggests that this is not a way in which any person would wish to be perceived. Frank was also someone who felt very strongly, in a general way, that welfare recipiency was contradictory to the norm of reciprocity, that it went against what it means to be a 'good' citizen:

'I thought everyone that looked at me said, "Oh, look, he's in welfare, we're keeping him."... I wasn't long on social welfare when I attempted suicide, because I didn't want to be around. I didn't want to be a burden ... people have to work to keep me today and that makes me feel like nothing.'

Clearly Frank has some very strongly held views about what it means to receive welfare and holding these views has had a very serious effect on him, even causing him to attempt suicide. It is also clear that, for Frank, these views revolved around being in a position where he felt as though he was a burden, someone who was in essence 'taking while not giving'. While it is true that Frank presents an outlier in the sense of just how badly he was affected by his own preconceived ideas, he nevertheless expresses a theme that was common to all those affected by the inherent expectations of social reciprocity. At one point he talks about people he feels "have to work to keep" him, and for most of the participants affected by this particular phenomenon, this was where the major fault line tended to occur. Many of the participants here suggested that social resentment, based on a sense of unrequited generosity from those in work to those receiving welfare, was something that they had encountered or were at least aware of. Some participants managed to resist this narrative, although others tended to internalise and even accept it.

My taxes are paying your welfare: the darker side of social reciprocity

Being the beneficiary of somebody else's taxes was a very prominent theme for many of the participants, whether they were overtly negatively affected by it or whether it was just a general perception (see Coughlin [1980] for a discussion of the same). For example, Trevor references the resentment that he feels may flow from the 'taxpayer' towards the welfare recipient: "It's probably just resentment that they're having to pay taxes and they think their taxes are paying someone else's [welfare]."

This was also something that Harley referenced:

'I think that with a lot of those things, like, you know, looking for help, especially financial when it's taken out of people's pockets as taxes, I think that like, you know, you feel like you're an extra burden sometimes and it's terrifying.'

Harley directly references the notion of taking money from "people's pockets" in the form of collective taxation. She also talks about feeling like a burden, something she describes as "terrifying". This was something that Alan was also conscious of, although he was at least inclined to challenge the simplicity of this suggestion:

'And, you know, you have, you know, the working population pay taxes and resent people who don't work as hard as they do ... there's very little nuance shown to the fact that maybe somebody is only out of work for a few months. You know, there's usually – in my experience anyone I've ever met who's on welfare there's usually a reason for it, you know.'

Alan challenges the notion of a tax-paying majority being responsible for the upkeep of an intentionally unemployed population, suggesting the argument lacks nuance. Patricia too has an awareness of an ongoing social narrative surrounding taxes and social welfare and describes an encounter during which her brother was verbally accosted on that very basis: "... my brother was in the local shop and he said that he was going on holidays and the shopkeeper turned around to him and said to him, 'Oh, is it taxpayer's money that's taking you on the holiday?'"

Patricia describes a very public confrontation experienced by her brother and delivered on the basis that, as a welfare recipient, he should not be going on a holiday due to the fact that his income represents a portion of collective taxation. While this must have been unpleasant for Patricia's brother, Patricia herself did not appear to be too badly affected by this particular social narrative. Others were, however. James, for example, talks about the shame he feels as a welfare recipient and links this directly to a sense of 'taking and not giving': "Well, I feel kind of sorry or sad, you know, because, you know, I wish I had work, you know. It's kind of shameful to be taking the money, you know."

James, who has severe and chronic, cognitive and mental health difficulties, has not worked for almost all of his adult life, and, based on the information he submitted at the time of interview, was unlikely to be in a position to do so at any point in the future, at least not in formal paid employment. Nevertheless, he describes a sense of shame in "taking the money". The effects of an inverted norm of reciprocity are apparent here: James does not experience the benefit of giving, and is left with the shame of taking (Titmuss, 1997; Parsell and Clarke, 2020). Grace also describes something very similar and, again, she specifically uses the word "shame":

'I feel that people think that they shouldn't be funding me, if you want to call it, or whatever, like. I suppose the shame is also that I haven't kind of done it. Like I don't have a job that pays me well or whatever and I don't have a job at the moment. I mean, we all want to eventually have a living wage, you know, and it's disappointing that I haven't yet been able to do that. So I suppose that's kind of – the fact that I'm on social welfare means I haven't done that, you know.'

Grace describes feeling that others are "funding" her, once again denoting the sense of 'taking while not giving' that accompanies the receipt of welfare for so many of the recipients here. She goes on to describe it as a type of shame; the fact that she is not working or earning her own wage appears to trouble her deeply. Scarlett makes a similar point about what it means to receive welfare and when one should seek social assistance:

'I believe that people should have assistance when they need it and I don't believe that people should have assistance when they don't need it. And if I'm working full-time or, you know, I can support myself, I don't need that and I wouldn't go looking for that.'

Scarlett is categorical about what it means to work and to support herself. Again, it is possible to read into what she says in order to get a sense of how she sees welfare as 'taking while not giving' – something she will only do should she absolutely have to. Inherent in the cases of James, Grace and Scarlett are perceptions of what it means to contribute to society. Each of them feels that they are taking while not giving and, as a result, they are not contributing to society in the way they would like to be contributing. This is also something that Mary has articulated very well:

'I suppose at the moment what I'm on, like, I don't feel like – you know, I'm not really contributing to anything and that kind of has the effect then as well, like, of thinking that, you know, you should be doing better kind of thing, like.'

Mary clearly suggests that, due to her status as a welfare recipient, she feels as though she is not adequately contributing. There is also a strong sense of shame or unhappiness in what Mary describes, particularly in how she feels that she 'should be doing better'. It is certainly clear that there are many strong feelings surrounding deservedness, welfare recipiency and what it means to be 'taking while not giving' for many of the participants mentioned so far. However, of all of those interviewed, none appeared to be as badly affected by the thought of 'taking while not giving' as Frank or, at the very least, and without wishing to denigrate or demote the feelings or experiences of others, none articulated this phenomenon quite so strongly. It was earlier established that Frank was quite deeply affected by the work ethic and that not working, or not being in a position to work, engendered a strong sense of shame in Frank. It is not altogether surprising then that he would also be deeply affected by the concept of social reciprocity. Like others, Frank is deeply affected by the concern that he is effectively being supported by the taxes of those in work: "I'm taking other people's money who have to get up early in the morning, go out to work, and they're doing it for me." He is also deeply affected by being, as he sees it, no longer able to adequately contribute to society: "I'd love to be working, because when you're working there's nothing like it, because you're paying your taxes, you're giving to society. I'm giving nothing. I'm taking everything, I'm giving nothing."

Frank is explicit, equating the payment of taxes with "giving to society". He also suggests that, due to his status as a welfare recipient, he is "taking everything" and "giving nothing". He, like others, is also aware of what he perceives to be social resentment of those receiving social welfare by those in work:

'They think that anyone that doesn't work is a cheat and robbing the state. And they feel we paid in for these people to be on the dole or on social welfare or whatever kind of social welfare they're on. We've worked all our lives and here they are they're just enjoying our money. That's how I feel about those people. That's the way they think.'

Although Frank is short on detail here in the sense of not being clear about who "they" are, he has nevertheless had some direct experience with which to bear out such assertions, on a personal level at least. However, it could also be argued that Frank is engaging in an act of othering here based on a 'common-sense' analysis of working people and their concerns about welfare recipients. Ultimately, Frank feels that his reliance on welfare means that, in essence, he has let down those closest to him:

> 'I let me kids down. Always feel I let me kids down. I don't know about other people, I only know about me, and about me, like I said, I feel guilty I'm taking social welfare. I feel guilty that I'm not working so my kids can say, oh, my dad's doing this, my dad's doing that. I feel guilty that I can't give them the things that other parents can give their children.'

It is clear from Frank's experiences that a reliance on welfare, which engenders for the recipient feelings of 'taking while not giving', can be very powerful. Frank, like others, feels that he is not adequately contributing to society, something that working had previously afforded him the opportunity to do through the payment of taxes. He suggests and appears to have internalised the idea that those in work harbour a natural resentment towards him and others here have made reference to this perception too.

Hurtful stereotypes or harmless fun?

In briefly exploring the origins of the perception of welfare recipients that those in work resent them based on their own feeling of involuntarily supporting 'idle' welfare recipients through collective taxation, it appears that it takes the form of a social discourse, and is something that many of the participants have experienced directly, albeit almost always cloaked in humour. Lisa, for example, describes just such an experience: "I suppose sometimes people crack jokes about oh, I'm paying your wages, you know, the tax.... But that's quite a common one and, like, you know, I'm not going to take offence to that, like."

Here Lisa describes experiencing jokes that are targeted at her and rooted specifically in the assertion that those in work are "paying" her "wages" by virtue of paying tax, but essentially she brushes it off, in effect considering it permissible. Peter also experienced something very similar: "When I wasn't working a bit of slagging off from my friends, like – 'I have to go to work, pay tax to pay you.' A bit of slagging."

Peter describes something very similar to Lisa's experience. Like Lisa, he is specifically the target of 'humour', and, again, the specificity of this permeates from notions around work, taxes and welfare recipiency. Also, like Lisa, he appears to shrug it off. Trish also describes experiencing something similar, in a humorous way, from her brothers: "My brothers maybe have a little snide but they'd be having a laugh more than anything else."

However, she also describes coming in for negative attention from her sister, whose circumstances are vastly different from those of Trish, in a way that is devoid of humour:

'A lot of snide remarks, you know.... She'd just rip a hole in me, to be honest. She'd be great working for the government. She would find the dole cheats, you know. One of them ones, you know. Looks down on everyone.... It would annoy her, people on social housing, and if something came on the radio she'd have to turn it off because she'd go red in the face ... when it comes on the radio now she gets so mad, you know. "Social, and you're getting houses and I have to pay for mortgages and they getting that." You know?'

Trish describes how her sister directed "snide" remarks towards her. Her later description of her sister's reaction to hearing radio coverage relating to welfare recipiency and social housing suggests that, for some people at least, there is truth in the assertion that those who are in work and who pay tax appear to harbour a resentment towards those in receipt of various forms of social welfare. In attempting to assess the pervasiveness of this social discourse, the fieldwork data drawn on here is ultimately insufficient. Nevertheless, it may be argued that when something becomes acceptable enough to be continuously couched in and delivered through humour, it is likely to be very widespread indeed.

In conclusion, this chapter has shown that discourses surrounding deservedness and who deserves to get what are deeply impactful and efficacious, and, alongside having a long history (see Whelan, 2021b), also form part of the contemporary welfare experience, judging by the comments of the participants interviewed for this study. By drawing on cognate literature throughout, the chapter also suggests that much of what our participants have recounted here is likely to feature as part of the welfare experience in other liberal welfare states, thus demonstrating the 'shared typical' nature of these experience types. With respect to how an awareness of a deservingness discourse manifests in particular types of practice, as well as voicing awareness and opinions as they relate to deservedness in general, many of the participants tend to deal with the question of their own deservedness in particular ways and using a particular set of strategies. The chapter has demonstrated how this devolves on a tendency to engage in the othering of other welfare recipients, followed by a distancing and justification of one's own welfare recipiency. The psychological permutations involved in this are clearly complex and the sociology of how this plays out is messy. This is not least because of the fact that engaging in the othering of other welfare recipients often denotes a value position that may be out of sync with or contradictory to the personal circumstances of those engaged in othering, hence the subsequent need for self-justification.

Closely related to views surrounding deservedness is the question of social reciprocity and many of the participants tend to characterise welfare recipiency as 'taking while not giving', in effect engaging in a process of questioning their own deservedness. Opportunities to reciprocate are arguably something that human beings desire strongly and this certainly appears to be borne out in the data presented here and elsewhere (Parsell and Clarke, 2020). As a result, when opportunities to reciprocate are out of reach or do not readily present themselves, this can have a devastating effect on welfare recipients or on those receiving aid, charity or benefits in general (Titmuss, 1997; Parsell and Clarke, 2020). Ultimately, then, this chapter has shown that welfare recipients are deeply affected by the question of deservedness in a general sense and by their own deservedness in particular, and this certainly forms a key part of lived experiences in the context of welfare recipiency in a way that is likely to be 'shared typical'. As a way of combatting this, many participants tend to engage in othering coupled with self-justification and self-distancing. Ultimately, however, this practice encapsulates a contradictory value position, leaving those who engaged in it attempting to do a 'psychological double-step' to condemn the very act that they themselves are 'guilty' of committing. Finally, many of the participants are troubled by their own deservedness in the context of social reciprocity and this is denoted by a tendency to conceptualise receiving welfare as 'taking and not giving'. In the next and final empirical chapter drawn from this study, I take these ideas forward by exploring the idea that receiving welfare has ultimately come to be thought of as something nefarious or simply 'bad'.

Welfare is 'bad': bringing it all together

This chapter sets out to encapsulate and affirm all of the empirical materials that have been presented so far in a way that draws together all the different and complex strands. For this reason, it revisits much of what has been recounted already, including some of the most pertinent data excerpts. The aim of this chapter is to suggest that the contemporary 'welfare imaginary' has shifted irrevocably, particularly in the time since the embedding of the post-war welfare commons, and to show that, because of this, there is a persistent and pervasive tendency within the liberal welfare regimes of the Anglosphere for welfare provision – a social good originally imagined as something positive and necessary – to be thought of as inherently 'bad'. I suggest that the contemporary 'welfare imaginary' is badly damaged and that the sociology of this drives lived experiences in the context of welfare recipiency. This break or schism in the 'welfare imaginary' is something that has been addressed elsewhere. Jensen and Tyler (2015: 471), themselves drawing on a range of sources, note this in the context of the UK in a way that is worth recounting:

> It is difficult to remember from a contemporary perspective that the Keynesian welfare state was imagined by its original architects as a 'cradle to grave' safety-net for citizens: a 'welfare commons' of 'shared risks' which would function to ameliorate economic and social hardships, injustices and inequalities (see Timmins, 2001; Lowe, 2005; Glennerster, 2007). The landmark publication of the Beveridge Report in 1942 saw people queuing outside government offices in their desire to get their hands on a copy of this blueprint for a new welfare state (Page, 2007: 11) and the report sold over 100,000 copies within a month of its publication.

More recently, Fitzpatrick and colleagues (2019) return to T.H. Marshall's idea of a basic minimum standard of social and economic security as a facet of social rights. Drawing on Hoxsey (2011), and with recent reforms in the UK in mind, they make the following observation:

> These developments beg the question whether social citizenship is entering a post-Marshallian phase, or returning to a pre-Marshallian form; even whether, as Hoxsey suggests of Canada, citizenship is taking

on an individualistic and marketised form shorn of its social element. (Fitzpatrick et al, 2019: 5)

Others have also written in a way that attempts to reclaim and re-emphasise the value of a strong welfare state or welfare commons (Beresford, 2016; Glennerster, 2017) or that points to the damaging effects that the poverty, created by welfare reforms, is having on the social fabric in liberal welfare regimes (Armstrong, 2017; Alston, 2019; Lister, 2021). There has also been an acknowledgement within the literature that the contemporary 'welfare imaginary' begets a landscape that is alive with myths and populated by folk devils (Jensen and Tyler, 2015; Baumberg and Meueleman, 2016; Crossley, 2017, 2018). Armstrong (2017: 12), in particular, notes the potential for damage to the texture of social life when the safety net provided by a strong welfare offering is eroded:

> Because the welfare system is the foundation on which many of the most admired achievements of our society are founded – affluence and the growth in tolerance of different ethnicities, faiths, gender and sexual orientation – it follows that, if social protection can be eroded, nothing else is safe.

It is against this backdrop that lived experience plays out, and much of the literature that captures this is clearly replete with contexts that demonstrate the effect of a damaged 'welfare imaginary' that suggests that to claim welfare and to be a welfare recipient is somehow 'bad', 'morally questionable' or even somehow 'deviant' (for example, Boland and Griffin, 2016, 2018; Patrick, 2016, 2017; Whelan, 2020a, 2020b, 2021a; Finn, 2021). Essentially, then, as will be seen, for many of the participants, it has become just 'normal' to feel bad about receiving welfare. Furthermore, the idea of a reliance on welfare being somehow 'bad' appears to be largely expected and, as a result, accepted. Interestingly, what has shown up quite strongly for many of the participants here is how discourses such as these tend to permeate and become reproduced in the online space. Many of the other themes explored here throughout contribute to this overarching narrative of welfare as 'bad'. The valorisation of work and the proliferation of the work ethic as a measure of what it means to be 'good' feeds into the overall production and presentation of welfare as 'bad'. The conditions attached to the legitimate receipt of welfare are indicative to those who must attempt to comply with them that receiving welfare is 'bad'. This is arguably further exacerbated by the nature of ongoing receipt, which is a heavily scrutinised process conducted under ongoing suspicion. Questions surrounding deservedness, engagement by welfare recipients in the practice of othering and self-justification, and the conflictual nature of social reciprocity all also feed into a sense that welfare is 'bad'. As with previous chapters, I suggest that by positioning the experiences described as 'shared typical' (McIntosh and Wright, 2019; Wright and Patrick, 2019) in nature, they are likely to resonate with the experiences of welfare recipients in other, similar welfare regimes.

Before presenting the empirical materials for this chapter, I note that by approaching this theme in this way and by couching the analysis in the idea of a damaged 'welfare imaginary' I am not suggesting that there has not always been, to some degree, an anti-welfare narrative in broad social discourse (Powell, 1992; Dukelow and Considine, 2017; Whelan, 2021b). Rather, the suggestion is that this sense of a reliance on welfare as being 'bad', immoral and even deviant is something that the participants in the study keenly felt. I note that the idea of a self-sufficient and wholly beneficent post-war welfare commons is itself a problematic proposition and that it has indeed been problematised, particularly recently, in the literature (Bhambra and Holmwood, 2018, 2021; Bhambra, 2020, 2021). However, a deeper look at this line of analysis is beyond the scope of this book, which devolves, in the main, on lived experience.

Welfare is just 'bad'

Many participants denoted a sense of seeing social welfare and the receipt of social welfare as 'bad'. This was something that was often imparted to them directly as well as being reinforced or experienced in a range of other ways, as exemplified by the following remark from Trish: "So he did try to teach us not to go to the Social Welfare but it was there for us if we needed it, you know."

Here, Trish talks about how her father attempted to teach her and her siblings "not to go to the Social Welfare". Inherent in this is the suggestion that social welfare is something bad, something to be avoided and something that parents should teach their children not to engage with if at all possible. Of course, this notion of welfare as 'bad' was something that was reinforced for Trish in intimate family relationships – "My sister would have given me a lot of snide remarks when you're on the dole...." – and in various public fora in the online space:

> '... all this "bum doleheads" and, you know, "all these fucking wasters" – da, da, da. To be honest I wouldn't go in and read them. I get mad when I go in there.... I think Facebook is a big thing anyway, you know, with the, I suppose bullying. It's kind of bullying on some level, you know, without actually knowing the person.... It is a public forum. It's like you're being lynched. You know, I felt like the comment[ator] had been lynched.'

The message inherent in what Trish describes encountering online is strikingly clear: social welfare is bad. Comments encountered online are, in the main, incendiary and hateful. Trish compares it to bullying and perhaps to a form of 'digital lynching' or 'piling on'. She suggests that she attempts to avoid consuming these narrative streams, but clearly she has been unsuccessful in avoiding them fully. Jennifer, like Trish, also experienced an overt negativity surrounding welfare recipiency in the commentary of those around her:

> '[a] particular girl now will always make comments, even on a night out, like, "Oh, look at them, now, look at them drinking, and what they're wearing, and they're probably drinking their social welfare money," and, you know, this kind of stuff.'

Again, the comments of Jennifer's companion evoke an overt sense of negativity surrounding welfare recipiency. It is interesting to note that these comments appear to have been delivered in proximity to Jennifer, despite her own personal circumstances.

This negative perception, this idea of welfare and any of association therewith being bad, is something that Alan has also experienced in a similar way to Jennifer and Trish: "To be honest even amongst friends and family I've found that there's a very negative perception around social welfare. I think it's everywhere really, you know." Like Trish, Alan has had negative experiences with close family members, or at least feels they have a negative perception of social welfare in general. He also describes what he feels is an overall negative perception that exists around social welfare, suggesting it may be 'everywhere'. Also, like Trish, Alan has encountered his own share of negativity in the online space:

> '... the comments section under like the *Journal.ie* or *The Irish Times*, oh my God it's *unreal*. And I think people feel safe. They can hide behind a pseudonym or, you know, a fake profile to say whatever they want, which is often horrible, you know, about – and yeah, like you say, often welfare recipients or anyone who is a recipient of, you know, the welfare state in any shape or form is the target, you know.'

Here Alan talks about encountering overt negativity online, suggesting that those who demonstrate a connection to welfare are often exclusively targeted for negative attention. Below, Alan talks about how this perception of welfare as 'bad' has affected him:

> 'There's layers and layers of ways that it kind of made me feel very negative. The first was to do with the stigma and it was the way people

treated me that kind of a sent me a very clear signal that I was bad in some way, you know.'

Alan describes there being "layers and layers" of negativity to contend with, ultimately feeling that his association with welfare, and the way in which people treated him because of it, meant that he was "bad in some way". This, again, speaks to the overall perception of welfare as being 'bad', meaning that those engaged in the act of receiving welfare are somehow 'bad' or tainted as a result. Here, Martin describes something similar: "… there's a perception there that oh, you're in the welfare system, then you're this kind of person, you know, then we just don't want to know you or, you know – there's definitely a stigma attached."

Again, Martin, like Alan, suggests that there is an overt negative 'perception' surrounding welfare and welfare recipiency and that an association with it can call into question the type of person you are. Welfare is 'bad' and therefore stigma in the context of welfare is normal, expected and accepted. This was something that Patricia also touched on, again suggesting that there is a general perception of welfare as being something inherently 'bad' along with a perception that the behaviour of those receiving welfare gravitates towards idleness:

'There is that kind of general thinking that oh, people are on social welfare because they choose to be on social welfare, they should get off their asses and do something to help themselves, when sometimes it's not always possible, you know.'

Patricia suggests that there is a general tendency to portray welfare recipients as possessing a responsibility deficit, a feeling that they should rescind their idle ways and 'help themselves', something that Patricia acknowledges is not always as simple as it appears. As with Trish and Alan, for many of the other participants, the space in which the proliferation of a negative welfare discourse was most concentrated and therefore most prominently reinforced was undoubtedly the online space.

There is nothing but echoes in this echo chamber: the continual reinforcement of welfare as 'bad' in the online space

If a similar study were to have been carried out even 20 years ago, it is unlikely that the stigmatisation encountered in the online space, so prominent a feature for so many of the participants of this study, would have offered much in the way of data at that time. On the one hand, this means that, with so much day-to-day activity being conducted in the online world, the participants in this study face a very different reality from that of their counterparts in the eighties, nineties and perhaps even the noughties. There is also the danger that, for many, depending on interests and inclination, space in the context of online life essentially consists of an echo chamber. People are likely to be drawn to that which reinforces their views. What this ultimately means for present-day welfare recipients is that the discourse suggesting that welfare is 'bad' now has wider reach, endless transmutability and, as a result, potentially much more potency. The effects of this have certainly been widely experienced by the participant groups here and across payment types. Below, Jane refers to this same phenomenon:

> 'Yeah, it's definitely societal discourse. It's what you see on, you know, *The Echo* and *The Examiner* and *Journal.ie*, where they're talking about oh, single parents who have everything and have cars that are 2018 or are in the best of gear and all this type of stuff.'

Jane speaks directly about what she considers to be a societal discourse that seems to be populated by welfare folk devils (Jensen and Tyler, 2015), containing not unfamiliar tropes. Like others, she references the comment responses to articles that have been published online. Ultimately, Jane suggests that being aware of this entrenched discourse does not affect how she sees herself. Nevertheless, she also admits that it is something she is constantly aware of:

> 'It doesn't affect how I view myself at all, no, but it's an awareness of judgement that other people might have. I mean, I don't view those people very highly when they have that judgement but I know it's there.... I am always aware, like I said earlier on, about the discourse around single parents that you read on the media. So I know it's there. I know certain people feel that.'

While Jane is clear that having an awareness of wider social perceptions does not affect how she views herself, it is hard to countenance that she remains completely unaffected. The very nature of remaining "always aware" of the negativity that surrounds her status as a welfare recipient is surely, in and of itself, deeply impactful in the context of Jane's lived experience. As shown earlier, Grace had also experienced an overt negativity surrounding welfare in the online space:

> 'There's just [a] little clause in one of the sentences in the big long article. And then in comments it's "Oh, social welfare" – you know, people are just tearing somebody to shreds over the fact that they get social welfare. And I suppose that affects me because I'm thinking they're all thinking that – they all would think that about me.'

Like others, Grace refers to the comment section that tends to follow many online articles. However, unlike Jane, Grace suggests that this is something that does affect her, leaving her wondering if she would be viewed in a similarly negative light as a result of her own reliance on welfare. This theme of encountering vitriol in the online space was apparent in Scarlett's experiences also:

'I would have had a little bit of an idea before when I had my daughter, but actually in the last few years it's really, like, gobsmacked me, since social media has just really blown up. You see under all these news posts that come up about social welfare in any form you have so many people under there with negative ideas of people on social welfare, especially single mothers. So I would feel that a lot of people believe that single mothers have children for income from Social Welfare or so that they don't have to work. That. I would feel a lot of people would believe I'm incompetent.'

Scarlett suggests that since becoming a single mother, her knowledge of the existence of a general negativity surrounding welfare recipiency has grown. Scarlett, perhaps not surprisingly given the context of her own experience, feels that mothers parenting alone tend to come in for particular criticism and again she suggests that much of this is manifested in the virtual world that is the online space. Scarlett has also experienced the effects of this general perception of social welfare as 'bad' much closer to home:

'And then there would have been my daughter's father. So again he is, you know, in college. He's also in a high-paying job and, you know, he has a long-standing impression that I am a scummy single mother and that I live in everyone else's pockets, you know.'

Scarlett feels that impressions such as this are often held due to a lack of understanding and an inability to empathise as a result:

'And unfortunately, it sounds awful, but these are just the people that haven't really had to have experience on the other side of it. I think it's just lack of experience.... I think it's hard sometimes for any human to have empathy for something if you haven't been in that situation, because you can't fully understand, do you know what I mean?'

This exposure to negative discourses denoting that welfare is 'bad' is something that Harley also referred to: "Like you'd see the articles online, you know, of, like, newspapers, like, talking about people on welfare, talking about like there's programmes where people are abusing it and stuff like that."

Like Jane, Alan, Trish, Grace and Scarlett before her, Harley refers specifically to encountering negative discourses in the online space. However, she also refers to more traditional forms of media through which these discourses are transmitted such as newspapers and, presumably, television. This was something that was also prominent for Mary:

'So you kind of, you know, you feel like kind of ashamed nearly that you're on it.… I think it's when you hear it on the radio or the TV and it's being kind of broadcast to everyone and everybody's hearing this and, you know, like, it's, you know, a thing that's been I suppose for years and years and years.'

Mary refers to hearing and seeing repeated negative portrayals of welfare recipients on radio and television respectively that have ultimately had the effect of engendering a sense of shame. She also suggests discourses in these media have been imbued with the quality of longevity. Mary had a particularly difficult and negative experience with close family members regarding their reactions to her becoming reliant on welfare. Much of the concern emanating from Mary's family members appears to have been grounded in a set of negative beliefs with respect to welfare recipiency that devolve on a sense that social welfare and the receipt thereof is somehow, intrinsically, 'bad':

'I don't know whether they were just kind of seeing or hearing about the negative things that people, you know, that some people who are on, you know, maybe Jobseeker's or, you know, or just social welfare in general are like, you know, people who are just like going out and they're drinking all day and they're spending their money on, like, whatever and they're just, like, you know, not making any effort to like actually look for work and things like that basically, like.'

Mary suggests that her parent's negative reaction to her revelation that she had signed on to receive social welfare may have been couched in their own preconceived ideas around social welfare and those in receipt of social welfare. Again, this suggests that an overt social negativity surrounds the concept of social welfare in general and that the overall social consensus largely seems to suggest that social welfare is 'bad'.

Resisting the negative

Although the experiences of almost all the participants here give rise to a sense of 'badness' or 'deviancy' in the context of welfare recipiency, some managed to resist this negativity. This social consensus, reinforced in multiple contexts and appearing to encapsulate ideas around social welfare and what it means, was also something that Olive mentioned:

'I think in society generally it probably comes from the — I suppose from the media portrayal of welfare as being almost a bonus that you get rather than something that enables you to eat and heat your house and feed yourself and whatever family you might have. And there was also a very strong feeling that in the recession, okay, lots of people were affected, lots of different areas of work, but you had to bounce back very fast or within a certain period, an acceptable period of time.'

Here, Olive, as was the case with many other participants, talks about there being a general sense of welfare as being something 'bad'. She also references the media and how it tends to portray welfare receipt. She also poses a very interesting question by contemplating an, arguably, more accurate and 'Marshallian' (Fitzpatrick et al, 2019) definition of the purpose of social welfare, suggesting that it functions to enable recipients to meet basic needs such as food, heating and so on. In defining the purpose of welfare in this way, Olive is also asking, what's the alternative? Grace also asked this question, and answered in a way that echoes much of Olive's assertion around meeting basic needs: "It covers the basics. And the alternative is that we just don't have anything at all and we just sit on the green outside and don't eat."

Olive also talks about the pressure that came on the Irish social welfare system during the recession following the 2007-08 global financial crisis. In doing so, she raises a further interesting point in relation to duration. She suggests that there is a perception that there is "an acceptable period of time" after which a reliance on welfare may become more problematic. This is interesting as it evokes an aspect of Pinker's (1970) depth, distance and time analysis of stigma, in the context of social welfare. Essentially, Pinker (1970) explores the effects of spending a certain amount of time in a 'dependent state'; the longer a person stays reliant on a benefit or benefits, the more likely for there to be a stigma attributed to them or for them to become aware of a stigma effect.

Clive also had an awareness of there being a general negative perception of social welfare:

'So, I mean, that's news. It's everywhere. I mean, how often do you hear it yourself about, you know, the people on social welfare, people, you know, perpetrating fraud, they're going to have to clamp down on it, you know?'

Like others, he suggests that the discourses propagating a particular image of social welfare are "everywhere", and he briefly refers to the news media.

However, not unlike Olive and Grace, Clive was capable of challenging the common-sense view of social welfare in an interesting way:

> 'Yeah, you can see who's going down and who has to sign. And it's always perceived as a bad thing, you know. You hear people talking about, oh – this is a thing now, they're – how would you describe it – boasting themselves about. "I was never on welfare. I wouldn't go on welfare. I'd never fucking take a penny out of welfare, like, you know." That I often react to when people say it. Like, why, you bloody idiot? It's your right. You know, you should have. What's the glory in not accessing your rights? That's why the system is so bad is because you don't access your rights. There is a need for it. There's more need for it than the supply that's there and the service that is being provided. There's a need for a better service. And that's because people like that don't let it be known that, you know, when you're a worker you've a right. Make it your right.'

Clive suggests that the perception of those receiving welfare is generally bad. However, he goes on to broadly condemn those who would valorise the fact that they never have, or never would, access social welfare. In doing so he reconceptualises welfare as something people should treat as a right before going on to suggest that people should access welfare as and when needed in order to improve the manner in which welfare, as a service, is delivered. While the effects of a negative welfare discourse may be pervasive, importantly, Olive, Grace and Clive have shown that they can at least be resisted and even challenged by those with experiences of receiving social welfare.

In reaching its conclusion on the pervasive effects of a negative set of discourses surrounding welfare and welfare recipiency, this chapter also brings to a close the book's empirical content. This chapter, in particular, has served to bring multiple facets of the previous empirical chapters together in a way that shows that the overarching societal perception of welfare as something bad can and does have a negative effect on welfare recipients. The next chapter takes the reader forward. As detailed at the outset, the main materials presented in this work are drawn from the data arising from a study conducted in a pre-COVID-19 world and, albeit no less valuable for that, the texture of social life and of welfare receipt in particular, has changed, if temporarily, since the study was conducted. Some of these changes have been profound, others have been short-lived, and many have placed the nature of welfare and on what we need to provide by way of a social safety net at times of crisis firmly on the social, economic and political agenda. For this reason, it is worth visiting these themes briefly before drawing a final conclusion.

COVID-19: policy responses and lived experiences

In this chapter, I look briefly at the impact of COVID-19 in the context of welfare and at the effect this has had on lived experiences and on the 'doing' of welfare in the public consciousness. Writing this chapter is a tricky task as the situation remains very much live and therefore what is written here will inevitably age quickly. Nevertheless, there can be no doubt that the onset of the pandemic saw the idea of welfare and the role of welfare states come into sharp focus virtually overnight. In the face of the global developments arising out of the COVID-19 pandemic, the social contract was rapidly rewritten, and the social safety net rapidly expanded as emergency welfare payments were rolled out across jurisdictions (Hick and Murphy, 2021). In terms of what was offered in the context of welfare and particularly with respect to unemployment supports, I focus, in the main, on the Irish example. However, for context and to give a sense of the global picture, I offer some detail of the responses seen across jurisdictions. It should also be noted that responses across jurisdictions, in general, contained a range of measures, including wage subsidy schemes and supports for the self-employed. However, I focus on what would be generally constituted as 'out-of-work' or unemployment support benefits and so, in the Irish case, this means focusing on the Pandemic Unemployment Payment, commonly referred to as the PUP. First, however, to get a sense of what the welfare response has been internationally, Table 8.1 (adapted from Institute for Government [UK], 2021) provides an overview across nine countries.

In general, this table suggests that responses, in the main, have reflected the particular and embedded welfare logic of the countries involved in terms of how the various schemes have been administered and the level of support offered. Sweden, for example, falls back on a social insurance model and ties this to eligibility. Denmark, Germany and France all offered support based on previous earnings. The US operationalises the language of 'through no fault of their own' in terms of eligibility, which at once reflects a liberal welfare heritage and perceived degrees of deservingness. The UK uses its relatively new but nevertheless pre-exiting welfare infrastructure in the form of Universal Credit to respond but specifically targets low-wage earners and, again reflecting the logic of a liberal welfare regime, takes means such as the income of a partner and/or savings into account. With respect to the UK

Table 8.1: How different countries supported workers through the COVID-19 pandemic

	Ireland	UK	Australia	Canada	Denmark	France	Germany	Sweden	US
New welfare or benefit	Yes (PUP)*	No – generosity of existing benefit (Universal Credit) increased	Yes (coronavirus supplement to JobSeeker Payment)	Yes (CERB)**	No	No	No	No	Yes (PUA and FPUC)***
Level of unemployment benefits available to those who lose their jobs due to COVID-19	€350 (£310) per week	£410 per month (£90 per week) for a single, childless adult	AU$1,116 per fortnight (£310 per week) for a single, childless adult	CA$1,000 per fortnight (£290 per week)	90% of previous wage (up to a maximum of DKK 18,866 per month (£520 per week)	57% of previous daily salary or 40.4% plus €12 (£11) a day, whichever is higher (up to cap of €248 (£220) per day). Minimum €29 (£26) per day	60% (or 67% for parents) of previous net wages below €6,900 (£6,130) in West Germany and €6,450 (£5,730) in East Germany	70–80% of previous salary, with cap of 1,200 SEK (£100) per day for the first 100 days and 760 SEK (£70) afterwards. Those not eligible for A-kassa insurance receive 225–510 SEK (£19–£44) per day	Varies by state: $600 (£470) per week coronavirus supplement, on top of existing state UI**** payments (worth 25–50% of previous weekly wage). Total amount is roughly equal to the average wage in most states

(continued)

Table 8.1: How different countries supported workers through the COVID-19 pandemic (continued)

	Ireland	UK	Australia	Canada	Denmark	France	Germany	Sweden	US
Eligibility for unemployment benefits	Those employed at the beginning of March who have lost their job due to COVID-19 crisis	All unemployed and low earners eligible except those with >£16K savings, or with partner with higher earnings	Anyone with fortnightly earnings under AU$1,086 (£290 per week) who is unemployed, a gig/casual worker, sick, or caring for sick people	Anyone earning <CA$1,000 per month, who both earned >CA$5,000 (£2,930) in 2019 and due to COVID-19 is unemployed, sick or a carer	Member of recognised unemployment insurance fund for over one year	Anyone who paid contributions for four months in past 28 months and did not leave their job voluntarily	Anyone who has paid contributions for 12 of past 24 months and be seeking new job	Member of A-kassa insurance scheme who has worked a minimum of 60 hours per month for six of past 12 months to qualify for full insurance. Anyone who has worked can claim basic insurance	Anyone unemployed through no fault of their own, including casual workers. State-level work history requirements
Changes made in response to coronavirus	Entirely new benefit	£20 per week extra, made easier for self-employed to qualify	US$550 per fortnight (£150 per week) extra, partner income test relaxed and asset limits waived	Entirely new benefit	For benefits recipients, period 1 March–30 June does not count as a period where benefits have been received (essentially extension of benefits period)	All benefit claimants continue receiving benefits to 31 July if entitlement should run out before then	Eligibility period extended for a further three months	Cap and basic rates (ie for those who are not members of A-kassa) raised, work requirements reduced	Extra $600 per week for all UI claimants, UI duration extended, extension of UI-equivalent benefits to gig workers and those whose claims had expired (PUA)

Notes:

*PUP = Pandemic Unemployment Payment (Ireland).

**CERB = Canada Emergency response Benefit (Canada).

***PUA = Pandemic Unemployment Assistance; FPUC = Federal Pandemic Unemployment Assistance.

**** UI = Unemployment Insurance

Source: Adapted from Institute for Government (UK) (2021).

specifically, there is now some research emerging that gives a sense of how people experienced receiving welfare support during the pandemic there.[1]

There is also an interesting contrast to be found between countries that managed the crisis through and within existing welfare infrastructure and those that created something entirely new, Ireland, along with Canada being the only two examples of the latter, with the majority of countries opting for the former in various ways. With respect to Ireland, creating a new payment proved effective in terms of its immediate efficacy. The strength of Ireland's response through the PUP, and this is borne out further on through the lens of lived experience, has been the reasonable ease of access with which the payment was administered; effectively, you could get it quickly and without a means test if you needed it and, therefore, it worked (Hick and Murphy, 2021). However, there has arguably always been an apparent discomfort with the PUP in political circles, and this is evident in the many attempts that there have been to unravel the payment and realign it with existing welfare infrastructure since its inception (Cullen and Murphy, 2021; Hick and Murphy, 2021). Indeed, almost since the day it was introduced, there have been discussions about how it will be eventually 'wound down', with budgetary forecasts written as early as April 2020 predicting less reliance on the payment by the fourth quarter (Q4) of the same year, with an expectation that, by then, those still in need to support would be 'folded' into pre-COVID welfare infrastructure (see Parliamentary Budget Office, 2020). However, Q4 of 2020 has since come and gone, and, at the time of writing, the PUP continues to support those whose employment has been affected by the pandemic. There are, however, firm plans in place to discontinue the payment by early 2022 and so it is likely that by the time these words are printed, the welfare landscape will have changed again. New applications will cease to be accepted by end June 2021 and those still in need of support when the payment has been fully wound down are expected to revert to 'traditional' income support payments at a much-reduced rate of payment (see https://services.mywelfare.ie/en/topics/covid-19-payme nts).[2] Effectively, this will mean an eventual income 'cliff-edge' for those reliant on the payment. The top rate of PUP will be reduced from €350 to €300 from 7 September 2021 'provided progress on re-opening continues'. Two further phases of changes will take place over the following months – the payment will reduce to €250 on 16 November 2021 and be abolished on 8 February 2022. At this point, as noted, those still unemployed will revert to claiming unemployment benefits and be paid at a rate of €203 per week (see Department of Social Protection, 2021a). These plans remain broadly in place despite the fact that rising case numbers in November and December 2021 have seen the PUP scheme reopen to new entrants whose employment is deemed to be affected as a direct consequence of Covid (see Department of Social Protection, 2021b). Bearing in mind that, in 2019, the minimum disposable income needed for a single adult to stay above the poverty line stood at €252.11 (Social Justice Ireland, 2019), this will arguably see many of those who lost employment due to the pandemic have to contend with increased hardship, particularly where a still deflated labour market is not in a position to offer suitable job opportunities. Bearing this out, the Economic and Social Research Institute (ESRI, 2021) has recently published research that shows that many persons, and younger people in particular, face a particularly steep 'cliff-edge' effect that will undoubtedly result in much financial hardship:

> Those in the 18–24 age category and students are particularly likely to lose a significant proportion of their income when the schemes are wound down, if ample employment opportunities are not available. This finding is driven by the fact that students are eligible for PUP, but not the pre-existing unemployment payments. Those aged under 25 and not in education are eligible for JSA but at a rate 45 per cent lower than that of those over 25. (ESRI, 2021: 31)

Interestingly, and despite disincentive narratives about payment generosity, the report shows that 95 per cent of persons receiving PUP would be financially better off at work. This, of course, is grounded in the context of a healthy labour market where employment opportunities are available. Nevertheless, it strongly suggests that the narrative of an overly generous unemployment payment disincentivising a return to work is almost wholly false at worse and can be said to lack nuance at best.

Before going on to look at some of the lived experiences of those interacting with the Irish welfare state during the pandemic, it is worth making one further point. As noted earlier, one of the strengths of PUP was the ease with which it could be accessed by those who needed it. A further strength was the relative generosity of the payment at €350 per week. However, it is interesting to note that the payment was originally to be set at the rate at €203 per week, mirroring basic welfare rates. This was quickly increased, however, first to €305 per week and subsequently to €350 (Hick and Murphy, 2021). What this effectively did was create a 'two-tier' welfare system in Ireland, and, as Hick and Murphy (2021: 8) have noted:

> ... enhanced supports to those affected by COVID opened up new differentials between pandemic-era claimants and pre-pandemic social security claimants (most of whom, regardless of whether they were contributory or means-tested recipients were entitled to a maximum of €203 per week for a single person and an additional €135 if they had an adult dependent [sic]).

These differentials have arguably devolved, in the main, on perceived levels of deservingness that introduced what can only be described as a tacit favouring of the worker (productive) whose employment was 'through no fault of their own' affected by the pandemic, over and above the 'traditional' welfare recipient (unproductive), who, having been absent from the labour market ahead of the onset of the crisis, would continue to receive €203 per week.

Lived experiences in the context of COVID-19.

Having set the scene with respect to policy responses, I now focus briefly on lived experiences of welfare recipiency in the context of COVID-19 in Ireland. In particular, I offer a sweep of data that shows how people initially experienced the lockdown and the disruption to work, along with how supported they felt. I also demonstrate how respondents felt about the social welfare response in particular and specifically the 'two-tier' welfare system created by the introduction of PUP. I will also present some data that show that many respondents, ultimately, have come to value the security of a strong social safety net as encapsulated by the pandemic welfare response. However, many of the themes that emerged with respect to the pre-COVID-19/post-2007/08 global financial crisis data that make up the bulk of what is presented in this book, are also apparent in the more recent data, and this is particularly true in the context of notions of deservingness, including seeing some recipients as 'other' and therefore liable to abuse the system. These themes are also highlighted here. It should be noted that the intention here is not to mirror what has been presented with respect to the pre-COVID data; rather, it is to offer a 'snapshot' of the lived experiences of those who have come to rely on a form of state welfare because of the pandemic. The ultimate value in doing so is the insight given into how people view welfare through the lens of a crisis.

A note on this research

Before presenting some data that speaks to lived experiences, I briefly offer a context for when and how the research was carried out. The research presented in the following sections departs from the study that forms the bulk of this book, and takes up the findings of a project carried out from April 2020 through to 2021. This project, so far, has consisted of two long-form qualitative surveys that aimed to capture peoples' experiences of work disruption and receiving support during the pandemic in the Republic of Ireland. The research was conducted with colleagues from the School of Applied Social Studies (Fiona Dukelow) and the Department of Sociology and Criminology (Tom Boland), both at University College Cork. Each survey consisted of a set of questions designed to capture relevant participant variables (age range, gender, type of employment prior to work being disrupted, income range and support accessed) followed by five long-form questions. The first survey garnered 161 responses. The second garnered 42. As outlined in the early paragraphs of this book, the sample sizes quoted here are largely without relevance; the research was conducted with 'big Q' qualitative values to the fore, and, as such, the aim was depth of understanding, not generalisability through statistical probability. The first survey opened in April 2020 and remained open until November 2020. The vast majority of responses came in the initial weeks of the survey opening and so reflect vividly the early nature of the crisis and lived experiences of the welfare response. The second survey opened in January 2021, remaining open until June 2021 and the responses, which filtered in more slowly, give a broad sense of how people had begun to adapt to living through the pandemic along with more nuanced interpretations of the welfare response. In presenting some of the findings here, rather than using participant pseudonyms, I refer to the survey from which the excerpts are drawn (Survey 1 and Survey 2). It should be noted that what follows is not over-theorised and ultimately reflects a small sample of a rich dataset with which the researchers are still working. Nevertheless, it provides an overview of some emerging themes in the COVID-19 context.

Living through history: initial and longer-term experiences of work disruption during the pandemic

In the first instance, as the onset of the pandemic and the changes to the textures of life it so forcefully wrought became a reality for people, this was understandably a time of great uncertainty. Although some respondents found positivity in having more time available to them as a result of their usual routines being disrupted, many more struggled with this aspect of the pandemic and the subsequent lockdown. On the whole, the lockdown was something that some respondents found very surreal. This is captured in the following excerpt, which is taken from Survey 1 where respondents were asked to grapple with long-form questions about the experience of becoming unemployed: 'Surreal is the only word I can use to describe this whole experience. It's as if a Hollywood B movie suddenly became real.'

Others described the sudden, almost brutal, nature of what it meant to be suddenly out of work: 'I was told my contract would be terminated early with two weeks' notice. I was shocked as although I am on a contract I work in the civil service and I assumed I would be safe' (Survey 1).

Despite the sudden and intense nature of the lockdown, some respondents did find positives in having extra time available to them, as these two examples show:

I have been enjoying the extra time with the children, doing normal household tasks, gardening, allotment, exercising in the house etc. (Survey 1)

A lot of my time has been taken up with developing existing hobbies such as reading, baking, cooking, sketching, painting, cleaning and even a spot of gardening. (Survey 1)

However, others did struggle with the sudden isolation and the distance that the cessation of employment coupled with the lockdown put between them and some of the things they needed in their lives – things such supports that were suddenly unavailable: 'I have a mental health condition and it has worsened some days…. So, without the professional help I was gonna have, I needed to focus a lot in the present moment' (Survey 1).

As the lockdown continued through various stages of restriction, many of the difficulties people had to contend with appeared to have become exacerbated. This is seen in the following excerpts, all of which are drawn from Survey 2:

My mental health deteriorated after my job loss.
I have some health issues and have started to suffer with depression and anxiety. Not due to financial issues but the not knowing what's going to happen. I liked my job and not redundancies being put on hold etc.
Very negatively. Mental health has suffered. Had been making great progress in my career and loved what I was doing. Now I've no direction.

Both surveys undoubtedly conveyed a mixture of positive and negative sentiments with respect to how the shock to the labour market and the subsequent disruption to work was experienced. However, in Survey 2, which was conducted well into the life of the pandemic, much more negative sentiment, couched in increasing worry and concern as the pandemic continued to eschew any hope of certainty, became overtly dominant, as can be seen from the previous examples.

Receiving support through PUP

If the general uncertainty of the pandemic was a grinding and negative experience for many, the certainty that was offered to those who were able to avail of the PUP payment seems to have been a balm to soothe it. As noted earlier with respect to the policy response, once a rate of €350 per week was agreed, PUP did not require a means test and was reasonably accessible to those who needed it (Hick and Murphy, 2021). An appreciation of this was certainly something that was expressed across the sample, particularly in Survey1. What becomes apparent when moving from Survey 1 to Survey 2 is that gratitude for a fulsome and effective government response in the first instance becomes more nuanced. The payment is still greeted favourably in the main, but this positivity is qualified with assertions about those who may perhaps be seen as less deserving of the support. As such, a form of othering creeps into the narrative in a way that was largely absent from the responses to Survey 1. As can be seen from the following excerpts, in the early stages of the pandemic, the Irish government's response through the introduction of PUP was something that respondents perceived very positively.

> I think the government has done pretty well so far by setting the emergency payment as 350 a week, I think it's more than enough for most people that don't have any major expenses at the moment. I also think the applications for this payment were processed v quickly which was good. (Survey 1)

> I have been impressed at how the government handled this so quickly and in the early days offered a subsidiary payment to anyone who lost their job, even the self-employed. (Survey 1)

> Overall the response has been excellent. It is reassuring to know that the government has put the welfare of the people first, whilst also trying to support businesses and the economy. The covid unemployment payment goes a long way to help me. (Survey 1)

All three of these responses are clearly very complimentary of the government response through the introduction of PUP in the early stages of the pandemic. The rate of payment and the efficiency with which payment claims were processed are both noted as being particular indicators of a satisfactory and adequate policy response. This type of sentiment does continue through to Survey 2, but it is now often considerably more nuanced, creeping, at times, into a form of othering, as can be seen in the following examples drawn from Survey 2:

> The PUP was mainly good but was set up in a way that allowed large scale fraud.
> I think the PUP was a good idea for the most part, when all this started we didn't know how long it would go on for or anything, so I think it was the best thing they could do at the time. However, I think just relying on people's honesty to stop it themselves was silly because of course people won't stop it.
> They should force people in the 20–35 age group to take jobs whether they like that job or not.

It is clear from these excerpts that sentiment towards PUP, albeit still generally positive, has nevertheless taken on a new form, a form of 'qualified' positivity. In the main, this appears to devolve on the idea of an 'other' who, much like the folk devils spoken about in Chapter 6, is seen as potentially fraudulent and somehow less deserving of support. Young people, in particular, come in for censure. In this way, a latent dissatisfaction with some of the terms of PUP appears to manifest. This, arguably, shows that even during times of existential crisis, deeply ingrained tendencies surrounding welfare and deservingness are wont to emerge (Whelan, 2020b).

In setting out the policy response earlier in this chapter, I posited the idea that through the introduction of PUP at a rate of €350 per week, the Irish government inadvertently created a 'two-tier' welfare system, at least on a temporary basis, via the fact that pre-COVID-19 welfare recipients would continue to receive €203 per week. A sample of the latter group was captured, primarily in Survey 2, and, in general, these respondents expressed a clear dissatisfaction with PUP with respect to their own particular circumstances. It is to this cohort and this area in general that I next turn.

A 'two-tier' welfare system?

Creating a system whereby one group is receiving a form of income support far above that of another effectively does two things that are of sociological relevance. First, by fixing pandemic supports beyond standard or mainstream rates of payment for an adult welfare recipient, there is an obvious, if tacit, acknowledgement that the standard or mainstream rate is unacceptable for the vast majority of people. Second, the spectre of deservingness is conjured through the tacit suggestion that some (the productive worker) are more deserving than others (the idle welfare recipient). This is certainly something that respondents who had been reliant on welfare before the pandemic felt very keenly, as demonstrated by the following excerpts from Survey 2:

> I was on the Jobseekers before the pandemic started. I then watched 20 year olds get an extra 150 a week for doing nothing. If they can get 350, why not give the same amount to unemployed or vice versa.
>   I think it is good, but I have seen people who earned 100 per week, get 350 per week covid payment, while I continue to receive 156 per week JA. My expenses are at least as high if not higher than theirs, but govt. has no consideration for people in my situation.

Alongside people who had direct experience of receiving the lower rate of welfare during the pandemic, there were others who, while not necessarily receiving the lower rate, expressed solidarity with those who were:

> I think it's unacceptable to have a two-tier welfare system for unemployment. It's an acknowledgment that the €203 rate isn't enough to survive on and feels punitive in comparison. (Survey 2)

Too much of a discord. I don't understand why those who have lost work due to Covid-19 have greater need than those unemployed for other reasons. (Survey 2)

However, this is clearly a complex area and one in which, perhaps echoing the logic of ancient debates (Whelan, 2021b), opinions were very much varied:

I think it is quite fair. In most cases people who were made redundant during the pandemic were making much more than €200. Therefore a higher payment is necessary to accommodate lifestyle choices that may have come with that e.g higher rent, more children, loan repayments. (Survey 2)

The complex debates being played out through the lens of pandemic supports are arguably indicative of the embeddedness of particular logics of welfare that precede COVID-19 by many centuries (Whelan, 2021b). Yet, to witness these debates fluctuate and play out in real time in the microcosm of welfare policy responses, themselves located in a macro catastrophe, tells us that debates about the 'doing' of welfare and indeed, how we would intend to 'do' welfare potentially in the face of greater existential crises to come, are far from settled. Nevertheless, many respondents to both surveys did express, both directly and indirectly, their recognition of the value of a strong social safety net, and so before concluding this chapter on empirical materials depicting lived experiences of welfare recipiency during the COVID-19 pandemic, I offer some final observations in this respect.

The value of a safety net

For many, PUP ultimately ends up being a barrier to impending hardship and potential destitution. The strength of the payment in terms of its relative generosity is also a stark reminder to those receiving it of what life could be without it. Receiving PUP is therefore tinged with a sense of uncertainty, liminality and precarity. This is something that is apparent in the following excerpts, both taken from Survey 2:

Without the pup ... I would be destitute.
I think the PUP has been a lifesaver for many, including myself. It has highlighted how little social welfare payments normally are.

If the lived experiences of welfare recipients during a pandemic can meaningfully illustrate the value of a strong social safety net, then this also arguably captures an argument towards the same in a general sense. The fact that this may not be the only pandemic we face in the coming decades, and that ongoing climate catastrophe will likely signal more social upheaval, seems to indicate that bells are tolling loudly, ringing out in strident tones the need for a strong and preventative social contract. There is, then, much learning to be had from how governments have responded during the COVID-19 pandemic. However, lessons given do not always translate to lessons learned. It is hoped that the data briefly visited here, while far from exhaustive, will go some way at least towards constructing such lessons, although whether or not they will be lesson learned remains to be seen. Having provided a flavour of the lived experiences of welfare recipients in context of the COVID-19 pandemic, I build on these observations in the next and final chapter, and close the book with some concluding thoughts.

Conclusion

When Michael Lipsky (2010 [1980]) set out his stall in *Street-level bureaucracy: Dilemmas of the individual in public services* in 1980, his project was one that offered a lens through which research could be conducted while also being a 'project of improvement' (Brodkin, 2012). In Lipsky's (2010 [1980]) case, the project of improvement with which he was concerned centred on the idea of 'redeeming public bureaucracies' (Brodkin, 2012). While the work that has been presented at length in this book has not been directly concerned with a street-level view of bureaucracies in action from within bureaucracies, it has nevertheless illustrated research conducted at street level, concerned with the experiences of those who have had to engage directly with the bureaucratic in the form of the Irish welfare state. In this respect, this too has been an undertaking with two concerns. The first of these, which has been made plain throughout, has been to forefront and showcase lived experience as a form of knowledge. This has hopefully been achieved. However, in as much as what has been revealed may tell us something of the challenges those receiving state welfare can face, it is hoped that it can also begin to add to a growing body of scholarly literature that, when taken together, can be seen to be part of a project of improvement aiming to 'redeem public bureaucracies' (Brodkin, 2012) by illustrating some of the challenges of those who interact with them. For this reason, in this final chapter, I offer some thoughts and suggestions for what a project of improvement in the context of welfare might comprise. Far from exhaustive, these following paragraphs are intended to open up a conversation about the 'doing' of welfare, and about how it can potentially be done better and for the benefit of those who may need it at different times in the courses of their lives. The discussion, then, is necessarily broad, but, in the main, focuses on the research context. However, the general principles laid out will have relevance to other welfare states and particularly to those liberal welfare states of the Anglosphere, and so I retain the 'shared typical' lens used throughout the book. I start this conversation by introducing the idea of 'stigma of public burden' before moving to illustrate the possibility of a 'developmental welfare state'.

The stigma of public burden

If Pinker (1970; 175) has suggested that '[t]he imposition of stigma is the commonest form of violence used in democratic societies', then this imposition is arguably made manifest through ideas that largely revolve around the notion of public burden. It has been plainly shown throughout this book that those who receive welfare face considerable hardship and social stigma. It has also been shown that this is itself multi-layered and complex, manifesting both through the administration of benefits themselves, which Spicker (2011: 16) has noted can be intensely 'humiliating and degrading', and through wider social phenomena such as ideas around work, social liminality and marginality, deservingness, practices such as othering, and common-sense understandings of welfare as 'bad'. Yet, when COVID-19 struck and emergency welfare measures were introduced, the stigma of public burden was largely absent from public discourse and broad and supportive welfare measures were roundly welcomed. This was certainly the case in Ireland where PUP, discussed in Chapter 8 and paid at a rate of €350 per week, was welcomed both publicly and politically, initially at least (Hick and Murphy, 2021).

What, then, does this tell us? Arguably, it suggests that when not tainted by the stigma of public burden, a taint that is arguably actualised through the processes of welfare conditionality, welfare as a social good can be both desirable and almost universally endorsed. Yet, when such approval occurs during a time of great crisis, is the stigma of public burden reassigned to those who seek or receive welfare once welfare states return to 'normal' and emergency benefits begin to be retrenched? Work on the historical development of social policy and welfare states suggests that the return of deeply embedded logics is likely to be the case (Powell, 1992, 2017, Boland and Griffin, 2021; Whelan, 2021b). Is there, however, a way in which this could be offset? That is, is there a way of 'doing' welfare that removes or reduces both the stigma of public burden and the associated hardship? In the following paragraphs. I intend to present what I feel are some of the potential answers to these questions by drawing on some broad plans or outlines for welfare and on the work of others to effectively describe a new 'welfare imaginary'. First, however, I draw attention again to the work of Richard Titmuss and, in particular, to his conception of the stigma of public burden as being created, in the first instance, through the way in which welfare is administered in liberal welfare states. Effectively, then, Titmuss (1968: 134), argues that:

> If all services are provided – irrespective of whether they represent benefits, amenity, social protection or compensation – on a discriminatory, means-tested basis, do we not foster both the sense of failure and the stigma of public burden? The fundamental objective of all such tests of eligibility is to keep people out; not to let them in.

If we take this as a baseline or a first principle of the 'doing' of welfare in a way that eschews the stigma of public burden, we are very simply left with the idea of universality within welfare states; that is, we are left with a type of redistributive justice that seeks to meet needs unequivocally and not through the mechanism of selection. It is therefore a social democratic vision of welfare in the main. It is not a new idea; it is not even an untested idea (see Esping-Anderson, 1990; Larsen, 2006 for more). Yet it may be an idea whose time has come, particularly as we begin to exit one crisis at a time when others may yet sit over the next horizon. To make this project 'doable', the required shift in liberal welfare states arguably requires a double movement, the first of which is a task for social policy and for how policies are designed. It is, therefore, at the very least a task in which social policy must seek to guide the sociological experience, and, in turn, shape the sociological imagination. The second movement follows and necessarily encapsulates a shift in public consciousness that sees welfare repositioned as a desirable, holistic and inclusive social good, as opposed to a tainted social good bearing the mark of failure, deviancy and public burden.

Citizenship and inclusivity

In a report on the future of the Irish welfare system, the National Economic and Social Council (NESC, 2020) revisited the following key principles as part of a vision for what a welfare system could and should be about:

1) Belief in the dignity and right to personal development of the individual, and in the value of bonds of mutual obligation between all members of the community.
2) The importance of fair shares within the community, including in particular the right of access of all people to adequate income, housing, education and health services.
3) The securing of these rights within a democratic framework (NESC, 2020: 76).

In actual fact, these principles were originally proposed by NESC in 1981 and were also reflected in the 1986 report of the Commission on Social Welfare. The principles, mentioned briefly in Chapter 1, focused on three financial objectives of social security:

- the prevention of poverty;
- redistribution – with the redistribution of income addressing the impact of distribution generated solely by market forces. This redistribution by the social security system takes place in tandem with the role of taxation and the provision of public services;
- income replacement – with social security to go beyond poverty relief to include replacement of income, with an earnings-related dimension.

Both these sets of principles underpin the vision set out in the 2020 document, which focuses on adequate payments, redistributive justice, welfare as an expression of solidarity, a comprehensive social safety net, and a simple system for both claimants and administrators to traverse. Ultimately, this amounts to a vision for what NESC has termed a 'developmental welfare state', or DWS (see also NESC, 2005). Of the DWS, NESC (2020: xxii) notes:

> A key element of the DWS is the fusion of economic and social policy: good economic performance can support good social policy, and good social policy provides a strong basis for economic development. Recognising the focus of Ireland's social welfare system on income supports, the DWS argued for the radical improvement of services such as education, health, childcare, eldercare, housing, transport and employment services. Services and income support should also be complemented by activist measures (i.e. novel approaches to provision, such as community/group projects, which address emerging new needs). These three overlapping areas (services, income support, activist measures) make up the core structure of Ireland's welfare state.

This description of an inclusive and developmental welfare state does two things. In the first instance, it provides a vision of a comprehensive welfare state not unlike the post-war vision of a welfare commons, a vision in which economic and social policies are not at odds but, rather, are constitutive of one another. The focus then shifts away from social welfare as the province only of income supports, to a system that encompasses caring, education, health and employment services. Where strings of conditionality exist, they are more likely to foster and promote inclusivity and citizenship as opposed to being punitive measures focused on the labour market and based on sanctions. What is perhaps most instructive, however, it that this report (NESC, 2020), and the work it builds on, aptly demonstrates that when it comes to how Ireland might 'do' welfare, there has never been a lack of imagination. This is evidenced by several discrete visions given over many decades and culminating in now further calls for a DWS. Yet NESC does not have a monopoly on visionary thinking in the context of welfare and I offer this here as only one example. Indeed, by picking out NESC as one vehicle through which a vision of the welfare state has been proffered, I perhaps do an injustice to the espousers of other, equally valid, visions in the Irish context (see, for example, Social Justice Ireland, 2021, which focuses on a universal basic income [UBI]). In fact, it could be argued that the idea of a DWS, as given by NESC, is not the most radical departure, with its 'middle-of-the-road' social democratic orientation. This perhaps best evidenced by the fact that the report (NESC, 2020) stops short of a call for the introduction of UBI. Utopia, this is not. What is also striking is that many of the report's recommendations echo the historical foundations on which many welfare states were built. For example, when read through the lens of the Beveridge Report, authored in 1942, it does not appear to stray overly far from a vision to ameliorate or eradicate want, ignorance, squalor, idleness and disease. When read through a vision of social rights, as given by T.H. Marshall (Marshall and Bottomore, 1992), it appears that the pendulum of progress for envisioning a modern and inclusive welfare state has not had to swing overly far. Perhaps the fact that calls for such a vision persist tells us that it is a vision never adequately achieved in the liberal welfare states of the Anglosphere; perhaps it tells us how far from such a vision we have wandered. Either way, what it does suggest is that although much may have changed since the inception of the post-war welfare state, a vision of welfare based on citizenship and inclusivity has not.[1] Such visions still contain the same basic building blocks, the same ideas about the social rights of citizenship set out by T.H. Marshall, and still effectively devolve on a 'right to welfare' so that people can at least be said to possess the right to 'a modicum of economic welfare and security', a right through which they may be entitled to 'the life of a civilised being according to the standards prevailing' (Marshall and Bottomore, 1992: 8).

In the context of the research documented in this book, realising a vision of welfare based on citizenship and inclusivity means we would need to take steps to ensure that being in receipt of welfare is a less marginal and socially liminal experience for recipients. We would also need to reappraise our sense of the work ethic and its value, and, indeed, what we value as, and what constitutes, work. We would need to think deeply about how the current practices of conditionality affect welfare recipients, and we would need to reappraise what it means to be deserving. Importantly, we would need to challenge and disrupt the framing consensus when it comes to how we 'do' social welfare. A vision of welfare ensconced within a DWS seems like an adequate place to start. In finishing, then, I take up this vision of a developmental welfare state by suggesting, based on what has been presented here in the form of lived experiences, what might need to be considered in order to move towards it. In order to do so, in the following paragraphs, I concentrate on the first principle set out by NESC (2020), and divide this into two separate strands that relate back to the research presented in this book.

'Doing' welfare differently: spaces and places

To begin with, let us take the first part of the first guiding principle set out by NESC (2020: 76) and described earlier (emphasis added): '*Belief in the dignity and right to personal development of the individual,* and in the value of bonds of mutual obligation between all members of the community.'

This might be said to suggest something about how we ought to 'do' welfare and welfare conditionality in particular. Effectively, it suggests that we would honour the individuality of those who cross the threshold of a welfare office in a way that is person-centred and not process-centred. This 'process-centeredness' was certainly something that many of the research participants encountered in these pages commented on directly. In the following excerpt, for example, Scarlett notes that the process can take precedence over the individual: "I feel like they stick – there's an awful lot of them who stick to the very specific system and they're not looking at you as a person in front of them but somebody who is that statistic and needs to be this, that and the other." And here, Martin talks about how his interaction with the administrators of welfare could be limiting: "I found it very limiting. It just seemed to me closing down the possibilities rather than opening up any doors or any progression."

Moving away from 'doing' welfare on a purely procedural basis, from what Finn (2021) has termed 'systemic indifference' – an approach that can be more about 'box ticking' and is therefore limiting – would mean honouring people's hopes, dreams and ambitions while also asking them what they have or what they would like to contribute. One way to do this might be to consider how we design welfare, both socially and physically, in the first place – to consider the 'spaces' (the reality of being a welfare recipient) and 'places' (the physical infrastructure of the welfare state) that make up the social and physical topography of welfare states. Space in terms of social space was something that did come up and was perhaps most apparent in data surrounding the marginal and liminal nature of welfare recipiency: let us remember Lisa, for example, who noted that: "It's not a pleasant, encouraging space that kind of helps you to develop into a fully functioning human being, like, you know."

In this way, 'space' is presented as an intangible aspect in the experience of welfare recipiency. Place, on the other hand, is meant in the sense of actual physical and hard geography and was perhaps most apparent in data that described welfare conditionality as part of a 'compulsive geography' of the welfare state, into which claimants were repeatedly required to enter to both establish and maintain welfare entitlements, and in which they were further compelled to engage in activities necessary to meet their entitlement requirements. It is also notable that, in recent years, the compulsive geography of the Irish welfare state has broadened via the 'insertion' of private job-matching services into the infrastructure of the Irish welfare state via the JobPath initiative. Entities such as Turas Nua and Seetec add a corporate visage to the physical geography of the Irish welfare state and, evidence suggests, eschew an approach that would honour the individual by reinforcing the compulsive 'any job is better than none' approach to welfare conditionality (Boland and Griffin 2015a, 2016, 2021; Wiggan, 2015; Collins and Murphy, 2016; Dukelow, 2021; Finn, 2021; Murphy, 2021; McGann, 2021; McGann and Murphy, 2021; Johnston and McGauran, 2021).

Building on the idea of 'shared typical' experience types as one foundation for a particular type of knowledge, space and place are undoubtedly something that feature in the critical literature on welfare. Boland and Griffin (2015a, 2015b, 2016, 2018, 2021) have addressed the idea in multiple instances, but perhaps most particularly in work that constitutes the welfare space as liminal. Liminality, for Boland and Griffin (2015a: 38), is as much about identity as it is about physical geography for the welfare recipient: 'Noneconomic elements of identity such as nationality or gender remain, but in the "meantime" the individual is no longer what they are, and not yet what they hope to become'. Boland and Griffin (2015a) specifically refer to jobseekers here, and the idea of 'becoming' or of 'reformation' is something they have since developed considerably (2021). Relating this to the work presented in this book, use of the word 'meantime' is particularly interesting. It arguably conjures up a sense of intangible space, denoting an 'in-between-ness' – the time or space between time in the past and time in the future – essentially describing a category of person 'in-between'. This is something that Boland and Griffin (2018) take further, going so far as to theorise jobseeking and the accompanying conditionality as constituting a purgatorial ethic. These authors have also articulated the compulsion that resides within the geography of the welfare state (Boland and Griffin, 2015a). There are also examples of cognate literature from further afield. For example, Crossley (2017) is representative of those who have made a distinct contribution to a much broader conception of spaces and places with respect to poverty. In doing so, Crossley (2017: 98) unpacks the complexity of space and place as being psychosocially intertwined while also addressing the 'concrete settings in which the state engages poor and marginalised individuals, families and communities', thus noting how these have become sites of compulsion. With respect to the idea of a developmental welfare state that honours the dignity and worth of individuals, such compulsive spaces, these places of 'reform' and of 'reformation' (Boland and Griffin, 2021), would need to be radically overhauled so that an interaction with the welfare state is shaped positively from the outset. This would mean changing both geography and processes in a way that removes the stigma of public burden. By changing geography, but more importantly, by changing process and policy, an opportunity to change the welfare imaginary arises. A DWS, then, must start with an overhaul of hard, physical places to foster less uncomfortable psychosocial spaces.

Framing welfare differently

If we are to '*do*' welfare differently, if we are to begin to foster better, more welcoming and more holistic spaces and places, we also need to begin to think about how to *see* welfare differently, to frame it differently. Here

I draw attention to the second part of the first principle as given by NESC (2020: 76) (emphasis added): 'Belief in the dignity and right to personal development of the individual, *and in the value of bonds of mutual obligation between all members of the community.*'

If we are seriously to move towards a space where we honour the bonds of mutual obligation, if we are to foster the vision of a 'welfare society', we must consider how we talk and think about welfare generally. This is arguably a question of social framing. If 'welfare framing' is the process that makes up and contributes to the 'common-sense' notions of social welfare inculcated into public consciousness (Jensen and Tyler, 2015), this is plainly shown to be at play in the work presented in this book through the way in which the documented experiences transmit a keen awareness of welfare as a social issue and further recognition of how this manifests in extremely negative terms and across different media. Alongside this work, and with one eye again towards the 'shared typical' in Ireland, Boland and Griffin (2015a, 2015b, 2016; 2021), Millar and Crosse (2018), Murphy (2020), Gaffney and Millar (2020), Whelan (2020a, 2020b, 2021a), Finn (2021) and McGann and Murphy, (2021) have all variously found this to be the case. The separate yet overlapping work of these authors pays varying degrees of attention to the plethora of folk devils and caricatured characters that populate the stage in the politically crafted pantomime that represents the welfare-framing consensus in an Irish context. Perhaps, however, the most blatant recent example of forging this consensus at a political level is to be found in the Welfare Cheats Cheat Us All campaign of 2017, which was mentioned by several of the participants who took part in this research. It has also been given space in the literature by Devereux and Power (2019, who undertook a critical discourse analysis of the media discourses concerning the Welfare Cheats Cheat Us All campaign in the Republic of Ireland, with a view to illustrating the media's role in articulating 'disgust' discourses focused on 'welfare fraud', poverty and unemployment. Ultimately, their work contributes to an understanding of how discourses concerning social welfare fraud are created, disseminated and perceived. In the work presented here, the very real awareness that many of the participants had of the Welfare Cheats campaign chimes with the work of Devereux and Power (2019) by adding detail derived from lived experience, thus showing the real effects of the discourse creation Devereux and Power (2019) are concerned to expose.

Again, focusing on the idea of the 'shared typical' in the Irish context, there is a corpus of literature emanating from further afield with which the work presented here will also resonate. With the likelihood of omitting more than one contribution, Jensen (2014), Jensen and Tyler (2015), Patrick (2016, 2017, 2019), Wincup and Monaghan (2016), Crossley (2017, 2018), Tyler and Slater (2018), Scambler (2018), Brady (2019) and Redman (2019) have all, to varying degrees, addressed the nature of the welfare-framing consensus in the UK. The work of Jensen and Tyler (2015), who consider 'benefit broods', arguably stands out in terms of documenting the nature of cultural and political crafting in the context of the UK and, because of this, many of the other authors cited here tend to draw on their work. Moving on to consider how the framing consensus described by Jensen and Tyler (2015) affects the lived experiences of welfare recipients in the UK and considering also how this may be viewed as 'shared typical', it is the experiences of the participants in Patrick's (2016, 2017) study, with which the lived experiences documented here resonate most acutely. Patrick's project, of course, differs from that of Jensen and Tyler (2015) and others by entering the territory of lived experience, an area to which the work presented here speaks directly. In addressing the lived experiences of welfare recipients in the UK, much of what Patrick (2016, 2017) uncovers reveals similarity and common ground with the findings of this study despite jurisdictional differences, thus demonstrating 'shared typical' knowledge.

In the Irish context, where others have described how the welfare-framing consensus is discoursed (Boland and Griffin, 2016) and others still have demonstrated how such discourses are crafted and disseminated (Devereux and Power, 2019), the work presented here has shown how these things are experienced by welfare recipients directly. Moreover, it has shown how potent and damaging the welfare-framing consensus can be – how it can become inculcated in public consciousness, how it can function as an aspect of stigma, thus driving behaviour such as othering and impression management, and how it undermines social solidarity and sows social division. All of this suggests that a campaign to 'reframe' welfare as a positive social good is a necessary step in reclaiming welfare in an overall sense. It also suggests that if we are to launch a serious project that seeks to value the bonds of mutual obligation as part of a developmental welfare state, we must seriously challenge how we currently think about, talk about and see welfare. While this may be a call echoed many times throughout history, it may be more pertinent now than ever.

Crises to come? Why we need welfare: a note to finish on

In *Why we need welfare: Collective action for the common good*, Alcock (2016: 2) notes that: 'We ... depend on others to meet our needs for welfare. The provision of welfare is intrinsically and inevitably a collective, not an individual matter.' In *Understanding the cost of welfare*, Glennerster (2017: 3) notes that: 'State welfare policies are ... designed to ensure that all individuals' basic needs are met, whatever misfortune affects them and whatever their age.' Moreover, Armstrong (2017), quoted in Chapter 7, has argued that welfare systems are of fundamental importance to the overall social health of any society. These are just three examples of authors who have espoused and argued for the importance of a strong social safety net in different ways. There are, of course, many other examples of similar calls going back over many years, calls too innumerable to list in full, although perhaps Richard Titmuss should get an honourable mention. What characterises the more recent of these calls is that they were made on the broad cusp of a crisis that was as yet unimagined – the COVID-19 pandemic. In this respect, they represent strong arguments for social welfare as a social good in a time before the onset of a crisis during which welfare responses were required overnight and the necessity of a functioning social safety net was amply demonstrated. In a sense, then, recent history has only made such calls seem even more pertinent, even more pronounced. In terms of empirics, if we take the fact that the unemployment rate in Ireland during the most stringent restrictions of the pandemic hit highs of near 30 per cent (CSO, 2021) and that the UK's benefit claimant count increased by 113.2 per cent from March 2020 through to February 2021 (ONS, 2021), this clearly demonstrates the need for a functioning social safety net as a means of ameliorating hardship during times of acute crisis. We now sit at a point where exiting the crisis seems a real possibility, albeit, at the time of writing, we are not clear of the crisis yet and the global response has been patchy and uneven. On the basis that we may exit the crisis in some shape or form, and before we return to 'business as usual' with respect to the 'doing' of welfare, perhaps it can now be suggested that we should consider that the current crisis may only be the first of many. So what about as yet unspecified crises? Could more pandemics follow this one? Returning global travel, continued urbanisation, the ongoing onslaught of climate change, increased contact between humans, wild animals and the natural environment, and a general global shortage of health and social care workers certainly suggest that this is likely (see GAVI, 2021). Notably, alongside the potential for further pandemics sits the spectre of climate change, surely the most eminent existential threat humanity currently faces and something that groups such as the International Labour Organization have continually warned will engender huge levels of job displacement and therefore the necessity for a huge welfare response in the years to come (see ILO, 2018). Surely, then, this – along with the COVID-19 pandemic – is enough to suggest that investment in welfare infrastructure *must* form an essential part of any strategy that governments the world over put forward to ensure the continued well-being of citizenry and populations in general? On the basis of what is offered in this book, I strongly argue that if such plans are drafted, lived experience, as a valuable and valid form of knowledge and expertise, must form part of the picture.

Notes

Introduction

[1] All payment scheme information mentioned throughout comes from www.gov.ie/en/category/social-welfare/. Payment information, rates and criteria may have changed marginally since data collection. Changes are likely to be marginal.

[2] Primary carer simply means that the child or children concerned spend more time on average with the payment recipient.

[3] The Tús initiative is a community work placement scheme providing short-term working opportunities for unemployed people. The work opportunities are designed to benefit the community and are provided by community and voluntary organisations in both urban and rural areas.

Chapter 1

[1] De Valera had a particularly romanticised vision of what a new Ireland should and could look like, and this vision is perhaps best represented in the work of anthropologists Arensberg and Kimball (2001), who undertook a study of Irish culture in Clare in the early 1930s and developed a sociological 'consensus' model to describe how rural Ireland functioned. A classic work, it has nevertheless been heavily criticised for promoting too sympathetic a view of Irish rural life that takes no account of conflict or class structures.

[2] Beveridge (1879–1963) was a British economist who was also a noted progressive and social reformer. See Williams and Williams (1987) for more.

[3] This was a group established in law in 1982 with a remit to advise the Minister for Health on the development of social services and to promote greater accessibility, coordination and public awareness of social services and to perform certain other functions in relation to social services. These included the encouragement of the spread in local communities of knowledge and advice in relation to social services and the promotion of the establishment and development of voluntary social services in such communities and to provide for connected matters.

[4] Celtic Tiger (Irish: An Tíogar Ceilteach) is a term referring to the economy of the Republic of Ireland from the mid-1990s to the late 2000s, a period of rapid real economic growth fuelled by foreign direct investment. The boom was dampened by a subsequent property bubble that resulted in a severe economic downturn.

[5] The post-2008 Irish economic downturn in the Republic of Ireland coincided with a series of banking scandals, and followed the 1990s and 2000s Celtic Tiger period of rapid real economic growth fuelled by foreign direct investment, a subsequent property bubble that rendered the real economy uncompetitive, and an expansion in bank lending in the early 2000s. An initial slowdown in economic growth amid the international financial crisis of 2007–08 greatly intensified in late 2008 and the country fell into recession for the first time since the 1980s. Emigration, as did unemployment (particularly in the construction sector), escalated to levels not seen since that decade. See Donovan and Murphy (2013).

[6] Child Benefit, also known as Children's Allowance, is a monthly payment to the parents or guardians of children under 16 years of age. It is paid for children under 18 years of age if they are in full-time education, full-time training or have a disability and cannot support themselves. Child Benefit is not paid for any child dependent aged 18 or older, even if they stay in education or training.

[7] Fuel Allowance is a payment under the National Fuel Scheme to help with the cost of heating your home during the winter months. It is paid to people who are dependent on long-term social welfare payments and who are unable to provide for their own heating needs. Only one Fuel Allowance is paid to a household.

Fuel Allowance is generally paid with your social welfare payment on the same day. You can choose to get Fuel Allowance paid weekly or to get your total allowance paid in 2 lump sums.

[8] The Household Benefits Package is a package of allowances that helps with the costs of running a household. The package is available to everyone aged over 70 and to people under age 70 in certain circumstances. There are two allowances in the Household Benefits Package: the first concerns utilities and the second grants a free television licence.

[9] Launched in 2012, Intreo was and is billed as being a single point of contact for all employment and income supports. Designed to provide a more streamlined approach, Intreo offers practical, tailored employment services and supports for jobseekers and employers alike. It arguably represents a 'case management' management approach to unemployment.

[10] JobPath was billed as an approach to employment activation that caters mainly for people who are long-term unemployed (over 12 months) to assist them to secure and sustain full-time paid employment or self-employment.

[11] Seetec Limited and Turas Nua Limited provide JobPath services in two contract areas based on the department's divisional structure. Seetec covers the West, Midlands North, North East, North West, Dublin Central, Dublin North and Dublin South; Turas Nua covers Cork Central, South East, Mid-Leinster, Mid-West, South West and Midlands South. Turas Nua is a joint venture between Ireland's national recruitment agency FRS Recruitment and leading employability and skills provider Working Links. They oversee the delivery of the Department of Social Protection JobPath scheme in the southern counties of Ireland. Seetec Employment and Skills Ireland deliver JobPath and Welcome to Work employability and skills programmes across Ireland. The Seetec Group claims to have over 30 years of expertise in working with people who are unemployed and states that it is fundamentally about 'helping them to aspire, achieve and make sustainable positive changes to their lives through employment'.

Chapter 2

[1] While it is true that liminality can be constructed and seen as overtly negative, it must also be acknowledged that this view devolves on the researcher's own analysis and interpretation of the data. It is equally possible to view or construct liminality in a far more positive way. As an example, an article by Wilhoit (2017) constructs routine liminality, via the daily commute as 'sacred time', thus demonstrating the multiple applications of the concept.

[2] Widow's or Widower's pension.

[3] A popular Irish field sport.

[4] In Ireland, a person is generally considered to be long-term unemployed after a continuous period of 12 months has elapsed since their previous employment.

[5] It didn't help that Martin was one of the interviewees I met in a community setting and that the office I interviewed him in was right across the hall from an office occupied by an official from the DSP.

[6] A food delivery service.

[7] A well-known nightspot.

[8] A children's play centre.

[9] For various examples, see Batty and Flint (2013); Chase and Walker (2013); Shildrick and MacDonald (2013); Tyler (2013, 2018, 2020); Baumberg (2014, 2016); Jensen (2014); Walker (2014); Garthwaite (2015a, 2015b, 2016); Jensen and Tyler (2015); Runswick-Cole and Goodley (2015); Patrick (2016, 2017, 2019); Seabrook (2016); Wincup and Monaghan (2016); Armstrong (2017); Crossley (2017, 2018); Scambler (2018); Tyler and Slater (2018); Redman (2019); Welfare Conditionality (2019); Lister (2021).

Chapter 3

1.   Carer's Allowance is a payment to people on low incomes who are looking after a person who needs support because of age, disability or illness (including mental illness).
2.   Of Cork city.
3.   Persons aged between 18 and 24 receive a reduced rate of JA. This increases at age 25 before reaching the full adult rate at age 26.
4.   Academics in Ireland have since entered this space. See Devereux and Power (2019).
5.   Fine Gael is the Irish political party in power at the time writing. It was founded in 1933 by Eoin O'Duffy, W.T. Cosgrave and Frank MacDermot.
6.   Fine Gael TD and Tánaiste at the time of writing, Leo Varadkar.
7.   The National Learning Network provides training and specialist support to people who, for a variety of reasons, may find it difficult to gain employment.
8.   Turas nua is a 'results-driven' actor, the presence of which reflects a broader structural shift towards neoliberal, managerialist reforms within the welfare sphere. This undoubtedly fuels the organisation's own performativity culture. To give a brief sense of how this works, a recent publication by the Irish National Organisation for the Unemployed (2019: 2) states: 'An initial payment is made to the contractor when they complete a Personal Progression Plan for each client. If the unemployed person takes-up a job for at least 30 hours per week, the JobPath provider receives another payment if the person remains in employment for 13 weeks. Further "job sustainment" payments may be made when the person remains in employment after 26 weeks, 39 weeks and a final payment after 52 weeks.'

Chapter 4

1.   The Welfare Conditionality project ran from 2013 to 2018 in the UK during which time interviews with 481 people living in Bath, Bristol, Edinburgh, Glasgow, Greater Manchester, Inverness, London, Peterborough, Sheffield and Warrington were conducted. Following initial interviews, participants were interviewed twice more over time, to explore the long-term effects of conditionality. See www.welfareconditionality.ac.uk
2.   An online food delivery platform.

Chapter 6

1.   The ash cloud was caused by eruptions from the Eyjafjallajökull volcano in Iceland. Although relatively small for volcanic eruptions, they caused enormous disruption to air travel across Western and Northern Europe over an initial period of six days in April 2010. Additional localised disruption continued into May 2010.
2.   This combination of the word 'Romanian' with the slur 'gypos' suggests that this expression by the participant is aimed at the Romany Gypsy community. While it makes for uncomfortable reading, it is kept for authenticity of voice.
3.   Of Cork city.
4.   A suburb of Cork City.

Chapter 8

1.   See Welfare at a social distance for example: https://www.distantwelfare.co.uk/
2.   Information accurate at the time of writing.

Conclusion

1.   I am deeply aware that this is a somewhat simplistic narrative and, as such, is being and needs to be problematised, particularly with respect to how the British post-war welfare state was funded; see Bhambra (2020).

References

Alcock, P. (2016) *Why we need welfare: Collective action for the common good.* Bristol: Policy Press.

Alighieri, D. (1995 [132]) *The divine comedy.* London: Everyman.

Alston, P. (2019) *Visit to the United Kingdom of Great Britain and Northern Ireland: Report of the Special Rapporteur on extreme poverty and human rights in Britain and Northern Ireland.* Geneva: UN. Available at: https://undocs. org/A/HRC/41/39/Add.1 [Accessed 22 June 2019].

Arensberg, C.M. and Kimball, S.T. (2001) *Family and community in Ireland.* Clare: Clasp Press.

Armstrong, S. (2017) *The new poverty.* London: Verso.

Aspalter, C. (2011) 'The development of ideal-typical welfare regime theory'. *International Social Work*, 54(6), 735–750.

Batty, E. and Flint, J. (2013) 'Talking 'bout poor folks (thinking 'bout poor folks): perspectives on comparative poverty in working class households'. *International Journal of Housing Policy*, 13(1), 1–19.

Baumberg, B. (2014) 'Benefits and the cost of living: pressures on the cost of living and attitudes to benefit claiming'. In Park, A., Bryson, C. and Curtice, J. (Eds) *British social attitudes 31.* London: National Centre for Social Research, pp. 95–122.

Baumberg, B. (2016) 'The stigma of claiming benefits: a quantitative study'. *Journal of Social Policy*, 45(2), 181–199.

Baumberg, B. and Meueleman, B. (2016) 'Beyond "mythbusting": how to respond to myths and perceived undeservingness in the British benefits system'. *Journal of Poverty and Social Justice*, 24(3), 291–306.

Beresford, P. (2016) *All our welfare: Towards participatory social policy.* Bristol: Policy Press.

Beveridge, W. (1942) *Social insurance and allied services report.* Available at: www.ncbi.nlm.nih.gov/pmc/articles/PMC2560775/pdf/10916922. pdf [Accessed 14 December 2021].

Bhambra, G.K. (2020) 'Colonial global economy: towards a theoretical reorientation of political economy'. *Review of International Political Economy.* DOI: 10.1080/09692290.2020.1830831.

Bhambra, G.K (2021) 'Narrating inequality, eliding empire'. *British Journal of Sociology.* 72(1), 69–78.

Bhambra, G.K. and Holmwood, J. (2018) 'Colonialism, postcolonialism and the liberal welfare state'. *New Political Economy*, 23(5), 574–587.

Bhambra, G.K. and Holmwood, J. (2021) *Colonialism and modern social theory.* Cambridge: Polity.

Boland T. (2018) 'Seeking a role: disciplining jobseekers as actors in the labour market'. *Work, Employment and Society*, 30(2), 334–351.

Boland, T. and Griffin, R. (2015a) 'The death of unemployment and the birth of job-seeking in welfare policy: governing a liminal experience'. *Irish Journal of Sociology*, 23(2), 29–48.

Boland, T. and Griffin, R. (2015b) *The sociology of unemployment*. Manchester: Manchester University Press.

Boland, T. and Griffin, R. (2016) 'Making sacrifices: how ungenerous gifts constitute jobseekers as scapegoat'. *Distinktion: Journal of Social Theory*, 17(2), 174–191.

Boland, T. and Griffin, R. (2018) 'The purgatorial ethic and the spirit of welfare'. *Journal of Classical Sociology*, 18(2), 87–103.

Boland, T. and Griffin, R. (2021) *The reformation of welfare: The new faith of the labour market*: Bristol: Bristol University Press.

Bonoli, G. (2011) 'Active labour market policy in a changing economic context'. In Clasen, J. and Clegg, D. (Eds) *Regulating the risk of unemployment: National adaptions to post-industrial labour markets in Europe*. Oxford: Oxford University Press, pp. 318–332.

Brady, M. (2019) 'Conceptualizing activation policies targeted at single mothers: a case study of Australia and the United Kingdom'. *Social Politics*. Available at: https://academic.oup.com/sp/article-abstract/28/2/290/5512313.

Bratton, M. (2015) 'Welfare discourse and the subjectivity of social assistance recipients: understanding classism as a barrier to justice'. *Canadian Social Work*, 17(1), 40–56.

Braun, V. and V. Clarke. (2006) 'Using thematic analysis in psychology'. *Qualitative Research in Psychology*, 3(2), 77–101.

Braun, V. and Clarke, V. (2012) 'Thematic analysis'. In Cooper, H. Camic, P., Long, D., Rindskopf, D. and Sher, K. (Eds) *APA handbook of research methods in psychology. Vol. 2: Research designs: quantitative, qualitative, neuropsychological, and biological*. Washington, DC: APA Books, pp. 57–71.

Braun, V. and Clarke, V. (2013) *Successful qualitative research: A practical guide for beginners*. London: Sage.

Braun, V. and Clarke, V. (2016) '(Mis)conceptualising themes, thematic analysis, and other problems with Fugard and Potts' (2015) sample-size tool for thematic analysis'. *International Journal of Social Research Methodology*, 19(6), 739–743.

Braun, V. and Clarke, V. (2020) 'One size fits all? What counts as quality practice in (reflexive) thematic analysis?'. *Qualitative Research in Psychology*. Available at: https://doi.org/10.108 0/14780887.2020.1769238

Braun, V. and Clarke, V. (2021a) 'The ebbs and flows of qualitative research: time, change, and the slow wheel of interpretation'. In Clift, B.C., Gore, J., Gustafsson, S., Bekker, S., Batlle, I.C. and Hatchard, J. [Eds] *Temporality in qualitative inquiry: Theories, methods and practices*. London: Routledge, pp. 22–38.

Braun, V. and Clarke, V. (2021b) 'To saturate or not to saturate? Questioning data saturation as a useful concept for thematic analysis and sample-size rationales'. *Qualitative Research in Sport, Exercise and Health*, (13)2, 201–216.

Brodkin, E. (2012) 'Reflections on street-level bureaucracy: past, present, and future'. *Public Administration Review*. November/December, 940–949.

Browne, N. (2007) *Against the tide*. Dublin: Gill & Macmillan.

Bryman, A. (2012) *Social research method*. Oxford: Oxford University Press.

Burr, V. (2002) *The person in social psychology*. London: The Psychology Press.

Butler, J. (1988) 'Performative acts and gender constitution: an essay in phenomenology and feminist theory'. *Theatre Journal*, 40(4): 519–531.

Carey, S. (2003) 'Theorising welfare state development: a case study of social insurance in the Republic of Ireland'. PhD thesis, Trinity College Dublin.

Carey, S. (2008) 'Social security in Ireland 1939–1952: the limits to solidarity'. *International Journal of Social Welfare*, 17(3), 274–275.

Chase, E. and Walker, R. (2013) 'The co-construction of shame in the context of poverty: beyond a threat to the social bond'. *Sociology*, 47(4), 739–754.

Cinnéide, S. (1970) *A law for the poor: A study of home assistance in Ireland*. Dublin: Institute of Public Administration.

Clasen, J. and Clegg, D. (2007) 'Levels and levers of conditionality: measuring change within welfare states'. In Clasen, J. and Siegel, N.A. (Eds) *Investigating welfare state change: The 'dependent variable problem' in comparative analysis*. Cheltenham: Edward Elgar, pp. 166–197.

Cohen, S. (2011) *Folk devils and moral panics*. Abingdon: Routledge.

Collins, M.L. and Murphy, M.P. (2016) 'Activation: solving unemployment or supporting a low-pay economy?'. In Murphy, M.P. and Dukelow, F. (Eds) *The Irish welfare state in the twenty-first century: Challenges and change*. Basingstoke: Palgrave Macmillan, pp. 67–92.

Commission on the Relief of the Sick and Destitute Poor (1925) *Report of the Commission on the Relief of the Sick and Destitute Poor*. Available at: www.lenus.ie/handle/10147/238535 [Accessed 15 December 2021].

Coogan, T.P. (1966) *Ireland since the rising*. New York, NY: Praeger.

Coughlin, R.M. (1980) *Ideology, public opinion and welfare policy: Attitudes towards taxes and spending in industrialized societies*. Berkeley, CA: California Institute of International Studies.

Cousins, M. (2003) *The birth of social welfare in Ireland, 1922–52*. Dublin: Four Courts.

Cousins, M. (2005) *Explaining the Irish welfare state: A historical, comparative, and political analysis*. New York, NY: Edwin Mellen Press.

Cousins, M. (2016) 'The Irish social protection system: change in comparative context'. In Murphy, M.P. and Dukelow, F. [Eds] *The Irish welfare state in the twenty-first century: Challenges and change*. Basingstoke: Palgrave Macmillan, pp. 37–65.

Crossley, S. (2017) *In their place: The imagined geographies of poverty.* London: Pluto Press.

Crossley, S. (2018) *Troublemakers: The construction of 'troubled families' as a social problem.* Bristol: Policy Press.

Crouch, M. and McKenzie, H. (2006) 'The logic of small samples in interview-based qualitative research'. *Social Science Information,* 45(4), 483–499.

CSO (Central Statistics Office) (2021) 'Release archive 2020' [Online]. Available at: www.cso.ie/en/statistics/labourmarket/archive/releasearchive2020 [Accessed 13 July 2021].

Cullen, P. and Murphy, M.P. (2021) 'Responses to the COVID-19 crisis in Ireland: from feminized to feminist'. *Gender, Work & Organization.* Available at: https://doi.org/10.1111/gwao.12596

Curry, J. (1998) *Irish social services* (3rd edn). Dublin: Institute of Public Administration.

Department of Finance (2010) *Summary of 2011 Budget Measures,* Available at: www.budget.gov.ie/budgets/2011/Documents/Summary%20of%20 Measures%20Combined.pdf, [Accessed 2 March 2019].

Department of Public Expenditure and Reform (2011) 'Minister for Public Expenditure and Reform Brendan Howlin, TD. Address to Dáil Éireann on expenditure estimates 2012' [Online]. Available at: http://budget. gov.ie/budgets/2012/EstimateStatement.aspx#section9.1 [Accessed 3 March 2012].

Department of Public Expenditure and Reform (2012) 'Minister for Public Expenditure and Reform Mr Brendan Howlin TD. Address to Dáil Éireann on expenditure estimates 2013' [Online]. Available at: http://bud get.gov.ie/budgets/2013/EstimateStatement.aspx#section6.1 [Accessed 3 March 2019].

Department of Social Protection (2021a) 'National Economic Recovery Plan – social protection supports and services' [Online]. Available at: www. gov.ie/en/press-release/f89bc-national-economic-recovery-plan-social-protection-supports-and-services [Accessed 13 July 2021].

Department of Social Protection (2021b) *Minister Humphreys announces details on the reopening of PUP to workers impacted by the latest restrictions.* Available at: www.gov.ie/en/press-release/2c0eb-minister-humphreys-announces-details-on-the-re-opening-of-pup-to-workers-impacted-by-the-latest-restrictions/ [Accessed on 13 July 2021].

Department of Social Welfare (1986) *Report of the Commission on Social Welfare.* Dublin: Stationery Office.

Devereux, E. and Power, M.J. (2019) 'Fake news? A critical analysis of the "Welfare Cheats Cheat Us All" campaign in Ireland'. *Critical Discourse Studies,* 16(3), 347–362.

Dignan, J. (1944) *Social security: Outline of a scheme on national organisation.* Sligo: Champion Publications.

Donovan, D. and Murphy, A.E. (2013) *The fall of the Celtic Tiger: Ireland & the EU debt crisis.* Oxford: Oxford University Press.

Dukelow, F. (2011) 'Economic crisis and welfare retrenchment: comparing Irish policy responses in the 1970s and 1980s with the present'. *Social Policy & Administration*, 45(4), 408–429.

Dukelow, F. (2018) '"Some sort of super welfare state"? The "rediscovery of poverty" and Irish welfare state change in the 1970s'. In Eklund, E., Oppenheimer, M. and Scott, J. (Eds) *The state of welfare: Comparative studies of the welfare state at the end of the long boom, 1965–1980.* Oxford: Peter Lang. pp. 61–84.

Dukelow, F. (2021) 'Sacrificial citizens? Activation and retrenchment in Ireland's political economy'. *Administration*, 69(2), 43–65.

Dukelow, F. and Considine, M. (2014a) 'Between retrenchment and recalibration: the impact of austerity on the Irish social protection system'. *Journal of Sociology and Social Welfare*, 41(2), 55–72.

Dukelow, F. and Considine, M. (2014b) 'Outlier or model of austerity in Europe? The case of Irish social protection reform'. *Social Policy & Administration*, 48(4), 413–429.

Dukelow, F. and Considine, M. (2017) *Irish social policy: A critical introduction* (2nd edn). Dublin: Gill & Macmillan.

Dunphy, R. (1995) *The making of Fianna Fáil power in Ireland, 1923–1948.* Oxford: Clarendon.

Dwyer, P. (2000) *Welfare rights and responsibilities: Contesting social citizenship.* Bristol: Policy Press.

Dwyer, P. (2016) 'Citizenship, conduct and conditionality: sanction and support in the 21st century UK welfare state'. In Fenger, M., Hudson, J. and Needham, C. (Eds) *Social policy review 28: Analysis and debate in social policy, 2016.* Bristol: Policy Press, pp. 41–62.

Esping-Andersen, G. (1990) *The three worlds of welfare capitalism.* Cambridge: Polity.

ESRI (Economic and Social Research Institute) (2021) *COVID-19 and the Irish welfare system.* Dublin: ESRI. Available at: www.esri.ie/system/files/publications/BP202202.pdf [Accessed 13 July 2021].

Etzioni, A. (1997) *The new golden rule.* London: Profile Books.

Eurostat (2019) 'Social protection spending as a percentage of GDP' [Online]. Available at: https://ec.europa.eu/eurostat/tgm/graph.do?tab=graph&plugin=1&language=en&pcode=tps00098&toolbox=type [Accessed 23 June 2019].

Ferguson, H. (2011) *Child protection practice.* Basingstoke: Palgrave Macmillan.

Ferriter, D. (2005) *The transformation of Ireland, 1900–2000.* London: Profile Books.

Ferriter, D. (2013) *Ambiguous republic: Ireland in the 1970s*. London: Profile Books.

Ferriter, D. (2015) *A nation and not a rabble: The Irish Revolution 1913–1923*. London: Profile Books.

Finn P. (2021) 'Navigating indifference: Irish jobseekers' experiences of welfare conditionality'. *Administration*, 69(2), 67–86.

Fischer, C. (2018) 'Gender and the politics of shame: A twenty-first-century feminist shame theory'. *Hypatia*, 33(3), 371–383.

Fitzpatrick, C., McKeever, G. and Simpson, M. (2019) 'Conditionality, discretion and TH Marshall's "right to welfare"'. *Journal of Social Welfare and Family Law*, 41(4), 445–462. Available at: https://doi.org/10.1080/09649069.2019.1663016

Foucault, M. (1988) 'Technologies of the self'. In Martin, L.H., Gutman, H. and Hutton, P.H. [Eds] *Technologies of the self: A seminar with Michel Foucault*. London: Tavistock, pp. 16–49.

Frayne, D. [Ed]. (2019) *The work cure*. London: PCCS.

Frayne, D. (2015) *The refusal of work: The theory and practice of resistance to work*. London: Zed Books.

Gaffney, S. and Millar, M. (2020) 'Rational skivers or desperate strivers? The problematisation of fraud in the Irish social protection system'. *Critical Social Policy*, 40(1), 69–88.

Garthwaite, K. (2015a) '"Keeping meself to meself": how social networks can influence narratives of stigma and identity for long-term sickness benefits recipients'. *Social Policy & Administration*, 49(2), 199–212.

Garthwaite, K. (2015b) 'Becoming incapacitated? Long-term sickness benefit recipients and the construction of stigma and identity narratives'. *Sociology of Health & Illness*, 37(1), 1–13.

Garthwaite, K. (2016) 'Stigma, shame and "people like us": an ethnographic study of foodbank use in the UK'. *Journal of Poverty and Social Justice*, 24(3), 277–289.

GAVI (2021) '5 reasons why pandemics like COVID-19 are becoming more likely' [Online]. Available at: www.gavi.org/vaccineswork/5-reasons-why-pandemics-like-covid-19-are-becoming-more-likely [Accessed 13 July 2021].

Glennerster, H. (2007) *British social policy 1945 to the present*. Oxford: Blackwell.

Glennerster, H. (2017) *Understanding the cost of welfare*. Bristol: Policy Press.

Goffman, E. (1990a) *Stigma: Notes on the management of spoiled identity*. London: Penguin.

Goffman, E. (1990b) *Presentation of the self in everyday life*. London: Penguin.

GOI (Government of Ireland) (2012) *Pathways to Work: Government policy statement on labour market activation*. Dublin: Government of Ireland.

GOI (2013) *Pathways to Work: 50 point plan to tackle long-term unemployment*. Dublin: Government of Ireland.

GOI (2015) *Pathways to Work 2015*. Dublin: Government of Ireland.

GOI (2016) *Pathways to Work 2016–2020*. Dublin: Government of Ireland.

GOI (2021) *Pathways to Work 2021–2025*. Dublin: Government of Ireland.

Gronmo, S. (2020) *Social research methods: Qualitative, quantitative and mixed methods approaches*. London: Sage.

Hansen, M.P. (2019) *The moral economy of activation: Politics and policies*. Bristol: Policy Press.

Hansen, L.S. and Nielsen, M.H. (2021) 'Working less, not more in a workfare programme: group solidarity, informal norms and alternative value systems amongst activated participants'. *Journal of Social Policy*, 1–17. Available at: https://doi.org/10.1017/S0047279421000301

Harvey, D. (2007) *A brief history of neoliberalism*. Oxford: Oxford University Press.

Hays, S. (2003) *Flat broke with children: Women in the age of welfare reform*. New York, NY: Oxford University Press.

Henriques, J., Hollway, W., Urwin, C., Venn, C. and Walkerdine, V. (1984) *Changing the subject: Psychology, social regulation and subjectivity*. London: Methuen.

Hick, R. and Murphy, M.P. (2021) 'Common shock, different paths? Comparing social policy responses to COVID-19 in the UK and Ireland'. *Social Policy & Administration*. 55(2), 312–325.

Hoxsey, D. (2011) 'Debating the ghost of Marshall: a critique of citizenship'. *Citizenship Studies*, 15(6–7), 915.

ILO (International Labour Organization) (2018) *The employment impact of climate change adaptation: Input Document for the G20 Climate Sustainability Working Group*. Geneva: ILO. Available at: www.ilo.org/wcmsp5/groups/public/---ed_emp/documents/publication/wcms_645572.pdf [Accessed 13 July 2021].

Im, Z.J. and Komp-Leukkunen, K. (2021) 'Automation and public support for workfare'. *Journal of European Social Policy*. DOI: 10.1177/09589287211002432

Institute for Government (UK) (2021) 'Coronavirus: how have different countries supported workers through the crisis?' [Online]. Available at: www.instituteforgovernment.org.uk/coronavirus-support-workers-comparison [Accessed 7 July 2021].

Irish National Organisation for the Unemployed (2019) *Mapping the journey for unemployed people: Report on Phase Three of the Employment Services Research Project*. Dublin: INOU. Available at: www.inou.ie/download/pdf/inou_employment_services_report_phase_3.pdf [Accessed 1 September 2019].

Jackson, M.P., Stewart, H.R., and Bland, R.E. (1987). 'Appeals tribunals on Supplementary supplementary Benefitsbenefits'. *Social Policy and & Administration*, 21(1), 58.

Jayanetti, C. (2018) 'Punishment beatings by public demand – the truth about welfare reform' [Online]. Available at: www.politics.co.uk/comment-analysis/2018/06/07/punishment-beatings-by-public-demand-the-truth-about-welfare [Accessed 23 June 2019].

Jensen, T. (2014) 'Welfare common sense, poverty porn and doxsophy'. *Sociological Research Online*. Available at: https://www.socresonline.org.uk/19/3/3.html [Accessed 21 June 2019].

Jensen, T. and Tyler, I. (2015) ' "Benefits broods": the cultural and political crafting of anti-welfare common sense'. *Critical Social Policy*, 35(4), 470–491.

Johnston, H. and McGauran, A. (2021) 'Moving towards a more tailored Public Employment Service?'. *Administration*, 69(2), 107–125.

Jørgensen, M. (2018) 'Dependent, deprived or deviant? The case of single mothers in Denmark'. *Politics and Governance*, 6(3), 170–179.

Kingfisher, C. (1996) *Women and the American welfare trap*. Philadelphia, PA: University of Pennsylvania Press.

Kissová, L. (2021) *Framing welfare recipients in political discourse: Political farming through material need assistance*. Basingstoke: Palgrave Macmillan.

Konle-Seidl, R. and Eichhorst, W. (2008) 'Does activation work?'. In Eichhorst, W., Kaufmann, O. and Konle-Seidl, R. (Eds) *Bringing the jobless into work? Experiences with activation schemes in Europe and the US*. Berlin: Springer, pp. 415–443.

Larsen, C.A. (2006) *The institutional logic of welfare attitudes: How welfare regimes influence public support*. Aldershot: Ashgate.

Lee, J. (1990) *Ireland 1912–1985: Politics and society*. Cambridge: Cambridge University Press.

Leech, B.L. (2002) 'Asking questions: techniques for semistructured interviews'. *Political Science & Politics*. 35(4), 665–668.

Lewis, J., et al. (2014) 'Generalizing from qualitative research'. In Ritchie, J., Lewis, J., McNaughton Nicholls, C. and Ormston, R. (Eds) *Qualitative research practice* (2nd edn). London: Sage, pp. 347–366.

Lipsky, M. (2010 [1980]) *Street-level bureaucracy: Dilemmas of the individual in public services*. New York, NY: Russell Sage Foundation.

Lister, R. (2021) *Poverty* (2nd edn). Cambridge: Polity.

Lowe, R. (2005) *The welfare state in Britain since 1945*. London: Palgrave Macmillan.

Marshall, T.H. and Bottomore, T. (1992) *Citizenship and social class*. London: Pluto.

McCashin, A. (2004) *Social security in Ireland*. Dublin: Gill & Macmillan.

McCashin, A. (2019) *Continuity and change in the welfare state: Social security in the Republic of Ireland*. Basingstoke: Palgrave Macmillan.

McCashin, A. and O'Shea, J. (2009) 'The Irish welfare system'. In Schubert, K., Hegelich, S. and Bazant, U. (Eds) *The handbook of European welfare systems*. London: Routledge.

McCormack, K. (2002) 'Welfare (m)others: discourse, discipline, and resistance'. Doctoral dissertation, Boston College.

McGann M. (2021) '"Double activation": workfare meets marketisation'. *Administration*, 69(2), 19–42.

McGann, M. and Murphy, M. (2021) 'Introduction: the dual tracks of welfare and activation reform – governance and conditionality'. *Administration*, 69(2), 1–16.

McGee, O. (2015) *Arthur Griffith*. Newbridge: Merrion.

McIntosh, I. and Wright, S. (2019) 'Exploring what the notion of "lived experience" offers for social policy analysis'. *Journal of Social Policy*, 48(3), 449–467.

Mead, L. (1992) *The new politics of poverty*. New York, NY: Basic Books.

Mead, L.M. (1986) *Beyond entitlement*. New York, NY: Free Press.

Millar, M. and Crosse, R. (2018) 'Lone parent activation in Ireland: putting the cart before the horses'. *Social Policy & Administration*, 52(1), 111–129.

Mills, C.W. (1940) 'Situated actions and vocabularies of motive'. *American Sociological Review*, 5 (6), 904–913.

Milner, A. (2019) 'Class and class consciousness in Marxist theory'. *International Critical Thought*, 9(2), 161–176.

Molander, S. and Torsvik, G. (2021) 'In their own best interest: is there a paternalistic case for welfare conditionality?'. *Journal of Social Policy*, pp. 1–18. DOI: https://doi.org/10.1017/S0047279420000768

Murphy, M. (2020) 'Dual conditionality in welfare and housing for lone parents in Ireland: change and continuity?'. *Social Policy & Administration*, 54(2), 250–264.

Murphy M. (2021) 'Arguments for a post-pandemic Public Employment Eco System in Ireland'. *Administration*, 69(2), 127–147.

Murphy, M.P. (2012) 'Interests, institutions and ideas: explaining Irish social security policy'. *Policy & Politics*, 40(3), 347–365.

Murray, C. (1984) *Losing ground: American social policy 1950–1980*. New York, NY: Basic Books.

Murray, C. (1990) *The emerging British underclass*. London: Institute of Economic Affairs.

Murray, C. (1994) *Underclass: The crisis deepens*. London: Institute of Economic Affairs.

National Committee on Pilot Schemes to Combat Poverty (1981) *Final report: Pilot schemes to combat poverty in Ireland, 1974–1980*. Available at: https://www.lenus.ie/handle/10147/45862 [Accessed 15th December 2021] 22 June 2019].

NESC (National Economic and Social Council) (1981) *Irish social policies: Priorities for future development*. Dublin: NESC.

NESC (2005) *The developmental welfare state*. Dublin: NESC.

NESC (2011) *Supports and services for unemployed jobseekers: Challenges and opportunities in a time of reccession.* Dublin: NESC.

NESC (2020) *The future of the Irish social welfare system: Participation and protection.* Dublin: NESC.

Nielsen, M.H. (2021) 'Money, competences or behaviour? On the many worths of the unemployed'. *European Journal of Cultural and Political Sociology*, 8(2), 124–150.

Norris, M. (2016) *Property, family and the Irish welfare state.* London: Palgrave.

Ó Cionnaith, F. (2017) 'Welfare cheats campaign was a mistake, says official'. *Irish Examiner Online.* Available at: www.irishexaminer.com/ireland/welfare-cheats-campaign-was-a-mistake-says-official-464149.html [Accessed 22 June 2019].

ONS (Office for National Statistics) (2021) 'Labour market overview, UK: January 2021'. Available at: www.ons.gov.uk/employmentandlabourmarket/peopleinwork/employmentandemployeetypes/bulletins/uklabourmarket/january2021 [Accessed 13 July 2021].

Page, R. (2007) *Revisiting the welfare state.* New York, NY/Maidenhead: McGraw Hill/Open University Press.

Page, R.M. and Silburn, R. (1999) *British social welfare in the twentieth century.* Basingstoke: Macmillan.

Parker, L.D. and Northcott, D. (2016) 'Qualitative generalising in accounting research: concepts and strategies'. *Accounting, Auditing & Accountability Journal*, 29(6), 1100–1131.

Parliamentary Budget Office (2020) *The COVID-19 pandemic: Employment and unemployment supports.* Dublin: Parliamentary Budget Office, Houses of the Oireachtas. Available at: https://data.oireachtas.ie/ie/oireachtas/parliamentaryBudgetOffice/2020/2020-04-26_the-covid-19-pandemic-employment-and-unemployment-supports_en.pdf [Accessed 13 July 2021].

Parsell, C. and Clarke, A. (2020) 'Charity and shame: towards reciprocity'. *Social Problems.* Available at: https://doi.org/10.1093/socpro/spaa057

Patrick, R. (2016) 'Living with and responding to the "scrounger" narrative in the UK: exploring everyday strategies of acceptance, resistance and defection'. *Journal of Poverty and Social Justice*, 24(3), 245–259.

Patrick, R. (2017) *For whose benefit?: The everyday realties of welfare reform.* Bristol: Policy Press.

Patrick, R. (2019) 'Unsettling the anti-welfare common sense: the potential in participatory research with people living in poverty'. *Journal of Social Policy*, 1–20. Available at: https://doi.org/10.1017/S0047279419000199

Patrick, R. and Reeves, A. (2021) 'The legacy of an ideology: a decade on from benefits as lifestyle choice'. *European Journal of Public Health*, 31(2), 242–243.

Peillon, M. (2001) *Welfare in Ireland: Actors, resources, and strategies.* London: Praeger.

Pemberton, S., Sutton, E., Fahmy, E. and Bell, K. (2014) *Life on a low income in austere times.* Available online at: https://www.poverty.ac.uk/sites/defa ult/files/attachments/Life%20on%20a%20low%20income%20in%20aust ere%20times_final_report.pdf. [Accessed December 15, 2021].

Pierson, P. (2001) 'Post-industrial pressures on the mature welfare states'. In Pierson, P. (Ed) *The new politics of the welfare state.* Oxford: Oxford University Press, pp. 80–104.

Pinker, R. (1970) 'Stigma and social welfare'. *Social Work*, 27(4), 13–17.

Potter, J. and Wetherell, M. (1987) *Discourse and social psychology: Beyond attitudes and behaviour.* London: Sage.

Powell, F. (2017) *The political economy of the Irish welfare state: Church, state and capital.* Bristol: Policy Press.

Powell, F.W. (1992) *The politics of Irish social policy 1600–1900.* New York, NY: Edwin Mellen Press.

Prendergast, L. (2020) 'A self- governing reserve army of labour? The commodification of the young unemployed through welfare policy, practice and discourse'. *People, Place, and Policy*, 14(3), 262–281. Available at: https:// doi.org/10.3351/ppp.2020.4244896377.

Puirséil, N. (2007) *The Irish Labour Party, 1922–73.* Dublin: University College Dublin Press.

Rafferty, M. and O' Sullivan, E. (2002) *Suffer the little children: The inside story of Ireland's industrial schools.* Dublin: New Island Books.

Ratzmann, N. (2021) 'Deserving of social support? Street-level bureaucrats' decisions on EU migrants' benefit claims in Germany'. *Social Policy and Society*, 20(3), 509–520.

Redman, J. (2019) 'The benefit sanction: a correctional device or a weapon of disgust?'. *Sociological Research Online*. pp. 1–17.

Redman, J. (2021) ' "Chatting shit" in the Jobcentre: navigating workfare policy at the street-level'. *Work, Employment and Society*. DOI: 10.1177/ 09500170211024138

Redman, J. and Fletcher, D.R. (2021) 'Violent bureaucracy: a critical analysis of the British public employment service', *Critical Social Policy*. DOI: 10.1177/02610183211001766

Rorty, R. (2007) *Philosophy as cultural politics.* Cambridge: Cambridge University Press.

Runswick-Cole, K. and Goodley, D. (2015) 'DisPovertyPorn: *Benefits Street* and the dis/ability paradox'. *Disability & Society*, 30(4), 645–649.

Sage, D. (2019) 'Unemployment, wellbeing and the power of the work ethic: implications for social policy'. *Critical Social Policy*, 39(2), 205–228.

Scambler, G. (2018) 'Heaping blame on shame: "Weaponizing stigma" for neoliberal times'. In Tyler, I. and Slater, T. (Eds) *The sociology of stigma.* London: Sage, pp. 46–64.

Seabrook, J. (2016) *Cut out: Living without welfare.* London: Pluto Press.

Selbourne, D. (1994) *The principle of duty*. London: Sinclair Stevenson.

Shildrick, T. and MacDonald, R. (2013) 'Poverty talk: how people experiencing poverty deny their poverty and why they blame "the poor"'. *The Sociological Review*, 61(2), 285–303.

Simich, L., Maiter, S. and Ochocka, J. (2009) 'From social liminality to cultural negotiation: transformative processes in immigrant mental wellbeing'. *Anthropology & Medicine*, 16(3), 253–266.

Smith, B. (2018) 'Generalizability in qualitative research: misunderstandings, opportunities and recommendations for the sport and exercise sciences'. *Qualitative Research in Sport, Exercise and Health*, 10(1), 137–149.

Social Justice Ireland (2019) *Poverty focus 2019*. Dublin: Social Justice Ireland. Available at: www.socialjustice.ie/content/publications/poverty-focus-2019 [Accessed 13 July 2021].

Social Justice Ireland (2021) 'Delivering a basic income pilot – videos and presentations'. Available at: www.socialjustice.ie/content/publications/delivering-basic-income-pilot-videos-and-presentations [Accessed 13 July 2021].

Soss, J., Fording, R.C. and Schram, S.F. (2011) *Disciplining the poor: Neoliberal paternalism and the persistent power of race*. Chicago, IL: University of Chicago Press.

Spicker, P. (1984) *Stigma and social welfare*. London: Croom Helm.

Spicker, P. (2011) *How social security works: An introduction to benefits in Britain*. Bristol: Policy Press.

Timmins, N. (2001) *The five giants*. London: Harper Collins.

Titmuss, R.M. (1968) *Commitment to welfare*. London: Allen & Unwin.

Titmuss, R.M. (1974) *Social policy: An introduction*. London: Allen & Unwin.

Titmuss, R.M. (1987) *The philosophy of welfare: Selected writings*. London: Allen & Unwin.

Titmuss, R.M. (1997) *The gift relationship: From human blood to social policy*. London: New Press.

Torsvik, G., Molander, A. and Terum, L.I. (2021) 'The will to sanction: how sensitive are caseworkers to recipients' responsibility when imposing sanctions on non-compliance in a welfare-to-work programme?'. *International Journal of Social Welfare*. Available at: https://doi.org/10.1111/ijsw.12472.

Toupin, L. (2018) *Wages for housework: A history of an international feminist movement, 1972–77*. London: Pluto.

Treanor, M.C., Patrick, R. and Wenham, A. (2021) 'Qualitative longitudinal research: from monochrome to technicolour'. *Social Policy and Society*. DOI: 10.1017/S1474746421000270.

Tyler, I. (2013) *Revolting subjects: Social abjection and resistance in neoliberal Britain*. London: Zed Books.

Tyler, I. (2018) 'Resituating Erving Goffman: from stigma power to black power'. In Tyler, I. and Slater, T. (Eds) *The sociology of stigma*. London: Sage, pp. 26–47.

Tyler, I. (2020) *Stigma: The machinery of inequality*. London: Zed.

Tyler, I. and Slater, T. (2018) 'Rethinking the sociology of stigma'. In Tyler, I. and Slater, T. (Eds) *The sociology of stigma*. London: Sage, pp. 3–25.

Wacquant, L. (2009) *Punishing the poor: The neoliberal government of social insecurity*, London: Duke University Press.

Walker, R. (2014) *The shame of poverty*. Oxford: Oxford University Press.

Warner, J. and Gabe, J. (2004) 'Risk and liminality in mental health social work'. *Health, Risk & Society*, 6(4), 387–399.

Watts, B. and Fitzpatrick, S. (2018) *Welfare conditionality*. London: Routledge.

Welfare at a (Social) Distance (2021) 'Accessing social security and employment support during the Covid-19 crisis and its aftermath' [Online]. Available at: www.distantwelfare.co.uk [Accessed 7 July 2021].

Welfare Conditionality (2019) 'Final findings: WelCond project' [Online]. Available at: www.welfareconditionality.ac.uk/publications/final-findings-welcond-project [Accessed 21 June 2019].

Wendt, C., Mischke, M. and Pfeifer, M. (2011) *Welfare states and public opinion: Perceptions of healthcare systems, family policy and benefits for the unemployed and poor in Europe*. Cheltenham: Edward Elgar.

Whelan, J. (2020a) ' "We have our dignity, yeah?" Scrutiny under suspicion: experiences of welfare conditionality in the Irish social protection system'. *Social Policy & Administration*, 55(1), 344–50.

Whelan, J. (2020b) 'Work and thrive or claim and skive: experiencing the "toxic symbiosis" of worklessness and welfare recipiency in Ireland'. *Irish Journal of Sociology*, 29(1), 3–31.

Whelan, J. (2021a) 'Specters of Goffman: impression management in the Irish welfare space'. *Journal of Applied Social Science*, 15(1), 47–65.

Whelan, J. (2021b) *Welfare, deservingness and the logic of poverty: Who deserves?* Newcastle upon Tyne: Cambridge Scholars Publishing.

Whelan, N. (2011) *Fianna Fáil: A biography of the party*. Dublin: Gill & Macmillan.

Wiggan J. (2015) 'What variety of employment service quasi-market? Ireland's JobPath as a private power market'. In Irving, Z., Fenger, M. and Hudson, J. (Eds) *Social Policy Review*, 27, 151–170.

Wilhoit, D. (2017) 'My drive is my sacred time': commuting as routine liminality'. *Culture and Organization*, 23(4), 263–76.

Williams, K. and Williams, L.J. (1987) *A Beveridge reader*. London: Allen & Unwin.

Wincup, E. and Monaghan, M. (2016) 'Scrounger narratives and dependent drug users: welfare, workfare and warfare'. *Journal of Poverty & Social Justice*, 24(3), pp. 261–275.

Wright, S. (2016) 'Conceptualising the active welfare subject: welfare reform in discourse, policy and lived experience'. *Policy & Politics*, 44(2), 235–252.

Wright, S. and Patrick, R. (2019) 'Welfare conditionality in lived experience: aggregating qualitative longitudinal research'. *Social Policy and Society*, 18(4), 597–613.

Wright, S., Fletcher, D.R. and Stewart, A.B.R. (2019) 'Punitive benefit sanctions, welfare conditionality, and the social abuse of unemployed people in Britain: transforming claimants into offenders?'. *Social Policy & Administration*, 54(2): 278–294. Available at: https://doi.org/10.1111/spol.12577

Index